Library and Archives Canada Cataloguing in Publication data available upon request.

ISBN: 978-1-894773-40-9

Cover and contents designed by:
Peter Moller, Egg Press Co.,
Calgary Alberta, Canada •

Published by:
Calgary Spoken Word Society
1428A – 44th Street SW
Calgary, Alberta Canada T3C 2A6 •

The Banff Centre Press
Box 1020, 107 Tunnel Mountain Drive
Banff, Alberta Canada T1L 1H5 •

The Banff Centre
BANFF CENTRE PRESS

 Canada Council   Conseil des Arts   Canadian   Patrimoine
for the Arts   du Canada   Heritage   canadien

Printed in Canada by Marquis Imprimeur Inc.

RECYCLED
Paper made from
recycled material
FSC® C021757

THESPOKENWORD WORKBOOK

inspiration from poets who teach

edited by Sheri-D Wilson

spokenwordworkbook.com

TABLE OF CONTENTS

INTRODUCTION

By Sheri-D Wilson

The poetry rEvolution has been in full swing for 30 years, and spoken word is at the vanguard of this ground-breaking, earth-shattering transformation. As poetry moved from the page to the stage, there came a tectonic shift from obsolescence to state-of-the-art. Poetry has moved back to its roots, or its oral origin, and thus this new form has returned the voice of the people to the people. Poetry is no longer associated with ivory towers or stuffy elbow patches. Now, due to the inclusionary philosophy of spoken word, poetry has become a forum for everyone to share their words and stories. This up-rise of spoken word has made it possible for poetry to embrace all forms of creative expression.

The vision for this workbook and interactive website: spokenwordworkbook.com arrived to me as an epiphany. Pow! *Create an inspirational resource where people can explore their own poetry (through history, story, voice, and song). Construct a universe where individuals know they are not alone and give them the tools to manifest their own Spoken Word performances. Make creativity fun!* Wadj.

So it became my mission to create this resource, and I am thrilled with the outcome of the endeavour. It has surpassed any and all expectations I might have imagined. Throughout the process I have learned about life, writing, and performance from all of the contributors, and I have been moved on many occasions to experiment with the exercises they have submitted. What an adventure! Some of the passages in this book have been so humbling they have brought me to tears—others so authentically embody the struggles of the artist, I have responded with deep contemplation—others have sparked outbursts of laughter, and then there were those that made me question my own reality. But I must say that all of the contributions have been thought-provoking. It is my intention and sincere hope that everyone who participates in these exercises expands their perspective and the breadth of their possibilities—as writers, performers, and human beings.

What is spoken word?
It is a genre in transition, which I hope is always

so—for defining it, pinning it down, stating what it is, immediately puts restrictions on the possibilities of new vision and/or voice. I remember when I started down this path 30 years ago, before "Spoken Word" existed, and there would always be some poetry know-it-all who would say "that isn't poetry." As if they held some cosmic key or the holy rule book to what poetry is or could be. To them I say, "Crazy!" Poetry is for the outcasts, the unclaimed, the trail-blazers, the rule-breakers, the renegades, and the soul-dancers. Anyone who desires to write a poem should not live in fear of being arrested by the poetry police! Spoken word poetry lives everywhere and anywhere voices have something to say: on the street, in the bars, in artist-run galleries—words are read in basements, clubs, and cabarets, anywhere.

What is true now?
The term "Spoken Word Artist" refers to and encompasses all artists/poets working in the oral tradition. This includes: jazz, dub, hiphop,sound, slam, folk, mystic poets, and storytellers. It emulates the beat of the street. Spoken word includes the body, as memory vessel, and resonator. Gesture is an important aspect for punctuation and jubilation. Spoken word poetry is oration with rhythm, metre, and repetition, and often involves humour and social commentary. It is presented in the lingo of the people for the people and often references pop culture. Improvisation is used both in the development of work as well as in the performance.

Spoken word artists seek new and innovative forms to present their work, including new media. It is important to recognise the historical context of spoken word. Some claim the oral tradition originated with Homer, continued through to Shakespeare, Dadaism, Surrealism, and into the Beats. This is true for those of the academic persuasion, but the roots of the oral tradition originated in a diverse variety of cultures: African culture, Caribbean culture, North American Aboriginal culture, Islamic culture, Celtic culture, and every culture known to humankind. It doesn't matter how you look at it, it is an unarguable point—spoken word is the oldest form of poetry. It is no phenomenon that poets who practise the oral tradition continue to contemporize the presentation of their work to keep up with modern movements.

Spoken word may be theatrical or multi-disciplinary in nature, with a strong leaning toward cabaret. But all spoken word poetry is about taking action—it is about being part of positive change. It is about evolving and bringing transformation both to self, to the world. It is poetry that speaks about working together to make a better, more compassionate, place. This is achieved by having voice, giving voice, listening, and taking action in our own communities. The time has come,

So what is my action?

♥ Artist sheridwilson.com
♥ Founder/Producer/Artistic Director of The Calgary Spoken Word Festival calgaryspoken wordfestival.com (2003-present)
♥ Produce The Calgary Slam (2006-present)
♥ Produced The National Slam in Calgary (2008)
♥ Produced SWAN (Spoken Word Arts Network) (2005 & 2007)
♥ Founder/Director of The Spoken Word Program at The Banff Centre www.banffcentre.ca

Spoken word artists are the keepers of history. Write your history—be present—develop your own social commentary. It has been a great honour to create space for others to have voice, and the gift of poetry has been the greatest of all. When you set out to do something for others, it always returns tenfold! Spoken word poetry has given voice to itself; a voice of astute technical variation, dimension and diversity. It is a rEvolution. It is the voice of our time.

One of the first things every orator learns is this: a speaker is only as good as his or her material. Learn to write, and write well. Learn to live, and live well.

Learn to listen, and listen well.

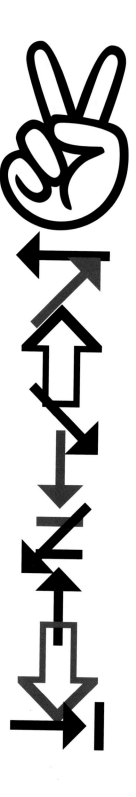

What's The Poem?

It's the weirdo in his nightgown,
            trimming the wick
            of an old-fashioned beeswax candle
and lighting a joint with a blowtorch.
            It's the shy girl straightening her hair
on the ironing board, with an iron.
            It's the guy in the suit with a career plan.
                        It erupts everywhere.

It's standing on the stage,
                                    your feet slightly apart,
            your weight centred on your solar plexus,
                        your *chakra*,
            your little pot belly....
whatever in hell's name you want to call it—
                        but it's centred.
And the voice comes out of the gut and it's a voice
                        of power,
rising,
            rising,
                        rising.
Quiet power,
                controlled
                            and uncontrolled power,
loud sometimes,
                        though not often.

Silence is much louder than a shout.

And sound came before the song.

The beat,
            the terrible beat of bones
                        and hands
                        and drums
                        and rocks
                        and power—
                        the power
                        of rhythm.

Start in a cave,
solo in a skyscraper.
Grunt and flex and live and watch your lover die.
Crash the cliff
and kiss the demon.
Demean yourself, but not your friends.

Sing
sing
sing
sing
and then sing again,
until you're ready to get it written.

Then you can form the first words,
give the codes weight and symbols and substance.
Rhyme everything and then forget rhyme.

When you come out of the cave
you will squeak a little bit,

maybe croak like a frog,
but you will find your voice,

standing on the stage,
legs apart,
centred,
the sound rolling out
of your mighty chest, or scrawny chest,
full breasted or breastless — that doesn't matter in the end —
only the voice like syrup and silence and birds greeting the morning.

Sing like the butterfly's wing,
the shark,
the shy entrepreneur,
the slutty big-toothed land developer,
the annoyed secretary,
the pompous professor.
Sing like the fencepost in a flood.
Sing like the virgin at the orgy.

Kill adverbs and adjectives,
and then revive them with a kiss.
Know a good noun when you see it
and the verb that needs no modifier.
And then ignore all advice
except the one that demands
THESE WORDS
IN THIS PLACE!

Now you are ready to write the singing codes
        some call poems,
        poems of desire
that will be meaningless to most of us
but grab the hearts of a few like an Aztec priest
        in the magic of sacrifice.

        It's easy.
        Just do everything.
        And then do it again,
        only better,
        and then again....

— Brian Brett ✪

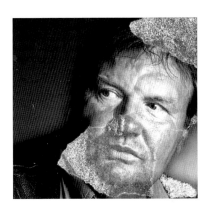

Brian Brett, poet, fiction writer, critic, journalist, is the author of 11 books of poetry, fiction, and memoir, including: *The Colour of Bones In A Stream, Tanganyika, The Fungus Garden, Coyote, Uproar's Your Only Music,* and the prize-winning best seller, *Trauma Farm.* As part of the Salt Spring Collective, he has also completed a CD of his "Talking Songs" called *Night Directions for the Lost,* produced and arranged by Ramesh Meyers at Allowed Sound Studios, and released by Tongue & Groove Records. He lives with his family on his farm on Salt Spring Island. brianbrett.ca ✪

Poète-performeur, né à Montréal de parents occitans.

15 recueils.
24 ans de publication.
35 ans d'écriture.
55 ans d'existence.

Les plus récents titres:

Une trilogie de recueils de poèmes intitulée *Critique de l'horizon pur*.

Le zéro est l'origine de l'au-delà, Editions Les Herbes rouges, 2011.

L'infini est moins triste que l'éternité, Editions Les Herbes rouges, 2009.
L'absolu est un dé rond, Editions Les Herbes rouges, 2006. ✪

Photo credit, Francine Alepin

Le futur intérieur

j'écrirai jusqu'à la nuit
où mes yeux cesseront
d'être une pluie sur le monde

deux soleils naîtront
je serai heureux de n'être plus
là pour les voir se donner la lumière

la lumière de ce qu'on a vu de beau
continuera toujours d'ouvrir
la blessure d'exister

j'aurai dit ce qu'il faut de faiblesse
pour avoir la ténacité de persister
à oublier ce qu'on attend de nous

quand le bonheur et le malheur s'entretuent
en tentant de nous faire croire des leurs
il vaut mieux être seul et ne pas dormir

j'ai assez attendu d'aubes
ces crépuscules de la nuit
pour savoir quand fermer ma lanterne

j'aurai raté très peu d'ivresses
contre la grisaille injectée
exigeant de nous le réalisme

j'aurai flotté entre conifères et corbeaux
ces bons connaisseurs de nuages
eux-mêmes grands maîtres du zéro

j'aurai accepté mon sous-sol schisteux
le seigle de mes cils le loup de mes yeux
et le lapis-lazuli de mes idéaux

j'aurai ouvert ma peau à mes os
mes os aux au-delà et mon ici
au nulle part ailleurs

j'aurai connu les formes du profond
le sans-fond des surfaces même
sans avoir la clé de mes mains

j'aurai confondu mégapoles et nécropoles
mots d'amour et amour des mots
béguins et bégonias

j'aurai compris les compromis
j'aurai banni les bannières
j'aurai honni les obséquieux

j'aurai très peu travaillé à la réalité
j'aurai élevé l'oisiveté à la contemplation
pour que parfois je voie la vue être vision

j'aurai réussi à m'étourdir
pour être saisi par l'évidence
personne n'est indéfiniment responsable

j'aurai poussé le bouchon
j'aurai repoussé les cuistres
j'aurai inversé les plafonds

j'aurai vu l'âme dont je suis l'ombre
j'aurai été touché par l'appel des mythes
jusqu'à la sphère du premier chiffre

j'aurai cru tous les oiseaux
et leur art de s'enlever de la terre
quand on veut les museler

j'aurai été un têtu du cœur
un puéril des paroles en péril
un garçon plein de douceur

et maintenant qu'un autre jour s'élève
qu'un autre train de vie siffle et passe
je me retire lentement de ce poème

et m'en vais me laisser boire par la lumière

—José Acquelin
Banff.25&27.05.2008 ✪

First appeared in *L'infini est moins triste que l'éternité*
2009, Les éditions Les Herbes rouges (Montréal)

ÉLEVER LA VOIX

Dans le roman traditionnel, en journalisme et à fortiori dans la conversation courante, la tendance générale est de simplifier la volonté d'expression par souci d'efficacité et vitesse de communication. Par peur de ne pas être compris, on dilue ce qu'on veut dire en usant de la convention la plus facile du langage.

Le poème, lui, fait exactement l'inverse : il concentre la profonde nécessité du dire en l'imageant, en le rythmant et en restant au plus près de la voix organique. Ceci afin de mieux faire sentir, en la re-sensorialisant, combien la voix, dans sa physicalité sonore et vibratoire, est déjà porteuse d'un message concret, immédiat que la parole essaie malhabilement d'interpréter.

Ainsi, la voix poétique, celle qui fait le poète, serait antérieure au code collectivisant de la parole — un peu comme le mime qui, par son tonus gestuel, énonce quelque chose que l'acteur jouant-parlant ou le slameur oublient trop souvent. — Elle, la voix poétique, pré-dirait, au sens fondateur du terme, ce que le langage quotidien tente de traduire; les mots, proférés uniquement pour leurs signifiés, n'étant dès lors que l'ombre de la voix elle-même. Et cette pré-diction devient encore plus flagrante dans le poème performé qui la porte significativement, vocalement, jusqu'au dépassement des mots écrits et appris.

MICROPHANIE DE LA VOIX DU POÈTE

(—phanie : du grec phainein «paraître».
Phanie : du grec phanos «lumineux».)

1. ♥ Prendre le micro, c'est d'abord accepter de donner sa voix et ce qu'elle porte : vulnérabilité, désir d'affirmation, besoin de reconnaissance et parfois, véridicité ou dire-vrai, tant dans sa tessiture assumée que dans sa textualité avancée. Quand il y a fusion de ces deux dernières composantes, il y a aussi manifestation de la pertinence de cette voix, d'une évidence de l'être l'émettant et qui le dépasse. La pause de la voix n'est une posture vocale juste que si elle se détache d'un contrôle trop marqué, donc craintif ou excessivement volontariste.

2. ♥ Car un bon micro éclaire: c'est une phanie sonore donnant accès au grain, au timbre, à la couleur de la voix. Et cette phanie s'avère en soi la première et ultime performance du poète, ou en tout cas la plus dynamiquement naturelle.

3. ♥ Certes, le poète peut s'adjoindre des musiciens, moduler le tempo et la hauteur de sa voix, parler-chanter ou même chanter pourvu qu'il ne trahisse pas le rythme propre, inhérent à son poème — il devient un des instruments du groupe ou de l'orchestre avec qui il est sur scène. — Donc un dialogue entre deux expressions artistiques et pas seulement un accompagnement musical. De telle sorte que le musicien est un poète des sons et le poète un musicien de la langue.

4. ♥ Le poète peut aussi avoir recours à des effets d'échos, de délais, d'échantillonnages et autres bidouillages : l'époque le permet et aime ça. Ces effets séducteurs peuvent aider à faire passer le message tant qu'ils ne le réduisent pas à une fioriture technique noyée dans l'ensemble. Le fond détermine la forme et non l'inverse.

5. ♥ Car, et là est le nœud de l'expérience poétique performée, si le propos du poème lui-même est dilué par son habillage—ne serait-ce que par une vocalisation forcée, timorée ou aux accents toniques déplacés—, on tombe dans le faux spectaculaire, la défaillance manifeste ou le démonstratif univoque. Bref on est à côté de nos pompes, hors champ, extérieur au chant particulier du poème, qu'il soit modal, atonal, mélodieux ou autre. On n'a qu'à le revivre en le vivifiant par la voix. Encore faut-il qu'il y ait poème.

6. ♥ Il y aussi la forme textuelle du poème. De nos jours, ses avatars prolifèrent : rap, spoken word, slam, hip-hop, etc…Toutes ces manières venant essentiellement du monde anglophone, pour autant qu'elles traduisent un polymorphisme des discours actuels, une polyphonie des virtualités sonores, m'apparaissent comme des expérimentations nécessaires—on vit bien quelque part et à une certaine époque—, mais pas forcément obligatoires. Sans compter qu'elles donnent souvent lieu à des facilités langagières, subordonnées à des impératifs sonores et rythmiques: rimettes, accumulations d'assonances ou de consonances, prosaïsmes cabotineurs, anglicismes surabondant. Il ne faut pas confondre sculpture et moulages préfabriqués, écriture et tags au pochoir, battements de cœur et beatbox, liberté et volonté de libération. Les deux modes ont leurs raisons d'être mais pas la même profondeur ou résonance humaine. Et puis, rien de si nouveau que ça à ces façons de rendre publiques les multiples voix possibles : il suffit de revenir aux sources de la poésie francophone, aux troubadours occitans, il y a de cela plus de mille ans. Je les imagine d'ailleurs facilement comme de sacrés performeurs de l'oralité et de la langue populaire, ces Guilhem de Poitiers, Jaufré Rudel, Bernard de Ventadour, Peire Cardinal. Des performeurs de la langue d'Oc, de leur cœur et de celui de leur époque.

7. ♥ Oui, le cœur, le bon vieux cœur fait la différence et il passe aussi par la voix et la langue. Cela peut paraître nunuche et suranné, j'en conviens, mais je crois encore à cette congruence entre la voie et la voix, dans une simplicité naturelle, une authenticité précaire mais résistante, dans le risque d'une pureté dépouillée : cette petite lumière de l'être, cette microphanie de la langue et d'une culture. Le souffle est un inspir-expir de l'être et le poème n'en est qu'une de ses traductions verbales. Et le poème performé, qu'un de ses recyclages vibratoires et aériens.

8. ♥ Avant de conclure, voici les dernières lignes d'un texte de Simone Weil, écrit en 1942 et intitulé En quoi consiste l'inspiration occitanienne? «Nous n'avons pas à nous demander comment appliquer à nos conditions actuelles d'existence l'inspiration d'un temps si lointain. Dans la mesure où nous contemplons la beauté de cette époque avec attention et amour, dans cette mesure, son inspiration descendra en nous et rendra peu à peu impossible une partie au moins des bassesses qui constituent l'air que nous respirons».

CONCLUSION

Non seulement chaque authentique poème est porteur de cette urgence du premier et dernier poème, d'une déclaration de naissance et d'un testament simultanément, mais il est ce chercheur qui sonde ce qui a précédé autant que ce qui pourrait dépasser la parole. Dès lors, on peut envisager le poème comme une transparole traversant la réalité ou ce que l'on convient d'appeler ainsi, ceci afin de proposer d'autres réels, d'autres dimensions de l'être et du non-être. ✪

The murmur of the pigeon

I am sitting on a park bench, my tired eyes searching further than the eyes of the old man sitting on the bench next to me. He stares at the flood of steel and humans on the road. This all is already a memory. A young, patient mother teaches her child to walk. Each with a project. Tell me, red-eyed pigeon, aren't you tired of digging garbage for food? Somewhere a clock ticks. The bird looks back at me, eyes wild, and says: "Come on, I'm not the only one eating from garbage bins. Many of your species dine as I do." Still, but is this an excuse…? The branch-dweller interrupts me: "The world is filled with answering-machines that do not know what they answer, nor why. Answering is all that matters to them." The bird concludes. The galaxy is riddled with conclusions, but we sink in hypotheses. The child falls on her bum and laughs, the mother laughs. The pigeon flies away. The old man greets a friend. I close my eyes and stare into a star.

Translated by Antonio D'Alfonso
The man who delivers clouds (selected poems), Guernica Editions, 2010

Le pigeon murmureur

Je m'assois dans un parc, les yeux fatigués de voir plus loin que ce vieil homme assis sur un autre banc. Il regarde le torrent de ferraille et d'humains qui passe dans la rue. Tout ça, c'est déjà des souvenirs. Une jeune femme apprend patiemment à son enfant à faire ses premiers pas. Le monde est plein de projets. Dis-moi, toi, pigeon aux yeux rouges, t'es pas exténué de chercher de la bouffe dans nos ordures? Le temps continue ailleurs pendant que l'oiseau me dévisage. Son œil vif me dit : «Tu le sais, je ne suis pas le seul, y'a de tes semblables qui font comme moi.» Bon, d'accord, mais ce n'est pas une raison… «L'univers est rempli de répondeurs qui ne savent pas ce qu'ils répondent ni pourquoi ils le font», me renvoie le ramier. «Ils répondent, c'est tout ce qui compte ici», finit-il par conclure. Les galaxies sont bourrées de conclusions mais nous n'en sommes qu'aux hypothèses. L'enfant est tombé sur le cul et rit avec sa mère, le pigeon s'envole, un ami est venu rejoindre le vieillard. J'ai fermé les yeux en regardant un soleil.

First appeared in *Là où finit la terre*
2009, Les éditions Les Herbes rouges (Montréal)

bill bissett

billbissett.com

born on lunaria far distant planet arrivd on erth on th first shutul 2 erth from th brite orange place wher we childrn provdid all th enerjee by combing sereenlee th yello orange lite evree morning   from th veree beginning eye wantid 2 write as owing 2 a sereez uv operaysyuns eye wasint abul 2 dance eye lovd putting books 2gethr wrote my first storee in an oxygen tent 11 watching th orange crush go thru tubes i was drinking it thru a straw go in n out uv my bodee   first reel pome black black n mor black aftr my first mothr went 2 spirit 14 deth deth n mor deth i was aware uv repitishyun n sound chanting eye was alwayze interestid in sound sylabul oktave leeps changes was n am alwayze wanting 2 xploor sound in poetree sound being poetree whn sound is th most important element uv th pome lungs throat mouth larynx beleef aksyun travl thruout canada n evreewher dewing reedings n art shows ther ar sew manee dimensyuns uv meening being not all uv them based on th transitiv verb or linear meening s cumming

most recent book *time* from talonbooks othr books *sublingual ths is erth thees ar peopul* also from talonbooks most recent cd *ths is erth thees ar peopul* with pete dako from blu loon prod

4thcumming book work in progress *th bear waiting 4 yu at th bottom uv th cave* now calld *novel from wch anothr versyun uv i get frenzeed just thinking abt it is time* th cd with pete dako n ambrose pottie n eric shenkman n penn kemp soon soon soon ✪

eye get frenzeed just thinking abt it   what

dont yu   what happend membr   that muskrat
time   eye need mor hed room   veree oftn n th
ferree ploughd on   4evr   thru th choppee   watrs
th zanee winds   n th back   ground catapulting   why
cud we see   2 know   is far 2   window   loud
eye did th   deposits   cries in th nite   citee all ovr
thru th evree   thing radiant th murmurs   defening yes
who at th atm   i saw mystakes   n th bop   entree spinach
caut them in   time evn at that sum   levl   sumtimez life
is sew much   like a trapeez   starring   yrselvs is b b
zee doubul u   w w wuh estern rangul   t t temspestuous
villagree raptyur   pithee jengmost scour   act evn th fansee
mer en jack   who asparagus wheet   road   gay sesamee
hey yu kno   triste or bettr th   cud sircumplex
koff koff both   th tunnul th play   sur cudint yu three
fold or tree   bold mooving ovr   th prairie   th cedars
n spruce fir   n willow sweeping   thru th hot yello orange
glow n planting   them selvs like   symphonee th ad such
yes mixtyur   alwayze changing   above a a th saphire
resounds   dusint it th prospektiv   land lord dusint pick
up chill   b ok or yes eye   hope orchids dis
n anchoves   n th wind cries thers   2 much sunshine
goblet   th jellee micro   fish   what they
yelld at each othr   rattuls my brain   pan fan dango creek
tremor n th watr   up gushing softr   n being yu wud think with
all theyr they cud   leev each othr   alone oh ward word n see
who can sat   say what way   triggerd they each in each
tried 2 solv   yes or no   its like an edmonton
wintr   ed mon ton   wintr morning eye sd th
sun n th kold   how it plays   on our minds n souls

—bill bissett ✪

sound poetree spokn word poetree in my life my historee with sound

in th crib uv kours we ar all dewing sound poetree th magik circus
uv manee alphabets   thn th kultur we ar born in2 tells us what n
what is alredee ther in our dna unkovrs itself n bcums operativ
my first memoreez as well as all that wer endless orange th colour
uv my first home planet lunaria   wher we childrn wud fold n en
fold th magikul orange lite that was evreewher 2 provide enerjee
4 all our homes   i wud wake up skreeming in remembrans uv that
life as i missd it sew much n erthling life seemd 2 me 2 b way 2
harsh 4 nothing

as i seriouslee bgan writing aftr my first n birth mothr went 2 spirit
deth deth n mor deth i wrote all ovr th page th sheet uv papr i was
aware uv vizual writing n that th onlee opsyun 4 writing need not b
in rektangular or versyuns uv square boxes   also th mesmerizing
sumtimes possiblee effekts uv repitishyun chanting mantra ovr n
ovr agen til th mind calms in its life alredee wrenchd from sew much
comfort th chanting can help make it seem sumhow tho tragikalee
acceptabul n is a plesyur in itself 4 th lungs throat larynx like
swimming also can b accompaneed as we go thru th watr with deep
breething enlarges our lung capasiteez our whol breething being

my best frend around 04 n erleer was arthur davis who much latr
as time can go in sum kind uv sequens wrote brillyantlee abt george
grant th brillyant philosphr n soshul historian who was a teecher
uv both arthur davis n myself n went on 2 b mor uv a teechr with
art as i had run away from home in manee wayze with my first boy
frend billie oliver   i was always looking 4 a way out uv solelee linear
logiks wch ar reelee based on traps 4 th self n othrs who wud follow
thos entangulments dew we evr wrest totalee 24/7 free uv   arts brothr
bob came back from studeez in europe   names picasso gertrude stein
jp sartre cocteau   huxley orwell richler his first novel was publishd ther
edith sitwell   records wer big thn n books 2 me aneeway i cud go 2 th
libraree th record store n get ee cummings ts eliot marianne moore
gertrude stein tennessee williams eugene oneil lillian hellman cather
capote n my hed heart n soul wer filld with all thees amayzing peopul
n sew manee othrs louis armstrong   reflections in a goldn eye all th
amayzing movee stars who had my familee 4 sew long n continuing

th first sound poetree spokn word recording i herd was edith sitwells
facade i was fascinatid n thrilld with it i was getting th idea that
poetree writing cud xist byond linear surface meening burroughs
joyce hart crane i livd in ths world matisse gris picassos lovrs
chagall on th walls listning as well 2 berg shoenberg bartok string
quartets kurt weil betrolt brecht lotte lenya three pennee opera
mozart brahms schubert chopin fats domino sarah vaughan ella
fitzgerald frank sinatra billy eckstein judy garland joni james th
ink spots frank lehrer whol worlds wer opning 2 me infinilee opn
ing 2 me no stoping as th chemikal brothrs 2day say thers no
stopping

n me n billy usd 2 walk thru th streets uv halifax all nite talking uv thees
peopul as well as carmen mcrae anita oday june christy johnny
mathis james baldwin giovanis room making plans 2 leev town n freeing
our minds 4evr sound n space in poetree michael mcclure allen ginsberg
denise levertov diane diprima ths kind uv bird flies backward a raisin in th sun
th whol world as we knew it was sew filld with possibiliteez reeding as well
marshall mccluhan sensing how th tradishyunal appul uv th narrativ was
falling in2 enriching peesus shares 4 evreebodee byond class n gendr
suprstishyuns n ordring langwages as cultural commands mor n mor n
mor n poetree was considrd a veree important part uv all ths reelee rev
olushyun uv consciousness

i was also reeding issak singer simone de beauvoir andre gide abert camus
jd salinger ee cummings gertrude stein stanzas in meditaysyun n ee cummings
wer my mentoring dreems   vizual poetree th space we write on can b fullee
xplooring all ovr th papr not onlee pomes in shapes uv things xcellent but as
well th innr shape uv th pome itself made outtr visibul n in sound th pome
can reelee b manee voices manee philosophikal linguistik loci not onlee
th trad transitiv verb kontrukts wch yeers latr i wrote abt in s th storee i 2
langwage is sound is not onlee th subjekt akting upon th objekt   yes yes

sew thats a littul bit uv my historee in sound poetree spokn word first time
4 me i was chanting plain delivree th ancient lord laydee uv th univers asks
us 2 b ovr n ovr agen n thn th sounds tuk off all ovr evreewher from evree
wher seemd like   that was in th advans mattress coffee shop on alma street
wch is spanish 4 soul n vancouvr around 1966 i had alredee startid n
thn from thn on i was well on my way n it keeps going dusint it yes ☺

kreeaysyun n writing

sew ium in vancouvr alone billy had returnd 2 halifax n working shelving books at th van publik libraree in th science n technolojee divisyun thn on burrard n robson wher hmv is now n writing spayshulee n a bit soundlee at leest spokn word n shy 2 find my own life with othrs trying thees pomes out with frends at work n rewriting n re writing n reeding thomas manns th magik mountain feeling thinking ium gonna b a writr i was maybe 18 by thn dewing mor n mor spayshul writing vizual writing

fast 4ward a littul bit sew creaysyun was always th result th end produkt 4 me uv writing n thn th next end produkt result uv writing 4 me was definitlee publishing living n writing with martina clinton n writing with lance farrell finding th sylabul th bottom line uttrans making pomes based solelee on that n thn a bit 4ward as nowun wud publish anee uv us n othrs like us in summr 62 startid blewointment press in vancouvr maxine gadd judith copithorne lance farrell martina clinton sam perry myself sew manee othrs who wer oftn politikul aktivists n poetree aktivists eye cud n did publish loving evree volume i wud had print sumtimes printing on old gestetenr milton acorn n dorothy livesay helpd us a lot as did earle birney n warren tallman

all ths help is veree oftn part uv th creaysyun n th development n th providid space manee manee isews uv blewointpress n likewise tish th prhaps mor universitee based publikaysyuns i lernd uv robert duncans writing uv wch ium huge fan n charles olson n othrs from ther th blewointment poets wer mor considerd th downtown poets nothing was 2 hard drawn we wud all meet at warren n ellen tallmans place jamie reid th thn gladys hindmarch her sew xcellent peter storeez manee othrs beth jankola david harris hart brody it was a thriving kultur within manee kulturs th thn daphne buckle who encouragd me a lot as well now daphne marlatt

kreeaysyun bring th work in2 being thru writing it n publishing it

all thees xcellent places 4 reeding out lowd flat five black spot cellar ad vans mattress koffee shop evenshulee van pub libraree robson square ubc simon frasr wher wuns maxine gadd ne me red on th same bill n 2gethr 4 hours n hours seemd like in th amayzing sun n sew manee peopul publishing getting it out n speeking words out lowd

spokn word out lowd making a nois taking it up n spouting it all out riding on a cadens riding on a riff a phrase a sylabul ridng on a song th rhythm not alwayze returning 2 th mnemonik centr or sides letting go uv alwayze evn i love thinking abt a pome i wrote erlee 60s calld th warmth uv human

companee wch bob cobbing in london england pickd 4 wun uv his publikay
syuns ther ths was big xcitement 4 me 4 all uv evreewher in th world as
spontaneous combustyun sound vizual konkreet poets wer rocking evreewher
d a levy cleveland okio bob cobbing clive fencott paula claire manee othrs yew k
dr wagner california dick higgins yew s poets in brazil chek poet ivro vroom
japan evreewher n we wud all write 2 each othr all th time n uv kours bpnichol
toronto who had previouslee his comox street pomes bin in vankouvr wundrfulee
he lovd gertrude stein as well n we wer both most proabablee neurologikalee
lyrik poets whos abiliteez ther cud transmute ourselvs in2 othr genres uv
writing as i did abt 7 approaches 2 writing lyrik narrativ non narrativ sound
vizual konkreet fuseyun poetree containrs seeing th pome in part as a containr
vessul his her storikaul writing politikul poetree conversaysyunal vois poetree
n sew on barry also was interestid in a wide range nothings bettr its all in how
we find our kreeaysyun s our vois es

sumtimes wun lettr or an entire sentens phrase on top uv each othr layerd
palimpsesting letting variaysyuns uv tapestreez yu cud say happn sum
times brekway from th line letting each lettr sylabul phrase fall down brek
up fall ovr spaces btween each word almost colums n brek up rising each
word lettr sylabul sentens phrase variaysyuns on all thees approaches
sumtimes creaysyun cums out uv th world wind thats oftn in our heds sumtimes
out uv it all being fallow in th hed n thn th outflowing th life uv th langwage
jumping spilling cawsing asserting cumming presenting lowd not arm
chairs poetree th ezt silent on th text but biting krackling devastating th well
worn upholstreez ther ar pickshurs in th lettrs lettrs in th images most langwages
wer ar originalee piktographik n thn all th sound poetree festivals that ar still
happning on th same bill as th four horsmen th best sound poetree group ther
evr was thn bob cobbing owen sound paula claire evreewun praktikalee iuv alredee
 mensyund heering othr great voices sheri -d wilson air plane paula n her pantees
 pome being sew rockd by thos kedrick james coleen thibadeau pony vega
heering myself being in a band mandan massacre 67 sonik horses 83 luddites
86-92 working n recordid as well as with thees othrs denis cornies pete dako
ambrose pottie gary shenkman penn kemp chris meloche bill roberts
ths all takes us in2 2011 yes how we moov our bouche 4 sound th titul uv our
next world tour adeena karasick n me bouche time a bouche in time its abt
bouche time we can n dew all rock each othr n th set lanwage patterns n get our
own thing stronglee out ther push let

th raging xcellent brillyant qualitees uv th word th langwage how sew manee wayze it
can happn writing n reeding with adeena karasick oral vokal festival 09 saskatoon
dewing sound poetree as well with penn kemp workman arts 09 n 08 its each lettr
sylabul phrase word pouring kaskading spillage uv lettrs langwage that dusint have
2 b kleend up is kleening up th poisonous sumtimes th dominas uv wun wayze onlee
uv using speech b b b b schkleeeeeeeeeeeeeeeeeeeeeee oshqwa yes what sounds
dew yu spontaneouslee make write down whatevr cums n sew yu dont get lockd in2
anee fixd posisyuns 2 much write down onlee say evree third word see n feel th
liberating effekt uv randomness admissyuns uv how much is reelee accidental th
loopholes chagrin n downfalls uv intensyunalitees steev mcafferty book north uv
intensyun wher we all live say ovr n ovr agen th origins or orangeness try it ✪

prformans praktise makes imperfekt n less intens relax in th zone

all thees things ar sew intrtwind each breth letting th breth go in2 th bottom uv th lungs n below mouth opn shaping th sounds dicksyun enunsiaysyun phrasing praktise makes imprfekt yr own wayze on uv all thees things wun time a littul whil aftr sum brain surgeree around 1970 reeding in warren tallmans class he was upset n stood up moovd 2 stop me whn i bgan chanting in non english words thn he realizd i was ok alrite n he relaxd n was fascinatid n enjoyd it i cudint stop th surprising 2 me at that time as well uttransing

if othr voices brek thru what yuv alredee prepard let them thos may b part uv uv kours what yu ar dewing if its a long song n yr with in a band thn thers lots uv cues bars counting uv kours alwayze wanting 2 b with yr reel vois 4 that song that chant as with each work it reelee may b diffrent eye startid 2 not want 2 smoke aneemor 2 xercise mor if its alredee writtn mostlee mewsik ium vokalizing sounding with ium wanting 2 find th vois from me 4 that work that serch may take qwite a few tries alone in my studio going ovr n ovr sum thing until it finds itself its important 2 remembr it reelee dusint have 2 b like aneething onlee itself mooving thru time n space n sound waves

wun time i was prforming with luddites n peter denny sd throwing down his mallets from his brillyant zylophone playing n sd out lowd 2 ovr 200 peopul bill bissett came in late no gerry collins th leed guitar playr sd he was not he was rite on th munee thr was a paws that seemd 2 long sew i went up 2 th mike n sd wasint that great wasint it convinsing we rehersd that well i noddid ovr 2 peter n gerry n murray favro rhythm guitar who seemd a littul xcellentlee dumfoundid n ther was xcellent applaws we wer all fine with it n continued playing by th time th band veree un4tunatelee was breking up eye had lernd all th cues prfektlee did i cum in late or was i on time weul nevr know n it dusint mattr but thats how strikt it can seem 2 get we did lots uv gigs 2gethr in southrn ontario it was a veree wundrful xperiens

th book is in yr hed workng with composr bill roberts in his apt in port colborne finding a vois 4 his mewsik rumours uv hurricane th recording studio was veree basik anothr wundrful xperiens we nevr did gigs 2gethr he wrote all his mewsik parts elektronikalee n his life was totalee changing as we wer working 2gethr thr was less rehersal thn wih luddites th work with that band is availabul *luddites* 86-91 on itunes *rumours uv hurricane* with bill roberts availabul thru red deer press but abt prformans feeling th thrill evree time in a band or not n th shaping uv phrases sounds oval

full wide opn sliding thru a half sound whatevr it is that is th closest 2 how
yu ar can b n what yu can dew with yr voice s let them out riff
 unlike luddites n bill roberts working with chris meloche also composr but
uv ambent mewsik no rhythm no melodee finding yr own uv thos if yu need
or want them n also going outside thos referenses yes 4 a whil its a wundrful
feeling also rainbow mewsik with chris meloche also with red deer press
did a 3 nite consert with mari osonai in london beautiful xperiens making
sounds singing chanting whil mari osoni was dansing ther rathr thn cues
keeping in synch with yu yrself n her th othr prson complementing n en
hansing inklewding sum randomness being th sound with th moovment
not see saw   2007

pete dako composr guitarist evree instrument also awesum 2 work with
am currentlee working with him a lot wev dun sum gigs 2gethr wun wndrful
yeer n wintr have brout out 2 cds 2gethr deth interrrupts th dansing from
red deer press ths is erth thees ar peopul coupul yeers ago with pete n
ambrose pottie we love jamming 2gethr strange how th phases go working
a lot a lot 2gethr n letting othr things happn prsonal work othr things
life etsetera same with th writing reelee not sticking 2 wun format with it
letting it change b interruptid allow finding serching   th tones n th
variaysyuns now wer working on time th nu cd complement 2 th latest
book *time* from talonbooks me n pete dako n ambrose pottie n eric
shenkman n penn kemp wer getting ther its cumming writing th words jamming
n fnding a maybe consistent versyun that can repeet itself with minor
changes n variaysyuns 4 gigs wch me n dermot foley nevr did but we had
a wundrful time his composing my words 4 sonik horses sumtimes i

reelee think i dont know sound song chant glips trops uv random nois
not evn trops sound lettrs stakatto yernng imploring improv roar
let th lettrs sing   we ar mooving in2 th futur in2 th futur now mor thn we
ar mor thn we can yet b from embrace wch is in time honey novick n me
a 20 min sound spokn word poetree work   4 canada speeks a hilary peech
producksyun honey novick n me n th stairs go n 4evr in hamilton art work
ellingtons in toronto manee places th wide opn possibilitees uv vois nuans
n evreething yu can dew with a sound poetree work partlee memorizd partlee
improv finding it 2gethr with th mewsik on cd uv chris meloche honey n me
n me by myself have also workd with helene ducharme an amasing opera
singr th three uv us dewing i dont want 2 such anee empire i just want 2
suck yu   n th 3 uv us at harborfront last sept 09 dewng eye hed galaxee song
from sublingual th nite uv th tribute 2 charles n jesse huiskin ths aint th rosedale
libraree she is a he is a she is a she is a heis a cum is a she is a cum he is a cum
he is a cum is a cummmmmmmmmmmmmmg n latr april 10 dewing spokn word
n sound poetree with th brillyant mewsik uv bowen mcconnie at th cabaret nite
uv th calgaree intrnashunal spokn word festival veree thrilling 4 me 2 b reeding
making sounds prforming with bowen mcconnies mewsik feeling sew in
synch with it with th mewsik in all thees xperiences thats 4 me th best whn
that happns on a theatr sound system ambient mewsik n like can happn
feeling evree second uv th xperiens a teeching 4 th rest uv our lives wer i
onlee 2 alwayze b knowing that each moment each moment each beet
beet each beet eee aaa ch ch see ch h h hu b b b eeeee t t t t

prompts

prompt 1 ♥

aftr sound poetree spokn word poetree in my life my historee with sound   try duets follo thru bcum
devotid 2 n with   chek out myself with honey novick in th embrace sound pome work 4 canada
speeks   on you tube being part uv a duet changes evreething n espeshulee yr usd 2 comfort zones
sew yu keep on exploring n enjoying n diskovring yes

prompt 2 ♥

aftr   kreeaysyun n writing   try riffing on enunseeating illusidating each lettr t t t
s s s go thru th alphabet out lowd allowing all th sound variaysyuns that can
happn with yu n yr xpressyun work

prompt 3 ♥

praktise makes imperfekt less intens   relax in th zone try out   b a part uv a band 4
a whil lerning th arrangement whn 2 cum in n go out   feelin at times yr vois es
merging n being distinktiv with instrumentz n th mewsik ✪

Regie Cabico is a poet and spoken word pioneer, having won the Nuyorican Poets Café Grand Slam in 1993 and taking top prizes in the 1993, 1994 & 1997 National Poetry Slams. Television appearances include two seasons on HBO's "Def Poetry Jam." His work has appeared in over 30 anthologies, including *Aloud: Voices from the Nuyorican Poets Café, Spoken Word Revolution & The Outlaw Bible of American Poetry*. He co-edited *Poetry Nation: A North American Anthology of Fusion Poetry* (Vehicule Press, 1998). He is a recipient of a 2008 Future Aesthetics Arts Award Regrant from The Ford Foundation/Hip Hop Theater Festival, three New York Foundation for the Arts Fellowships for Poetry and Multidisciplinary Performance, Larry Neal Awards for Poetry 2007 (third place) and 2008 (1st Place), a 2008 DC Commission for the Arts Poetry Fellowship. He received the 2006 Writers for Writers Award from *Poets & Writers* for his work teaching at-risk youth at Bellevue Hospital in New York. He is a former artist-in-residence at NYU's Asian Pacific American Studies Program and has served as faculty at The Banff Centre's Spoken Word Program, and at Kundiman, an Asian American Writers Retreat. As a theatre artist he has directed two plays for the 2007 & 2008 Hip Hop Theater Festival, *Elegies in the Key of Funk* and *The Other Side*. He received three New York Innovative Theater Award Nominations for his work in *Too Much Light Makes the Baby Go Blind. The Kenyon Review* recently named Regie Cabico the "Lady Gaga of Poetry."

He is the Youth Program Coordinator for Split this Rock Poetry Festival and is the artistic director of Sol & Soul, an arts and activist organization. He is the co-founder of Sulu Dc, a monthly Asian American Performance Series, and is the co-director of Capturing Fire: A Queer Spoken Word Summit. He is pleased to be returning as part of The Banff Centre's 2011 Spoken Word Faculty. ✪

Photo credit, Lestalusan

i got it bad
for nina simone

nina look at the sky april clouds hang a fat
sappy syrup on my saddest day
played you monday night
my day unbearable as a wool coat in april
came back to find my bed empty as a tire swing in winter

nina in my saddest hour
you have crooned me over a cruel block
of loneliness when unrequited love
is an italian bartender who flirts with you
from the torso and offers you
more lies than a tiramisu

yes nina, monday night i was so terribly sad
sadder than a parlour of long veils,
carrying groceries up too many flights of stairs

& the sound of your voice so full & broad-shouldered
made the day with all its drama into bangles & diamonds
nina you made me a culinary priestess
you placed a bojangling spell on me

crooning to the sizzling oil as i pranced like a tiger
among the tambourines & tin cans
the raindrops applauded & the single wine glass wept

because i found my inner nina
nina nubuan mona lisa woman painted
with egyptian mascara

you use silence the way a woman's figure
made jesus bend at the knees bend ache break
to the will of your beautifully blessed contralto

crackling bittersweet as you held a phrase
long enough for green finches to fly out the winter gloom
nina, the storyteller, nina a river lonely as hell,
nina tossed like an ark full of sparrows

you can honky tonk the bones of kali
& steal the lightning from her toes
listen nina, i think it's gonna rain again
human kindness is overflowing, flowing harder
even in the cruelest time

—Regie Cabico ✪

In 1992, I graduated, a semester early, from New York University's Tisch School of the Arts. With my BFA in Acting and Musical Theatre (and a minor in East Asian Studies & Journalism), I read *Back Stage Magazine* religiously. Call me a Filipino male version of Irene Cara's triple-threat diva, Coco Hernandez, in the movie *Fame*. A decade before I heard the caramel-coloured, multi-racial, diva belting, "Remember my name, Fame!" & singing Walt Whitman's, "I Sing the Body Electric," and it turned out to be the catalyst that *tour jeté-d* me from Washington, DC, to New York City.

✳

A year hanging out in New York's stand-up comedy clubs, cabaret bars, and at open mics left me unfulfilled. Where were my mentors and role models? Coco Hernandez was a screen persona. Were there any Filipino triple-threats? There were literally no parts for me except for a musical of Ghandi's life called *5 Guys Named Mo-hatma*. One day as I roamed the East Village looking for work, I stepped into the St. Mark's Bookshop. I saw anthologies of Asian American poets and queer writers. The 90s generated a multicultural democracy of diverse voices. What was happening in American literature was not reflected on film, television, or in the theatre. Should I write poetry, go to massage school, or get a law degree?

✳

The Poetry Calendar was an 11x17 sheet of coloured paper that listed every reading and open mic in "the city." I wrote poems and short prose, read my work and submitted it to The Writers' Voice Westside Y (Master Class). Jessica Tarahata Hagedorn was teaching fiction and Agha Shahid Ali was teaching poetry. These artists were writers whose work I'd read, admired and they were of the Asian-American diaspora—Jessica Hagedorn being Filipino. I submitted the same manuscript to both teachers, except changed the line breaks to

look like poetry. Though I was rejected from Hagedorn's class, I was accepted into Ali's.

✳

Essex Hemphill's poetry and essays fuelled me. Reading his poetry dealing with subjects like AIDS, HIV, loss and being an African-American gay man in Washington DC gave me the audacity to explore my own sexual identity candidly. ntozake shange's *for colored girls who considered suicide when the rainbow wuz enuff* taught me how rage, grief & poetry can soar in a black box. These poets gave me my two essential slam poems, "gameboy" and "Check One," published in *Aloud: Voices from the Nuyorican Poets Cafe*.

✳

In 1993, you'd have to be desperate, looking for crack, dodging bullets, or a homeless mole person hobbling up the sewers just to read your poetry on 3rd Street between Avenue B & C. With craggily poets hunched over wine, the tall ceilings and balcony was the church-like Alphabet City home for poets. There was something sacred and ornery about the Nuyorican Poets Café; poets of all ages and styles were downtown characters mingling in another universe. And this is what I never witnessed while I was an NYU student.

When I signed up to read in the Wednesday night open mic, I didn't know what the numbers were being called out for. When I found out that you could win $10, I thought: "I need ten dollars. I've got to win this." The idea of the poetry slam as a poetry competition written and performed for the people, and judged by the people, was the basis for Marc Smith's invention. A construction worker and poet, Smith gave poets three minutes to recite their original works without music, props, or costumes. Poets were being judged by people who didn't know anything of poetry. The motto goes: "if you want to be a judge, you're over-qualified."

I didn't know it then, but I was performing in what I call the end of the first wave of the poetry slam. Paul Beatty, Edwin Torres, Maggie Estep, Reg E Gaines, Hal Sirowitz, Willie Perdomo, and Dael Orlandersmith were some of the artists who defined the New York slam. The Nuyorican Poets Café named these artists their All-Stars and they were already touring internationally. Bob Holman, poet and poetry activist, was the Friday Night Slam host, and his zany style and love for words came through in his intros and outros for the slammers. (Holman was busy filming *The United States of Poetry* and some of the All-Stars were on MTV with 30-second poetry videos.)

After losing on four Wednesday nights, I finally won the slam and got to compete in the Friday night slot. There were usually five or six slam poets. That night Bob Holman put 12 poets on stage. It was a fierce line-up; I did a comic prose poem called "Benny's Burritos" about a fleeting gay romantic encounter, a poem about the lions coming to life at The New York Public Library and "Check One," a poem about Filipino America identity. The crowd went bozonkers, and I got a perfect score of 30. I felt like I won Olympic gold! A week later, *New York Magazine* released an issue called *The Beats are Back*, with Edwin Torres on the cover. Inside the magazine were slam poets, and placed in the centrefold with a staple through my face was my photo, labelled, "The Nuyorican Anonymous." I didn't care, I was just happy to be in the issue. My theatre classes at Tisch School of the Arts never prepared me for this kind of adulation. In fact, the drama teachers made me feel as if I couldn't act. But the slam wasn't about "acting," because it was about breaking the fourth wall, playing yourself, and writing the role that you were made to perform.

I was the first poet slammer to bring a theatrical polish to the genre. I incorporated what I developed from stand-up comedy and musical theatre onto the slam stage. I was off-book and if I needed to read a poem, I brought with me a big black binder with my poems in plastic sheets as if I were doing a staged reading. I looked at a slam poem as if it were a musical show-stopper. As this slam wave was ending, my poems were published in *Aloud: Voices from the Nuyorican Poets Café* edited by Miguel Algarin, Nuyorican founder and poet,

and Bob Holman. *My Grand Slam Finals* with Anne Elliott, Shirley Bradley LeFlore & Julie Patton were narrated by Algarin in the introduction. I won the slam and channelled my inner Coco Hernandez, not belting Whitman, but reciting my own, out-of-the-closet verses.

Other poets of colour with theatre backgrounds would find their way to the slam stage, most notably, Saul Williams & Sarah Jones. But also activists like Alix Olson and Carlos Andres Gomez who seemingly approach slam as a way to get their political messages across. Over the last two decades, I have seen the poetry slam become performance driven. We have reached and completed a phase which I call the Hollywood blockbuster slam poem. If you compared slam to cinema, and if in 1993 Technicolor was discovered and *The Wizard of Oz* was made, within a few years we reach the over-the-top performance styles, which are formidable and copy-able. We reached the Spielberg era of slam; the *Jaws*, the *Star Wars* era. I am not knocking Spielberg at all or any of these iconoclastic slam poets. Poetry evolves and so does the slam. A great slam poem is a great slam poem and stands the test of time.

In writing this history, I am reminded of a time when the poetry slam was an open mic for "writers." In those days, you could read from your journal and get a perfect score. And as this wave came to a close, another period did as well. Danny Hoch, a solo performance artist from NYU was making his debut at P.S. 122. I consider Hoch the last of the great performance artists that included Tim Miller, Karen Finley, Eric Bogosian, Spalding Gray & John Leguizamo. These artists, to varying degrees, have crossed over to a commercial level—Whoopi Goldberg, most notably, who won a Tony, a Grammy & an Oscar, was the centre square in *Hollywood Squares* and who continues to "slam" her political passions on *The View*. ✪

WRITING EXERCISE

EXERCISE 1 ♥

The List Poem
Write a list of "50 Things That Drive You Crazy."

A strong list poem has variety and general detail, i.e. people, places, things, days of the week, foods, cartoon characters, TV shows, etc. Use sensory details: Things that you smell, taste, see, touch, and hear. It's not important that you come up with 50 items but you should be trained to write for the allotted time that you give yourself. I usually have the class write for 10-15 minutes.

Use a list of words or phrases. Break the images down: If it's dogs that drive you crazy, is it pugs or pomeranians? And is it pomeranians barking in the middle of the night, or is it pugs who stare at you?

Avoid abstractions: Racism, Homophobia, Poverty....Come up with an image. Instead of Poverty – Try: Shaking pennies from a piggy bank. Towards the last third of the writing time continue the list but shift to things that drive you crazy in a "good" way, i.e. tiramisu, Brad Pitt, Sunday afternoons, honorariums.

Below are some examples written by three students in the 2010 Spoken Word Program at The Banff Centre. It is the only spoken word program of its kind and the director is Sheri-D Wilson. These writings are by people who were in my workshop.

"the Canadian inferiority complex, hippies telling me "it's all good," beach culture, vertical suburbias, black licorice, people who talk big but never follow through, people who actually believe the world will end in 2012, fatalism in all forms, tragic attitudes, BOO TRAGEDY, self-sabotaging friends, March Madness, the Toronto Raptors, poetry slams, sunflower seeds, espresso, the essays of David Foster Wallace, shopping, etc."
Chris Gilpin

"techno music from the apartment upstairs, panty lines, reality TV, rain splashing on pants when walking in it, large egos, misogynists, people who don't smile, pedestrians who don't understand driving, drivers who don't understand pedestrians, bad grammar, know-it-alls, sloppy kisses, dark chocolate, my cat biting and rubbing her face in my hair, my cat sleeping on the radiator, my cat spooning with me, my cat on my lap, neck rubs, taking risks, Johnny Depp, making a film, coffee with Bette, hummingbirds, Sudoku Puzzles, meditation, etc."
Pippa Hirst

"lemon pledge scent in restaurants because it smells like someone died, high-pitched whistling of my brother, crowded places, people who don't respect your personal space in a crowded place, 2pm in the afternoon on a weekday at work, energy suckers as friends, sweatpants with "juicy" written on the butt, losing pens, plagiarism, a novel to read where you can lose track of the time when reading it, cuddling, plunging my hands into a basket of soft wool, the feeling of taking an ice-cold drink of water and feeling it move down your throat, watching the stars, being in the rain, being the first person to break the surface of the water in the pool, grilled cheese sandwiches, riding in a zodiac on the ocean, whale watching, etc."
Mary Pinkowski

EXERCISE 2 ♥
"The Urge" Poem

With the list generated, write an urge poem. Start each line with, "I have the urge to…" and then incorporate the images and phrases from the crazy list. Consider verb choices and focus on image and specificity. For example, "I have the urge to lie. I have the urge to cry. I have the urge to ask why…" doesn't give me a picture… add details, specific wheres? whats? & with whoms? "I have the urge to drink cold beer from your hands…" evokes something sensory.

EXERCISE 3 ♥
Create a Variation

The basic form of performance poetry and lyrics is the list. Anne Elliott, is a slam poet who performed with me in the first wave of slam. Her influences are seen in the performance art confessional texts of Karen Finley. horehound stillpoint, of San Francisco, uses the list with queer punk rock audacity. I have included their poems here. Please reference A LONE LITANY, by Anne Elliott and note what sections, "THINGS THAT DRIVE ME CRAZY/URGE" have resonance.

DISCUSSION ⇢
You have created a unique list that provides a strong reaction, positive or negative, in you. These triggers are important in slam. Now, take one of these images and break it down, explaining your love or hate. What's the conflict? In a slam poem there is an enemy, an antagonist. And if not, ask yourself who, "Who is the hero?" Odes to rock stars, or to the attractive guy or girl behind the Starbucks counter are great fodder for a slam poem. What's the conflict? What's the message? The crazy list has a simple, clear sometimes humorous message. ✪

PERFORMANCE EXERCISE

EXERCISE ♥

Whisper, Scream, Sing – Dive into Poetry

There is no simple method or exercise to inspire an honest, committed poetry performance. In working with students, especially beginners, it's key to note to them that as a poet performing a poem, you are diving into the world of the poem.

Think about what you need to be doing in the world of the poem you are about to perform. Are you breaking up with someone? Finally telling someone that you have a crush on them? Are you saving the world from racism, homophobia, or apathy? Are you convincing someone to leave his or her job, glorifying or paying homage to a deceased loved one?

Especially in the poetry slam, you must raise the stakes; perform from the most up against the wall, climactic moment you can conjure. Your poem is an aria without singing, the Broadway showstopper you were meant to perform. Your job is to relive the emotions you went through as you wrote the poem.

Keep in mind that performing a poem is not the recitation of words; the poem has a complex series of emotional colours and levels that you can draw upon with voice, body gesture, and facial expressions. The poem is a series of words, phrases, images for the audience to catch, hold, and take in.

Ask yourself: "Who am I?" in the poem. Poems require certain aspects of our personality: our presidential side, our truck driver, our inner wallflower, our lusty lush, our preacher pontificating our gospel truth.

(While working with a student who had no idea what to do with her hands or voice in a poem, the words "flower," "fire," and "hushed footfall" came up. I ask her to physical-ize the "flower" in her hand, hold the "fire" to let the sensation of "hushed footfall" rush through her body and see how the words affect her stance and vocals.)

I developed this exercise while teaching at New York City's Project Reach. First, I taped off a section on the floor that would indicate the stage. I showed the students centre stage; stage left (poet's left); stage right (poet's right); upstage (away from the audience); and downstage (towards the audience). Then I had poets make their entrance CENTRE STAGE and would have them whisper, sing, and shout a line of their poetry.

A whisper is a stage whisper, one that is breathy but also audible and articulate. Singing forces the performer to explore the vocal possibilities of pitch, sung vowels and staccato rhythms. Shouting has the poet explore her/his full vocal possibilities, being able to project to the back of the room and command a declamatory presence useful for slam performance.

This exercise also brings about an untapped sense of play for the poet and the opportunity to really "own" the stage along with the freedom from the page to make vocal choices. I also encourage poets to make physical choices with gesture.

Diving into the emotional world of the poem requires sense memory, whole-hearted commitment, and an ability to "read" the audience, acknowledging that they are there and that they will trust you on the poetic/storytelling journey that you are about to take them on. Think about where you yourself need to go emotionally in the poem, the arc and flow of the drama unfolding. From the first line to the end of the poem you should have been transformed, and so should the audience. ✪

George Elliott Clarke (OC, ONS, PhD) is the son of William and Geraldine Clarke, themselves descendants of African-American immigrants to Nova Scotia. A poet-academic, he received an Honours BA in English in 1984 (University of Waterloo), MA in English in 1989 (Dalhousie University), PhD in English in 1993 (Queen's University). In 1994, Clarke was appointed Assistant Professor of English and Canadian Studies at Duke University. Concurrently, he also served as the Seagram Visiting Chair in Canadian Studies at McGill University (1998-99). In 1999, Clarke accepted an appointment at the University of Toronto, where he is the inaugural E.J. Pratt Professor of Canadian Literature, a position established specifically for a poet-professor.

Clarke has issued nine poetry texts, three chapbooks, four plays in verse (and three opera libretti), a novel, a scholarly essay collection, and edited two anthologies. He has two titles in translation: in Chinese and Romanian. Clarke has also won laurels for his work as an anthologist and scholar of African-Canadian literature, a field of study that he has pioneered. His honours include: The Archibald Lampman Award for Poetry (1991), The Portia White Prize for Artistic Excellence (1998), A Bellagio Center (Italy) Fellowship (1998), The Governor-General's Literary Award for Poetry (2001), The National Magazine Gold Award for Poetry (2001), The Dr. Martin Luther King, Jr. Achievement Award (2004), The Pierre Elliott Trudeau Fellowship Prize (2005), The Frontieras Poesis Premiul (Romania, 2005), The Estelle and Ludwig Jus Memorial Human Rights Award (2005), The Dartmouth Book Award for Fiction (2006), The William P. Hubbard Award for Race Relations (2008), The Eric Hoffer Book Award for Poetry (2009), Appointment to the Order of Nova Scotia (2006), and Appointment to the Order of Canada (2008). Clarke also holds seven honorary doctorates. ✪

Hymn to Portia White (II)

Portia, oh Portia, oh Portia White—
Voice like silver and skin like night,
You made each song a flaming dart—
A meteor to light each heart.

Born for glory, never forget—
The day's not done when sun has set.
Behind you glimmers History;
Before you glitters Destiny.

Come out of Truro, Lil Zion,
Where Love is pure contradiction:
White-robed Baptists face white-sheet Klan,
Both preaching love for God and man.

Stroll through the Marsh, hear water speak
New Testament Hebrew and Greek.
Raise the church roof, raise it up high:
Watch Caesar Jesus stride the sky.

King Jesus rides a milk-white horse:
The Cobequid River, you will cross.
No man's a-gonna hinder you:
Let oceans cry all gospel blues.

Stand proud in a cold field of snow,
Tell Nova Scotia, you must go,
Sail to Cuba, fly to Brazil,
Entrance the crowds, enchant and thrill.

Take to New York, hear critics praise
Your voice that sets stone hearts ablaze.
Conquer London, and quake the Queen:
Beauty like yours, there's never been.

By and by, you lay down burdens:
Sweet Jesus heals all your hurtin.
You go home to our Lord and are free:
African Baptist prophecy.

Oh Coloured gal, our very own
Down-to-earth genius by God's Throne.
You're our glory, we, each freed slave:
The North Star is your lustrous grave.

—George Elliott Clarke ✪

I—INKING YOUR VOICE

If poetry is akin to song, what worth is a song unsung?
No good poem is silent.

To speak out, to be heard, to be a voice crying in the wilderness, or to be a voice shouting down injustice, you must first know who you are, what your voice is.

Every voice is unique, but the superb poet has a voice that is inimitable in authority and in his or her personal "signature" or style.

Who are you and what should you want to talk about?

To answer this question, you need to understand your own personal dictionary, that is to say, the words that come immediately to your mind when you let yourself think about just anything at all.

The reason is, your personality is a function of your vocabulary: You can't be—enact or embody—a social role unless you hold, deep within, the words that construct it.

Let's find out who you might be and fathom your most profound concerns.

CATALOGUE

On computer screen or plain paper, take several minutes—as many as you like—to list nouns—only persons, places, things—separated only by commas.

Do not form sentences; deny yourself verbs and adjectives.

I give you my own spontaneous example:

Tongue, train, coins, keyboard, stapler, window, coffee, tea, rat, bookmark, books, eagle, ocean, cup, fountain pen, ink, keychain, T-shirt, napkin, letter-opener, knife, CDs, black velvet, printer, clock, desk-lamp, photographs, chequebooks, Cuba, New Orleans, masks, seashells, stones, rocks, French fries, Nova Scotian flag, motorcycle helmet, scroll, parchment, filing cabinet, office chair, crucifix, voodoo doll, magnifying glass, briefcases, wastepaper basket, garbage can, pastel paints, DVDs, canvas bags, CD player, audiotape cassettes, suits, urns, candleholders, goblet, wine, beer, milk, wife, chocolate, tiger, documents, sculptures, candles, pyramids, motorcycle, Mom, Dad, ribbons, daughter, false teeth, pencils, hardwood floors, sunlight, dusk, angel, paper clips, file folders, garage, grass, roses, blackberries, lilac bush, clothesline, crows, squirrels, leopard-spot patterns, envelopes, Violence in the Arts, *The Scofield Reference Bible*, long-gun registry, electric fan, rum, Mauritius, tape recorder, table, photo album, posters, Eric Kroll's *Beauty Parade*, Bloor Cinema Membership 2011, *The Hermit of Africville*, sandals, Sappho, *Riding with Rilke*, Duke University, University of Toronto, shadow, ice, apple blossoms, whip, pulp, maggots, pears, wasps, grapes, wax, honey...

The purpose of the catalogue, the creation of which is an eternal process, is to tell you what nouns at any given moment in your life occupy your consciousness and define your being. Your duty is to make your literature—or orature (Chinweizu, Jemie, & Madubuike, 1983)—out of these constituent particles of being.

Example: Any one word or more can inspire a composition: The leopard-spot-patterned shadow upon the squirrel resembles sudden ink splattered from a fountain-pen—or coffee that has fallen like tears. You take rum until dusk overtakes you.

If you read a catalogue aloud, you'll discover that it possesses its own intrinsic rhythm, which will be—guaranteed—hypnotic. Try it.

MEMORIZE

The poetry recital/reading IS a performance, even if you are a heavily decorated, sedentary, literary critic. You must MEMORIZE the poem to OWN it and DELIVER it as you like. ✪

II—VOICING POETRY

I was 15 years old, in 1975, when I began to write "songs"; a year later, the rhymes turned into poetry, that is to say, "free verse."

It took another ten years to find my own "voice"; it took still another 15 years for me to feel comfortable with it, to accept it.

My voice is a fusion of Black Halifax working-class argot—guttural grammar, blues cusses, moans, slurs, stutters—the Bible, and British-oriented education. I try to write how the people talk—TALK; and the practice of Shakespeare and all the other writers is just gravy—or sugar—on top.

Poetry is emotionally and intellectually tense song and talk: Really the Blues.

Poetry is an aunt sayin, "Without Jesus, how could there be serendipity?"

Poetry is overhearing a man say, "He want nice stuff and he keen to stuff nice gals."

Poetry is overhearing a woman say, "That dirty slut is even wearing my underwear."

Poetry is slang and it's vulgar, just as much as it's high-falutin and political.

Poetry is every rhetorical trick in Richard A. Lanham's *Handlist of Rhetorical Terms* (1991).

Get some. Come wit the truth or leave your bitch-ass home!

What I like to do in my poetry is slam together different kinds of speech—just as I used to hear all around me as a Haligonian youth, "back in the day":

⇢To the Poet

(Pace Constance Garnett's translation of Alexander Pushkin's Russian verse)

>   Poet! Damn you if you crave public love!
> People clap raucously, then, fickle, stop.
> Fools don scholars' tassels, bray their critiques,
> While crowds' hoorays chill—or scald—your marrow.
>   Best to stand Caesar-calm, statue-austere:
> It's majesty, yes, to dwell distantly,
> Castled in your own soul, free and aloof!
> Perfect your flowers, distill their liqueur-dreams,
> Ignoring all praise of your past confections.
> Judge for yourself the success of your art:
> Your own strict taste dictates your flowers' vintage sweetness.
>   Do you want joy? Let the pack bay and howl:
> Let them snarl and spit on your altar's flames
> And breathe your temple's triumphant perfumes!

Every text is a performance text—if you can feel the emotion inside it.

Take Psalm 23. By stressing different words in the first phrase, you change the tone and even the sense of the prayer:

THE Lord is my shepherd: **There's only one.**

The LORD is my shepherd: **HE means business.**

The Lord IS my shepherd: **Fact can't be doubted.**

The Lord is MY shepherd: **He ain't available to anyone else. Nope!**

The Lord is my SHEPHERD: **He be pastoral.**

Depending on your mood, and what you wish to communicate, your interpretation of a poem—your performance of it—will move your audience. "Thy word is truth," declareth Christ. *Amen to that!*

First appeared in *20 Canadian Poets Take On the World: The Exile Book of Poetry in Translation*.
2009, Exile Editions

Do not be confused or mislead: the poetry recital IS a performance.

You should prepare as an actor prepares: know the 'script'! Know how to 'act' it out.

Props, costumes, add to theatricality, but are NOT mandatory.

Vocal inflections, facial expressions, posture, pose, 'attitude,' tone: All communicate as directly as do words.

Practice speaking into a microphone, and recording and playing your voice back: Learn how you sound—and how to project that sound.

YES: PROJECT! Sometimes you need to compete with bar-crowd noises, or windy conditions, or an air conditioner, or the raucous event next door. All proceeds best if you know how to PROJECT your voice over any din OR can convince the extra-noise sources to calm themselves or to be calmed (or turned off).

MODULATE your voice as you need: Be LOUD and soft, RAUCOUS and even, as the material demands. Every poem is a piece of theatre waiting to be embodied and spoken.

Wanna PLAY some music? Go ahead. BUT, usually, it's tricky for POET and musician to perform together UNLESS the musician plays 'under' the words, or the poet SINGS, or the musician only plays when the poet ain't SPEAKIN.

ENUNCIATE too—even slang—so that words and their parts can be heard distinctly. Thy poetry is LOST when thy words slur all over your tongue and teeth and lips.

The Reciting Poet is part-actor and part-singer: Have FUN up there, 'on stage,' reminding your audience of how ancient this MAGIC is.

A good SPEAKER of VERSE weaves an oral/aural universe that is—or may seem—more spontaneously emotive and actual than the 'real' world everyone calls home.

GOT a point to make, a song to unleash, a prayer to utter, a lover to praise, an enemy to chastise? Perform it in remembered and MEMORABLE verse.

You can BE funny, angry, reverential, 'cool,' nasty, sweet, dirty, wistful, nostalgic, prophetic, political, plain, mystical, meditative, analytical, scatological, funky, zany, etc.

THOU MUSTN'T BE libellous, slanderous, hate-mongering, panic-inducing, seditious (unless attacking undemocratic practices), etc.: IF in DOUBT / Leave it OUT.

Have NO fear. Preserve Freedom-of-SPEECH. THAT's poetry.

Thou, SPEAK-ING/SINGING, that's POETRY!

RHYME?!! It be GOOD. *Can I get a witness?*

✪

Marcia

Remember your lilac perfume the rain only magnified,
Your kiss like baked apples—cinnamon all over,
And the orange curving of your tensed thighs,
Your body, lean and warm as July.

Remember the merciless rose in your black hair—
And the black hair of your lord-have-mercy rose—
Cola-sweet, cashmere-soft, cocoa-scented.
We snoozed under stars that were … gold earrings.

Now I awake to stars like dried-up sunflowers,
Finger thorny words in spotlight darkness.

Oh girrrrllll, whaddya mean
You distrust these metaphors?

Bellissima mia,
We had another way of speaking...

When we were honest.

First appeared in *Sons of Lovers: An Anthology of Poetry by Black Men*
2000, Oyster Knife Publishing

Paul Dutton

Poet, novelist, essayist, and oral sound artist, Paul Dutton has been pushing the boundaries of literary expression for more than 40 years, in books, recordings, and live performances, solo and collaborative, in print and film, on TV, radio, and the Web. He has performed in literary and musical contexts throughout Canada and across the USA, Europe, and South America. Dutton's artistic focus continues to be the exploration of consciousness and perception through the creation of multisensory works, employing written poetry and prose, visual poetry, and the sonic dimensions of language and oral expression.

Dutton began publishing in Canadian literary magazines in 1965, and in 1970 joined fellow poets Rafael Barreto-Rivera, Steve McCaffery, and the late bpNichol to form The Four Horsemen, ubu.com/sound/four_horsemen.html, a group that revolutionized poetry readings, introducing elements of sound poetry, theatre, and music within the context of highly energized performances. The group issued records and books, and travelled extensively across Canada and into the USA and Europe, until the untimely death of Nichol in 1988. The group's ensemble and solo works were newly treated and interpreted in the 2007 play *The Four Horsemen Project*, which won awards in Toronto and toured in Canada and Europe.

A primary international exponent of sound poetry, Dutton has also maintained an output of writing for the page, accumulating credits in a multitude of literary magazines and journals, and publishing books of poetry and fiction. His essays have appeared in Canadian literary and scholarly publications, and his poems continue to be included in anthologies in Canada, the USA, and the UK.

In 1989, Dutton joined forces with the free-improvisation band CCMC, streamlined since 1993 to a trio, comprising Dutton, Michael Snow (piano and synthesizer), and John Oswald (alto sax). Other collaborations have included the sound-voice group Five Men Singing and the poetry-music group Quintette à Bras.

Books by Paul Dutton include: the poetry collections *Right Hemisphere, Left Ear* (Coach House Press, 1979); *Aurealities* (Coach House Books, 1991; on the Web at archives.chbooks.com/online_books/aurealities/); *Visionary Portraits* (Mercury Press, 1991); and *Partial Additives* (Underwhich Editions, 1994); and the novel *Several Women Dancing* (Mercury Press, 2002).

He also has two solo CDs, *Mouth Pieces* (OHM Editions, 2000) ubu.com/sound/dutton.html; and *Oralizations* (Ambiances Magnétiques, 2005), and his collaborative work can be heard on the CD *Five Men Singing* (Victo, 2004) and the CCMC CD *Accomplices* (Victo, 1998). ✪

Photo credit, Eberhard Dolinsky

Mercure

pois(s)on

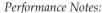

Performance Notes:
"Mercure" (mercury) is performed by using special vocal effects on the phonemes (units of speech-sound) of the French word *poison* (poison), which shifts at the climactic centre of the piece to *poisson* (fish). The phonemes of *poisson* are then performed with the same effects and in reverse order, providing a symmetrical structure, with the one difference of the *sss* sound of *poisson* rather than the *zzz* sound of *poison*. A video performance can be found at:
http://www.youtube.com/user/WordsAloud2#p/u/7/zCaCHyj4ozk

Begin by repeating a gentle, voiceless "bubble sound," done by bringing puckered, saliva-wet lips together and parting them with gentle release of air through saliva. Alter pitch by constriction and contraction of lip muscles, and play with various effects, moving the sound around the lips and the resonating mouth cavity, with occasional breath-bursts through the gentle suction, generally altering rhythm, volume, and intensity, gradually incorporating the percussive sound of the lips and explosions of breath, all voiceless until culminating in a forceful repetition of the voiced letter *p*.

Once the *p* is established, combine it with the phoneme *w*, first through pursed lips, eventually dropping out the *p* and slowly opening up the lips, ad libbing variations in rhythm, pitch, and duration throughout the process. Once the *w* is established, combine it with the phoneme *ah*, ad libbing play with *wah*. Eventually drop the *w*, and work with the *ah* for an extended period, gradually shifting location from the front of the mouth towards the back, first adding a nasal tone, then taking the sound into the throat and adding rasping and gurgling qualities to it.

With the *ah* established in the throat, move fluidly into a drone on the letter *z* (voiced sibilant), soon building rhythmic elements into it and eventually moving into a protracted nasalized drone on the phoneme *ohn*, using the tongue for rhythmic invention on the consonant sound while maintaining the drone, then sustaining the *n* and drawing it back into the throat with a fuzz effect, stopping suddenly and exclaiming very loudly and explosively:

PWA PWA PWA PWA [making the *A* raspy] // PWA-ZZZ PWA-ZZZ PWA-ZZZ PWA-ZZZ //
PWAZZZ-OHN PWAZZZ-OHN PWAZZZ-OHN PWAZZZ-OHN //
PWASSS-OHN PWASSS-OHN PWASSS-OHN PWASSS-OHN // PWA-SSS PWA-SSS PWA-SSS
PWA-SSS // PWA PWA PWA PWA

Brief pause—about as long as is required to take a deep breath.

Start a sustained drone on *n* in the back of the throat, with a fuzz effect, gradually introducing rhythmic play with that consonant and bringing in a simultaneous, protracted nasalized drone on the phoneme *ohn*. When it feels right (i.e., when the *ohn* drone is well established, and before it gets tedious), change to a rhythmic repetition of the phoneme *s* (unvoiced sibilant), gradually lengthening the rhythmic units until a sustained hiss is achieved. Thereafter move back in reverse order through the various sounds described in paragraphs four, three, and two, concluding with the repeated voiceless "bubble sound."

—Paul Dutton ✪

First appeared in *Additives*
1988, Imprimerie Dromadaire, Toronto

Becoming a Poet

I've always loved words, and from the age of nine wanted to be a writer, but only in my last year of high school did I start writing poetry, which at that time, for me, as for many beginning poets, was mainly an outlet for personal feelings. At university I gained a greater appreciation of the sonic dimension of poetry, especially in the writing of Gerard Manley Hopkins, Dylan Thomas, and E. E. Cummings.

In my early twenties I began publishing in poetry magazines, and was increasingly exploring the sound potential of words rather than just their immediate meaning, using them instead for purely rhythmic effect, for their colourful sound qualities, and for evocation instead of plain statement. I was beginning to feel the potential of language for expressing something outside my personal feelings and ideas, something both within language and beyond it, something I could sense but not quite put into words.

Me and Sound Poetry

Around that time, I met a fellow poet, bpNichol, from whom I learned, among other things, about visual poetry and sound poetry. When I first heard Nichol performing sound poetry, in a duo with David W. Harris (later David UU, pronounced "Double-U") in 1968, I found it an electrifying and (I'll admit it) a frightening experience. They wailed, stuttered, bellowed, and chanted, effecting direct visceral communication, with few words or none at all. It was loud, it was powerful, it was scary. But my excitement rapidly overcame my fear. Here was a new fusion of the literary and the musical, a hybrid medium that transformed both elements in a way that was rich with thrilling and adventurous potential. I had to try it. And when I did, I took to it very well; well enough that about a year-and-a-half later Barrie (that's bp) invited me to join him and two other poets, Steve McCaffery and Rafael Barreto-Rivera, in a poetry quartet bp named The Four Horsemen.

It was an exciting time, as we developed material and shared our discoveries and enthusiasms—not just in relation to sound poetry and poetry performance, but to poetry in general, including what was to me the exciting new world of visual poetry, or what I think of as "drawing with the alphabet." I continued (as we all did) to write syntax-based verbal poetry and prose (fiction and essays), but I had new tools to use for creation, radical new visual and sonic effects that had a profound impact on my whole approach to creative writing, especially to poetry, and also to language in general.

While I continued to create and perform sound poems in a literary context, I have, since the 1980s, worked extensively in the field of free improvisational music (just think of it as music without rules: no keys, time signatures, or preset structures), doing what I call soundsinging or oral sound, collaborating with instrumentalists and with other singers of sounds. For some time now, I've stopped composing pre-planned sound poems, focusing my sound-poetry efforts on an ongoing series called "The Antilyrics"—short, on-the-spot improvisations fashioned on the model of conventional free-verse lyrical poetry, but made up of completely nonverbal sounds.

But What Is Sound Poetry?

Sound poetry is better known now than in the 1960s, but it's still unfamiliar to most people (for forty years, audience members have been telling me they have never heard anything like it before), and there are misunderstandings about the term. First of all, sound poetry is *not* simply poetry where the sounds of the words matter more than their meaning, which is a feature of all kinds of poems. It is, in its strictest definition, poetry that doesn't use words at all, but sounds—which is why it's called sound poetry. But while much sound poetry is more about a poetic approach to sound than about a sonic approach to poetry, much of it also incorporates words in varying degrees, from very few words to nothing but words.

Although the category of sound poetry emerged only in the 20th century, elements of the genre have been around for ages: things like nonsense lyrics in folk songs, language-distortion songs, chanting, speaking in tongues (glossolalia), Scottish mouth music, Indian solkatu (orally rendered drum-rhythms), and various types of nonsense verse such as occurred in 13th-century Europe and 17th-century Iceland.

The Beginnings of Sound Poetry in the 20th Century

But none of that was in the minds of the artists—poets, painters, dancers, musicians—who began the tradition of sound poetry in the 20th century. These were the Italian and Russian Futurists, who emerged around 1910, and the Dadaists in Switzerland and Germany, who came along during and after the First World War. While the Italian Futurists glorified the machine and romanticized war, the Swiss Dadaists—who weren't Swiss, but expatriate Germans, Spaniards, Romanians, and others—were dedicated to pacifist principles and, horrified by the war, which they saw as the outcome of European middle-class values, did everything they could to undermine those values and outrage the people who held them. One of their tactics was *Verse ohne Worte* (poetry without words), as one of the artists, Hugo Ball, called it.

German Dadaist Kurt Schwitters' *Ursonate* (composed 1922–1932), a four-movement phonetic composition in the sonata form, is an early classic of sound poetry, revered and performed to this day. Notable among many versions is that by Dutch sound poet and musician Jaap Blonk, excerpt at youtube.com/watch?v=JgNL8-FdG-k.

The Growth and Development of Sound Poetry

Sound poetry sort of lay quiet during most of the 1930s and '40s, then took off again, starting in the '50s in France and Germany, until by the '70s poets and musicians (composers and singers, who called what they did "text-sound composition" and "extended vocal technique") were getting into the act all over Europe—England, Sweden, Italy—as well as in Russia, Canada, and the USA. There was enough going on to keep the International Sound Poetry Festival running for about a dozen editions through the '70s and '80s. Since then, the field has continued to expand, and today sound poetry, or elements of it, can be heard in work by a great variety of artists—whether or not they've ever heard of sound poetry—in everything from rock to chamber music, in performance art, audio art, video art, film, dance, theatre, jazz, free improvisation, stand-up comedy, and beat-boxing.

One important aspect of sound poetry that bears mention is the impact of technological developments, first tape recording, and then digital devices, all of which have facilitated a broader range of body-based sounds through tape manipulation (speed changes, cutting and splicing), contact microphones, and electronic treatment. Some of us, though, have stuck to purely acoustic voice and mouth sounds. Personally, I'm still discovering new oral sounds I can make, both with and without the voice (but more of that in my "Writing and Performance" section, which follows).

Where to Hear Sound Poetry

It's all well and good to *read about* sound poetry, but what's the point if you can't hear it? Well, fortunately, today there's the Internet, and while nothing equals the experience of a live performance, you can at least encounter the technological traces of past performances, from the genre's earliest history right up to the present day. A wealth of sound poetry can be encountered through the Web's rich store of audio files and videos. The most thorough resource for sound poetry (and sound art in general, including film and video) is ubu.com. There's a more specialized focus on sound poetry at epc.buffalo.edu/sound/soundpoetry. And a vital Web magazine of contemporary sound poetry is *As Long As It Takes*, aslongasittakes.org.

If you do go searching, and I heartily encourage you to, here are just a few artists I recommend listening to, in addition to those I've already mentioned in this account and in my biographical note: Henri Chopin (master of tape manipulation), Bob Cobbing, François Dufrêne, Carlfriedrich Claus, Christian Bök, Amanda Stewart, Lauren Newton, Gerhard Rühm, and Jörg Piringer. That should get you started, and on your way to discovering your own favourites. ✪

WRITING & PERFORMANCE

What's Needed for Making Sound Poems

Everybody, with few exceptions, comes readily equipped with everything required to create sound poetry: a body, a mouth, and a voice. Most of the effects used in sound poetry, even some of the most spectacular and strange-sounding ones, are used in everyday life, and most of them in normal speech. The difference is that in sound poetry—at least, *my* kind of sound poetry—the elements of speech and other human utterance are isolated, enlarged, and applied very differently from the way they're used day to day. For this lesson we'll be dealing mostly with the grunted, hissed, growled, or groaned nonword.

Getting Started, My Way

Today there are many types of sound poetry, and many different approaches to the art. It would take a whole book to teach all the various ways to create sound poems, so this lesson is constructed to introduce you to sound poetry the way I like to do it. A lot of the suggestions I make here will be illustrated in my Web videos at spokenwordworkbook.com, the site connected to this book, so be sure to check that out.

Now, the first thing I'd like to do is to show you a new way to approach how you hear yourself, which should lead into some new ways for you to make yourself heard. There'll be some things you're already expert in, and other things that will require practice—and those will not all be the same for everybody, because we're all built a little bit differently.

The two most important things to remember throughout these exercises are:

👓 **1.** The right way is *your* way.

It's your unique voice, your unique anatomical specifics, and your unique soul that you're working with. This isn't about carrying a tune or staying on pitch or accurately rendering some predetermined rhythms—though none of that's forbidden, if it's what you can and want to work with. But for now the focus is on sound, texture, and subjective, individual abilities. You'll be taking what you've got and developing it your way.

👓 **2.** No pain, no way.

If you're trying something and it hurts, stop. If it's something you really want to do, go back at it more quietly or more gently, gradually building up your capacity for it. You're basically using muscles, tiny though they may be, and you'll be exercising some of them more than you're used to. So go slowly, as you would with any new physical exercise. Beware of the "Feist effect"—that popular singer went so hard at singing punk rock that she damaged her vocal cords so badly she needed medical help to heal them.

Okay, the first thing to do is to get into some private, quiet, physical surroundings (by yourself, or with like-minded friends). It should be someplace where you can lie down fully and get totally relaxed, without any noise going on, if possible. Most likely, you'll be providing plenty of that yourself, sooner or later, so this should also be somewhere or sometime that will cause no disturbance to others, should you wind up getting loud. (Sound poetry doesn't have to be loud, by the way.)

Relaxing and Exploring Breath

Lie flat on your back, perfectly still, arms resting comfortably, unbent at your sides, legs uncrossed and unbent, eyes closed. Now let yourself become as totally relaxed as you possibly can, breathing normally and easily, mouth lightly closed or relaxedly open ever so slightly. Just lie there awhile listening to your breathing, not forcing your breath in any way: try to let the air breathe you, as it were, so it simply arrives at your lips, without being pushed there. Through all this, keep listening closely, noticing any little wayward sounds that might occur: barely audible wheezes or whistles, rustlings or sighings. After a while, when it feels right to you, begin exploring your breath, repeating on purpose those involuntary sounds you've noticed, exerting just a little effort to make them a bit more audible, but not using your voice-box (larynx) at all, and gradually breathing more heavily, more forcefully.

Next, start playing with those sounds, trying different sequences or patterns; and when you've had enough of that, start exploring other sounds that you can make with your tongue and lips (but not your voice; not yet), smooching and puffing, chuffing and hissing, whispering, swishing saliva around, squishing it in your cheeks, putting your tongue between your teeth and forcing air around it, putting your tongue to the roof of your mouth to force the airflow up your nasal passages (which should produce some interesting new sounds), doing all these things with your mouth sometimes open, sometimes closed. All the while, keep listening closely to sounds you find new and interesting; see how loud you can make them, and work them into rhythms and patterns.

The idea here is to play with sound, loosen up your inhibitions, have fun exploring and experimenting. Don't worry about being artistic at this point. For now, you're just establishing what you want to be artistic with, like a painter preparing her palette of colours. And I'm hoping you'll be able to come up with some things that haven't even occurred to me.

Exploring Voice

During this next phase, at whatever point feels comfortable or necessary, start slowly moving your limbs, hands, feet, and neck, roll your head, stretch, and gradually get into first a sitting position, then up on your feet and moving about. All that time, keep making your sounds. Continuing at your own pace, start using your voice, beginning softly, not rushing, just warming up, gradually increasing volume if you'd like, either with sudden spikes or sustained loudness, or moving back and forth between quiet and loud periods of time.

Don't forget to stop and rest whenever you feel like it. You might want to get a little—or even a lot—boisterous during this process, but remember never to strain your vocal cords: keep your throat relaxed and use your diaphragm and your stomach muscles to increase volume. If you decide to pursue this kind of voicework more deeply, you'll reach a point where you'll want to stretch beyond where you've gotten to (again, as you would in developing any set of muscles), but never forget the no-pain principle.

Maintain the ongoing attitude of exploration, experimentation, and fun, really cutting loose, freeing up any vocal inhibitions, trying not to care how silly or strange you might sound. Now's the time to try out different voice characteristics, like squeaking, rumbling, growling, muttering, grunting, making short sharp sounds, long droning ones, nasal ones, squawking, muttering, giggling, sounds like sobbing, like laughing, doing mock speech, shouting, screaming, shrieking, howling, making gravel-voiced sounds, gargling sounds, lib-burbling, and anything else you can think of. And keep varying the volume, intensity, duration, rhythms, and patterns of any and all the effects you achieve. Also, find out what difference in sound characteristics occur with the mouth held open in different shapes and varying degrees of wideness.

Once again, during all this, remember not to strain your vocal cords, being very careful with raspy, harsh sounds, working your way into them, and backing off if they start to hurt. And always support high volume with breathing from the diaphragm, using your abdominal muscles, keeping the strain off your throat. This is a whole-body endeavour, not an isolated throat-and-mouth event. And in that spirit, you could also try physical manipulation, like voicing sound while drumming on your chest or flubbing your lips with your fingers or squeezing your nostrils. And try out different tones of voice: angry, tender, excited, frightened—anything and everything that comes to mind. The sky's the limit. Oh, and there's no reason why you can't use words, too, if you're so inclined, but even there, try to keep the focus on sonic colour and texture.

A Few Unusual Sounds to Try

Here are a few suggestions, some easy to do, some not so easy. Also, some will be a snap to do for one person, while someone else might have to spend hours or weeks before finally succeeding, and a third person might just never be able to make the sound at all. It's a combination of individual anatomy and personal will.

- ✿ Press your tongue against the roof of your mouth, then pull it down to make a popping sound. The more forceful the pull, the louder the pop. Keep the tongue close to the teeth for lower pitches, further back for higher ones, and you can play melodies (very limited ones). It's a matter of strengthening the tongue (which consists mostly of muscles) by repeated practice.
- ✿ Blowing or sucking air through tightly or loosely held lips produces higher or lower pitches of nicely spattery sound. Get different qualities of sound by puckering your lips or spreading them wide. Blow or suck harder to make the sound louder. Again, it's all about strengthening muscles through practice. See if you can produce several simultaneous sounds at different points along the length of the lips, and if you can also get different pitches at different points.
- ✿ Start saying the syllable *wah* over and over, faster and faster, then nasalize the sound by tightening your throat muscles, forcing more air through your nasal passages, and listen for the two pitches, a lower one from your throat, and a higher one from your lips.
- ✿ Rolled *r*'s and *t*'s and *d*'s are produced by vibrating the tongue rapidly against the teeth while shaping your mouth for the respective consonants. Easy for some, requiring lots of practice for others.
- ✿ Drop your jaw as far as you can and shape your lips for saying the letter o. Now tap the fingers of your right hand on your right cheek and your left hand on your left cheek. Change the pitch of your two cheek drums by changing the shape of your mouth and making the opening smaller or larger. You can play all kinds of rhythms on your built-in drum. For added fun, make voice sounds at the same time.
- ✿ You know those rasping, scratchy sounds that blues singers, soul singers, and punk-rock singers use? Those are called multiphonics (more than one sound at once), and to be made safely, they have to be made carefully, to protect the vocal cords. The trick is not to make the scraping sound right in the larynx, on the cords, but to make it higher in the throat or off the soft palate or into the nasal passages. It will require some facial contortions and you might look weird, but you'll be saving your vocal cords. If you try this, go slowly and very carefully, building up your tolerance for it.
- ✿ A different kind of multiphonics is achieved by inhaled sound: breathing in while using your voice, as in a gasp of surprise, but sustained for a longer time. This is another technique requiring caution and a building of tolerance over time.
- ✿ Yet another kind of multiphonics is the production of two sounds at two different body sites. Try combining some nonvocal sounds—lip sounds, tongue-and-tooth sounds, tongue-and-lip sounds— with voicings, such as drones, rumbles, and growls.

Your Ongoing Personal Explorations

The preceding exercises are intended to get you started on your own exploratory development of your individual voice and your potential for expanded sounding. They are meant to be repeated as often as you feel it helpful to do so. You might find it more rewarding, and more fun, to carry out these exercises with a friend or friends. That will offer more learning possibilities, with the added opportunity of sharing discoveries and ideas.

There is something else I'd like to point out about delving into this kind of voicework. It can, depending on the individual, activate some very powerful, and sometimes overpowering, emotional states. That can, of course, happen with all kinds of artistic pursuits, art being very much about feeling. But it is especially true of voicework, and often even more true of the kind of voicework that I've proposed in this long-distance workshop I've laid out. Many of these techniques that I and others use in our artistic pursuits are used by workers in the helping professions as tools in the course of deep psychotherapy. So, depending on how much you get into it, be prepared for the possibility of the occasional bumpy ride.

Of course, deep emotional states can also be ones of intense pleasure, so keep that in mind, too. Sound poetry, like any art, can be used to explore a broad range of states of mind, emotion, and spirit — from lighthearted whimsy and humour to soul-scorching depths and soaring, joyous heights.

Creating Sound Poems

Well, no one can teach you how to do that. At the start of the lesson, I drew a comparison between doing the proposed exercises and a painter's preparation of a palette of colours. To carry on the analogy, once you're content with the palette of sound colours you've prepared, you can start doing some sound painting. You can do representational works (depicting literal events or states of mind) or abstract works (sound constructions that depict nothing except themselves). I myself am not too keen on representational sound poetry, preferring the abstract, which I find more suited to the kind of spiritual states that I'm attempting to gain access to through my work.

I'm often asked how I write my sound poems. Well, I rarely do. Most of them can't be written out at all, only roughly described, as I've done with "Mercure," the sample poem in this section of the book. A great many of them are improvised on the spot and aren't meant to be repeated. Most of the ones that are repeatable are worked up from sounds, with very idiosyncratic notes jotted down as I go, just to remind me of what to do when.

Some poets score out their sound poems, especially if the poems are made up of conventional syllables or phonemes. And this is a good point at which to note that not all sound poets use all the wild and wooly sounds I've covered in the first two pages of this section. Some work all the time exclusively with words, syllables and phonemes, carefully planned out well in advance of performance. Others create abstract alphabetical designs and then interpret them with sounds that the marks suggest to them. And then there are those who use electronic devices and instruments to treat the voice. I'm afraid I know nothing about that, but I do know that at least some of them write their compositions out somehow with some sort of notation.

All that being said, I will offer a few suggestions that might spark some ideas for you to build on. And I'll just add that you will likely get other ideas by listening on the Web to some of the sound poetry that's been produced (see "Where to Hear Sound Poetry" at the end of my "History" section). I've always found that the best way to find out how to do something is to experience how it's already been done.

❤ Create a complete sound poem out of those explorations of breathing, small mouth sounds, and whispers suggested in the "Relaxing and Exploring Breath" portion. Make a special effort to keep it as quiet as you can.

❤ Create a sound poem that makes use of simultaneous voiced and unvoiced sounds, combining mouth percussion (lip-smacking, tongue-popping, rolled *t*'s, *r*'s, and *d*'s, etc.) with drones, nasal whines, inhaled sounds, grunts, gargles, and other sounds from the throat.

❤ Start by pretending to laugh, and keep it up until you're *really* laughing, then imitate a variety of different kinds of laughs you've heard from different people, continuing with the sounds as you gradually remove from them any sense of mirth, until you're making just flat, unemotional laughter sounds. Stay open to where that might take you and see where you wind up.

❤ Use the letters, phonemes, and syllables of your name as the basic building blocks for an abstract sound composition or improvisation, rearranging the sounds into different patterns, using the letters to make other words to inject into the sound poem. If desired, you could do a whole series of sound poems in this way, using any other names you wish. ✪

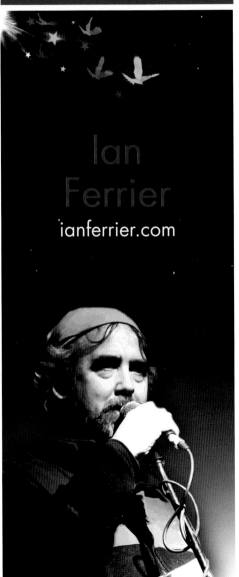

Ian Ferrier blends elements of poetry, song, and spoken word in his one-of-a-kind performance art, delivering a medley of literature and popular culture. Musically rooted in blues-driven inquiries into love, sex, and death, and poetically rooted in the cosmology of the Beats, Ferrier is also a founder of the spoken word label Wired on Words. He performs both as a solo artist and with the trance/improv music project *Pharmakon MTL*, mixing whispered and sung vocals, multiple guitars and drums into an absorbing voyage. Ferrier has released a CD/book *Exploding Head Man* (2004), and two CDs, *What Is This Place?* (2007) and *To Call Out in the Night* (2010). His poems have also been set on the page in anthologies from Montréal presses, such as Conundrum's *Impure-Reinventing the Word* and Vehicule's *Poetry Nation*. An active contributor to Montréal's literary community, Ferrier is a past president of the Quebec Writers' Federation (DN). ✪

Photo credit, Sandra Belanger, Quebec, 2009

Letters from the Ice Age

Cities buried   streets forgotten
warehouses ransacked and abandoned for the south.

We love   we breathe
light footprints of our passing through the snow.

What would we say? And how say it?
Who would we talk to? And how could they answer?

Buildings break beneath the ice
the bridges fall and there are less of us each year.

Like arctic animals we burrow through the wreckage
         of the city underground.

And high above where once the escalators climbed into the light
the tunnels terminate in breathing walls of ice.

Here in the dark
within the stone walls of the ancient hospital
below the copper roofs
and buried by the glaciers on all sides

Here in blood and wailing
anchored in breathing and inflexible resolve
we have sent this letter to the next world.

Archangel of the frozen colony
whose sign is fire   whose feet are locked in ice

We leave you more than this   than blowing snow
or permafrost a hundred feet below.

This is the breath of the last words spoken
bubbling up
the frozen evidence of love
like nitrogen in glass
our histories etched into the worlds
  we will not live to know.

—Ian Ferrier ✪

First appeared in *Exploding Head Man*
2000, Planet Rebelle Press

50

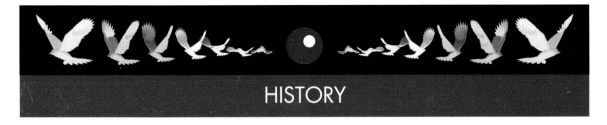

Imitations

I live in a part of the country where the French language is everywhere. Translation is incredibly important. But how do we translate when the very nature of the language we enter is different from our own?

The American poet Robert Lowell had a really good idea about this. He thought the attempt to translate was doomed. He could not hope to reproduce the power and delicacy of a great poem, as part of its greatness lay in the language in which it lived.

He did think he could imitate. By imitate he meant: Create a free translation which, while grounded and based in the original, attempted to reproduce in his own English, and with the tools and idiom he knew, the spirit and strength of the original poem. You can look at the results of this idea in his book *Imitations*. You can find out more about Robert Lowell at poetryfoundation.org/bio/robert-lowell.

I don't expect everyone to speak French, but I assume that most people reading this book have a reasonable command of the English language. If you don't, the ideas in this section can be used in any language.

I suggest that you go back and look into some of the classic poems of your language—for example English—and translate the English of Chaucer, of Shakespeare, of any poet you want, into *your* English language. These poems differ in time, place, idiom, and language. I suggest trying to make one a poem of *this* time, *your* location, and idiom. And like Lowell, forget word-for-word, and try to recreate the power and spirit of the original.

Ezra Pound did it with the Chinese poet Li Po (aka Rihaku, aka Li Bai) and came up with one of the most powerful poems in any language, "Exile's Letter." I tried to imitate Ezra's version in a poem I still perform under the same title.

Here's Ezra Pound's beginning:

To So-Kin of Rakuyo, ancient friend, Chancellor of Gen.
Now I remember that you built me a special tavern
By the south side of the bridge at Ten-Shin.
With yellow gold and white jewels we paid for the songs and
    laughter,
And we were drunk for month after month, forgetting the kings
    and princes.

And below is mine. The chancellor has magically become the narrator's old girlfriend, and China has transformed into the American South:

To Soo Kyin, old high school girlfriend,
now star musician on the stages of Europe
I think of when you found me that night club to run
south side of the levee in New Orleans.
With royalties and record deals we paid for months of song and
    laughter,

And we were drunk for whole seasons
forgetting money, career, family.

This is possible with any poem, from Chaucer to Shakespeare to a rapper whose work you like. It lets you interact with the original on a very intimate level, and find out how the poem derives its power.

Here's the beginning of trying to do it with Chaucer:

Whan that Aprille with his shoures sote
The droghte of Marche hath perced to the rote,
And bathed every veyne in swich licour
Of which vertu engendred is the flour,
Whan Zephirus eek with his sweete breeth
Inspired hath in every holt and heeth
The tendre croppes, and the yonge sonne
Hath in the Ram his half cours y-ronne
And smale foweles maken melodye,
That slepen al the nyght with open yë
(So priketh hem nature in hir corages),
Thanne longen folk to goon on pilgrimages,
And palmeres for to seken straunge strondes,
To ferne halwes, couthe in sondry londes;
And specially from every shires ende
Of Engelond to Caunterbury they wende...

When April with its sweet showers
Has pierced to the root the drought of March
And bathed every vein in a heady elixir
Engendering life in leaf and flower
When the sweet breath of the south wind
Has inspired the growth of the tenderest crops
And the young sun's course already carries it
halfway through Aries

(Fill in the rest. And feel free to change what I've done as well.)

Now why don't you try it with Shakespeare. And again, feel free to cross out anything I say:

Shall I compare thee to a summer's day?
Thou art more lovely and more temperate:
Rough winds do shake the darling buds of May,
And summer's lease hath all too short a date:
Sometime too hot the eye of heaven shines,
And often is his gold complexion dimmed,
And every fair from fair sometime declines,
By chance, or nature's changing course untrimmed:
But thy eternal summer shall not fade,
Nor lose possession of that fair thou ow'st,
Nor shall death brag thou wander'st in his shade,
When in eternal lines to time thou grow'st,
So long as men can breathe, or eyes can see,
So long lives this, and this gives life to thee.

If I compare you to a summer's day, who wins?
it's always you, more lovely, most beautiful
Rough winds shake the freshest buds of May...

What did you do with "And summer's lease hath all too short a date?" ✪

Poetry as a Cinema of the Imagination

One of the strongest ways poetry lives is through the creation of images that illuminate and change the way we see the world.

But in performance, how do we get those images across?

When you present an image to your audience you have to be able to see that image in front of you, or live within that image.

If you are doing neither, then there is no reason to expect your audience to be able to see it or live it. They won't. Your commitment to your images is what makes you a poet.

We also have at our fingertips the tools for a cinema of the imagination.

If you present images vividly enough, then people will see them as if they are on film. And they will see their own personalized film, in more than two dimensions: an internal journey for which you are the narrator, cinematographer, and all the actors. In which you are the person who carries them from one part of the journey to the next.

Which makes you not just the author, but the editor as well... how and when do you move from one image to the next? When and how do you juxtapose images? The answer to these questions is defined by your sense of juxtaposition, time, beauty, action, rest. These questions cannot be answered unless you are allowing each image you present enough time to live and register, which means—and I repeat—that each needs to be alive to you.

This is more than a desire. Rather it is a technique that affects the whole timing of what you do. If the image doesn't appear before you, how do you know how long to pause and keep it there before moving on to the next?

In this sense there is certainly as much to learn from film as there is from any other medium, including music or prose.

A Few Tips

For the most part, your audience will not have read or heard your poem before. They need more time than you for each image to appear and register.

And if they HAVE heard your poem before they need something else. They need you to make it as fresh and powerful as the first time they heard it.

So let's go to Samuel Taylor Coleridge and see how he does it:

Kubla Khan

      by Samuel Taylor Coleridge

In Xanadu did Kubla Khan
A stately pleasure-dome decree:
Where Alph, the sacred river, ran
Through caverns measureless to man
Down to a sunless sea.

So twice five miles of fertile ground
With walls and towers were girdled round:
And there were gardens bright with sinuous
rills,
Where blossomed many an incense-bearing
tree;
And here were forests ancient as the hills,
Enfolding sunny spots of greenery.

But oh! that deep romantic chasm which
slanted
Down the green hill athwart a cedarn cover!
A savage place! as holy and enchanted
As e'er beneath a waning moon was haunted
By woman wailing for her demon-lover!
And from this chasm, with ceaseless turmoil
seething,
As if this earth in fast thick pants were breath-
ing,
A mighty fountain momently was forced:
Amid whose swift half-intermitted burst
Huge fragments vaulted like rebounding hail,
Or chaffy grain beneath the thresher's flail:
And 'mid these dancing rocks at once and ever
It flung up momently the sacred river.
Five miles meandering with a mazy motion
Through wood and dale the sacred river ran,
Then reached the caverns measureless to man,
And sank in tumult to a lifeless ocean:
And 'mid this tumult Kubla heard from far
Ancestral voices prophesying war!

The shadow of the dome of pleasure
Floated midway on the waves;
Where was heard the mingled measure

Establishing shot; narrator's
   introduction; intro to dome; rhythm
   is 4 beats a line
First shot of caverns
First shot of buried ocean; 3 beat line
   holds and reverberates
We close in on pleasure-dome

Slow down the beat by lengthening
   the line
Settle on age of landscape; slow down

Closing in on raging river: major
diagonal

How long does this image stay?

Action sequence presented with a
series of images:
First shot of fountain

Close up
Another close up

Pull back

Return and repeat caverns
Return and modify sunless ocean

Foreshadow the death of all

This image is just managing not to
sink into the lifeless ocean

More detail on fountain and caves

54

<table>
<tr>
<td>

From the fountain and the caves.
It was a miracle of rare device,
A sunny pleasure-dome with caves of ice!

A damsel with a dulcimer
In a vision once I saw:
It was an Abyssinian maid,
And on her dulcimer she played,
Singing of Mount Abora.
Could I revive within me
Her symphony and song,
To such a deep delight 'twould win me
That with music loud and long
I would build that dome in air,
That sunny dome! those caves of ice!
And all who heard should see them there,
And all should cry, Beware! Beware!
His flashing eyes, his floating hair!
Weave a circle round him thrice,
And close your eyes with holy dread,
For he on honey-dew hath fed
And drunk the milk of Paradise.

</td>
<td>

Much later, after the action has peaked

Narrator reminiscing on the good old days

Recreates and has us leaf through the images he created earlier: dome, caves....
Instead of demon lover now we have the narrator.

</td>
</tr>
</table>

Now take one of your own poems and score it in the same way, putting the poem on the left-hand side, and the storyboard describing what each section does on the right-hand side.

<table>
<tr>
<td>

</td>
<td>

</td>
</tr>
</table>

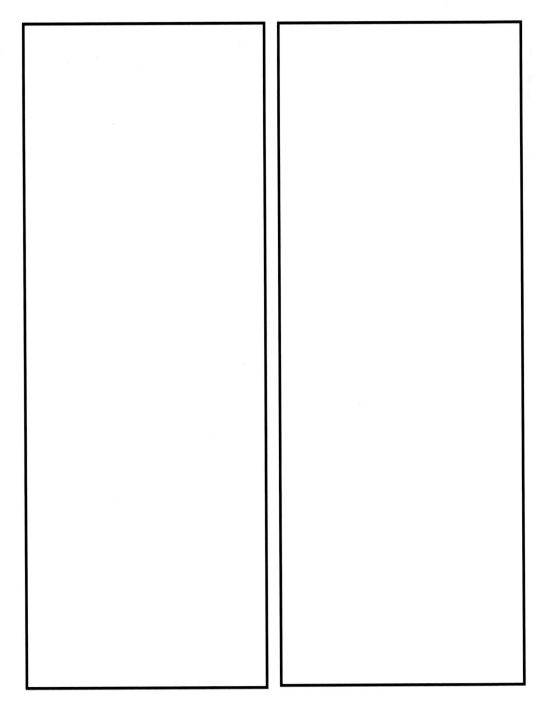

PERFORMANCE

Imagination Cinema with Soundtrack

Our sounds and chants—thrown together with primitive and not-so-primitive instruments—are always with us, from pop songs to hip hop, from African Griots to the troubadours singing the medieval news at each village they visited.

They are the beginning of recorded history, and yet so current that as I write this I have old cuts by Everlast—over 4 years old!—blasting through the speakers in my studio.

But I have turned off the sound now, and listen instead for a quieter soundtrack, one that might come up out of the darkness and fill a cinema of the imagination.

How could one build such a thing? What would its purpose be, and what tools would it use? And where do we go to find out?

None of these questions is trivial, and we won't have room here to answer all of them. What we can do is concentrate on some of the issues that affect any spoken word performance or recording with music:

Hear your Words

The first thing I want to talk about is volume. In the regular cinema, images are created by light on film and we watch them. The soundtrack can be as loud or as quiet as we like and there is no conflict. Image is being presented to our eyes and sound to our ears.

With spoken word this is not the case. The only thing we have to project images is voice.

This means that voice must always be heard and heard clearly.

Otherwise there is no cinema. We went to the cinema, and found ourselves in a music concert instead.

Which is why rappers have to yell, and even then we often can't pick out their lyrics.

How to be Heard

There are a number of ways to be heard with music:

♥ 1. TURN THE MUSIC DOWN.

That's the easiest. In words & music, the loudest thing is the most present, and it's as simple as that. If you want your images in your audience's mind, your voice has to be louder.

And you are not the judge of this, unless you're an expert. You already know every single word you're going to say, and could probably pick the words out even if the music was twice as loud. So find people you trust, who haven't heard the piece, and ask them to help you judge, get them to tell you when they can hear and follow everything you say clearly, and then add just a touch more volume to your voice.

PS Audio engineers are often not the best judges either. They're used to having a vocalist's song sit in the music, not on it. So unless they are experts in recording spoken word, add a bit of volume to what they say as well.

♥ 2. PUT THE WORDS WHERE THE MUSIC AIN'T.

There are two ways to do this. One is a simple matter of frequency. The human voice creates frequencies over a huge range of sound. Most of it lives in the mid-range, but there are both low and very high frequencies in most people's voices. So what you're doing in this section is picking sounds that will complement your voice without overwhelming it.

No Conflict

Bass guitar or plucked double bass will go great with your voice, almost no matter what. The fundamental frequency of all but the high bass strings is much lower than humans can produce. When a musician starts to bow a double bass, though, the wash of so many tones and overtones can overwhelm your voice if you're not careful.

High Frequency Voice

(female vocal; breathy male vocal; voices with lots of sibilance (sounds of ess, sh)).

If you have a high, breathy, sibilant voice (or if you whisper a lot like I do) you won't be heard at the same time as a flute, or a drum kit's cymbals, high hat, or snare. They all live in the high frequencies. Violin can also kill you, as can the higher notes on keyboard and guitar.

Instead, choose low drums, drums that thump, and pick a baritone sax instead of a flute. If you record the voice to a separate track, you can often fix this in the mix, either by making the voice louder, or EQ'ing the music so that it lets the voice frequencies through. Still, it's always better to have it working before you record.

Low Frequency Voice

If you have a low, resonant voice like James Earl Jones (Darth Vader) or Lauren Bacall, then most strummed guitar, bowed cello, or tenor sax will shut you out, as will low toms or djembes.

Frequency Matching and Mismatching

Guitar, piano, cello, and synthesizer can all create such a huge range of frequencies in the same area where voice lives that conflicts arise depending on where on the keyboard or fretboard the instrument is being played.

But the range is a gift, too.

- ☞ Record your voice with the melody played an octave higher or lower on the keyboard or fretboard.
- ☞ For the same amount of volume, which placement makes it easiest to hear your voice?

Sparseness

If the music is very full, then voice just has to be louder; there's no choice. But music doesn't have to be this way. Often instead of a full six-string chord on guitar I'll play only two or three notes, or mute the strings, and both techniques give the voice a lot more room to live.

Or if you or your musician is playing ambient (as opposed to rhythmic or repeating) music, then it's just a matter of putting your voice in the quiet parts of the music. Experienced musicians are usually very good at this, and if you ask them, they can help you, and design their music to work with you.

Working in Circles

Much music is circular or patterned. It repeats itself, and after a few repetitions you can pretty much predict when the end of a verse will come, and when we'll hear the chorus. We love this kind of predictability: It makes us feel like we know the future.

Musicians create patterns by setting up expectations and then fooling with them, putting the beat a little earlier or later, missing beats, or hitting them harder or softer.

And once any repetitive measure is established, it's a key to where and how we can place parts of a poem. As with music there are all kinds of ways you can approach this:

- You can have your poem stick with the pattern and start and end where the music does.
- You can start halfway through the verse and run right through the end of it and halfway into the chorus.
- You can jam your words in before a big downbeat (hip hop artists do this all the time.) "I wish you hadn't stolen all my (**DRUMTHUMP.**)"
- You can wait for the emptiness between beats, and put your words there.
- You can quiet or even cut the music for a few beats, and know that the audience will still have the beat or pattern going in their brain.
- You can seemingly ignore the rhythms the music is setting up, and have your words stick out because they do their own thing, regardless of music.

Listening

All of the ideas in this section are based on listening. The more you listen to the voice and the music, the better you'll get at figuring what goes with what and how to mix them together.

Silence

Strangely enough, one of the greatest gifts music gives a performer is the right to be silent. Because of music, you don't have to fill up every space with words. You can take a three second break, or repeat a line more quietly or more loudly. You can rest on a line and let it sink in while the music carries you. This is an amazing freedom. ✪

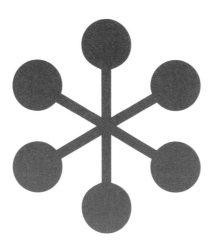

John
Giorno

John Giorno was born in New York and graduated from Columbia University in 1958. Four years later, when he became part of the experimental downtown arts scene, he met Andy Warhol, who became an important influence for Giorno's developments in poetry, performance and recordings. Giorno was the subject of Warhol's first film *Sleep*. He has collaborated with William Burroughs, John Ashbery, Ted Berrigan, Patti Smith, Laurie Anderson, Philip Glass, Robert Rauschenberg and Robert Mapplethorpe, and in the first decade of the 21st century, with Rirkirt Tirvanija, Pierre Huyge, Elizabeth Peyton, and Ugo Rondinone, who is his partner. Giorno is the author of 10 books, including the well-received *Subduing Demons in America: Selected Poems, 1962-2007*, *You Got to Burn to Shine*, *Cancer in my Left Ball*, *Grasping at Emptiness*, and *Suicide Sutra*. He has produced 59 LPs, CDs, tapes, cassettes, videopaks, and DVDs for Giorno Poetry Systems. John Giorno seeks alternative ways of writing and presenting his poetry: using the telephone (Dial-A-Poem), recordings (Giorno Poetry Systems), and multiples (poem prints). He founded the AIDS Treatment Project and is an important force in the development of Tibetan Buddhism in the West. ✪

Photo credit, Pepe Arrebato, Madrid, 2007

THANX 4 NOTHING

on my 70th Birthday in 2006

I want to give my thanks to everyone for everything,
and as a token of my appreciation,
I want to offer back to you all my good and bad habits
as magnificent priceless jewels,
wish-fulfilling gems satisfying everything you need and want,
thank you, thank you, thank you,
thanks.

May every drug I ever took
come back and get you high,
may every glass of vodka and wine I've drunk
come back and make you feel really good,
numbing your nerve ends
allowing the natural clarity of your mind to flow free,
        may all the suicides be songs of aspiration,
thanks that bad news is always true,
may all the chocolate I ever eaten
come back rushing through your bloodstream
and make you feel happy,
thanks for allowing me to be a poet
a noble effort, doomed, but the only choice.

I want to thank you for your kindness and praise,
thanks for celebrating me,
thanks for the resounding applause,
I want to thank you for taking everything for yourself
and giving nothing back,
you were always only self-serving,
thanks for exploiting my big ego
and making me a star for your own benefit,
thanks that you never paid me,
thanks for all the sleaze,
thanks for being mean and rude
and smiling at my face,
I am happy that you robbed me,
I am happy that you lied
I am happy that you helped me,
thanks, grazie, merci beaucoup.

        May you smoke a joint with William,
and spend intimate time with his mind,
more profound than any book he wrote,
        I give enormous thanks to all my lovers,
beautiful men with brilliant minds,
great artists,
Bob, Jasper, Ugo,
may they come here now

and make love to you,
and may my many other lovers
of totally great sex,
countless lovers
of boundless fabulous sex
countless lovers of boundless fabulous sex
countless lovers of boundless
fabulous sex
in the golden age
of promiscuity
may they all come here now,
and make love to you,
if you want,
may each of them
hold each of you in their arms
balling
to your hearts
delight.
balling to your hearts
delight
balling to
your hearts delight
balling to your hearts delight.

May all the people who are dead
Allen, Brion, Lita, Jack,
and I do not miss any of you
I don't miss any of them,
no nostalgia,
it was wonderful we loved each other
but I don't want any of them back,
now, if any of you
are attracted to any of them,
may they come back from the dead,
and do whatever is your pleasure,
may they multiply,
and be the slaves
of whoever wants them,
fulfilling your every wish and desire,
(but you won't want them as masters,
as they're demons),
may Andy come here
fall in love with you
and make each of you a superstar,
everyone can have
Andy.

everyone can
have Andy.
>everyone can have Andy,
>everyone can have an Andy.

>Huge hugs to the friends who betrayed me,
>every friend became an enemy,
>sooner or later,
big kisses to my loves that failed,
>I am delighted you are vacuum cleaners
sucking everything into your dirt bags,
you are none other than a reflection of my mind.

Thanks for the depression problem
and feeling like suicide
everyday of my life,
and now that I'm seventy,
I am happily almost there.

Twenty billion years ago,
in the primordial wisdom soup
beyond comprehension and indescribable,
something without substance moved slightly,
and became something imperceptible,
moved again and became something invisible,
moved again and produced a particle and particles,
moved again and became a quark,
again and became quarks,
moved again and again and became protons and neutrons,
and the twelve dimensions of space,
tiny fire balls of primordial energy
bits tossed back and forth
in a game of catch between particles,
transmitting electromagnetic light
and going fast, 40 million times a second,
where the pebble hits the water,
that is where the trouble began,
something without substance became something with substance,
>why did it happen?
because something substance less
had a feeling of missing out on something,
>not
getting it
was not getting it
not getting it,
not getting it,
imperceptibly not having something
when there was nothing to have,
clinging to a notion of reality;
from the primordially endless potential,
to modern day reality,

twenty billion years later,
has produced me,
gave birth to me and my stupid grasping mind,
        made me and you and my grasping mind.

        May Rinpoche and all the great Tibetan teachers who loved me,
come back and love you more,
hold you in their wisdom hearts,
bathe you in all-pervasive compassion,
give you pith instructions,
and may you with the diligence of Olympic athletes
do meditation practice,
and may you with direct confidence
realize the true nature of mind.

America, thanks for the neglect,
I did it without you,
let us celebrate poetic justice,
        you and I never were,
never tried to do anything,
and never succeeded,
        I want to thank you for introducing me to
the face of the naked mind,
thanx 4 nothing.

—John Giorno ✪

"Lorca, please help me?"

I was seventeen years old, and had just begun my freshman year at Columbia College in New York. About two weeks after I arrived, on September 14, 1954, Tuesday in the early evening, I was in my room sitting on the green leather armchair doing homework, reading for the Humanities Core Curriculum class tomorrow.

I was looking out the wide window from the 8th floor of Livingston Hall at the view over the Quadrangle, and the classic Georgian buildings designed in 1893 by architect Sanford White, who created a master plan in the grand style of great palaces and beautiful arrays of trees and English landscaping, and the broad green South Field. It was warm and balmy, hazy, a sylvan glade, and a vivid rose-grey sunset, heavenly, smack in the middle of New York City. It also seemed like a joke, a young man in an ideal situation reading Plato and the classics. On the surface it was idyllic, but beneath I was filled with anxiety, confusion and doubt. I was reading, had a hangover, and a depression problem.

There was a loud knock on the door, and John Kaiser, a new friend, who was also majoring in literature, came in and visited. "I just learned the most amazing bit of information," said John, "a monumental fact. Federico Garcia-Lorca lived here!"

"What?" I had no idea what he was talking about.

"Garcia-Lorca lived in John Jay Hall."

"What?" I was completely taken by surprise. I hadn't thought about Garcia-Lorca in a long time. "When?"

"In 1929 and 1930," said John.

"And wrote *Poet In New York*, his greatest work, here!"

"This is 1954. Twenty-five years ago," I said. When you are seventeen, twenty-five years ago seems like ancient history. I remembered Lorca had traveled to Cuba, and came to New York; and he was gay and I was gay. "Lorca did not live in a dormitory room in John Jay Hall! I don't believe it!"

"It's true! Garcia-Lorca lived here."

"For one night by mistake, because he couldn't get a hotel."

"For two years!" said John.

"In what room?"

"On the 12th floor of John Jay, room 1231."

"Garcia-Lorca did not live in a dormitory," I said. "It's not possible. I don't know where he lived, he lived in a god world!" It was very confusing. I did not want Lorca living in my dumb middle-class, bourgeois, fucked-up world. He would hate it. It would be horrible for him, and cause him suffering. Anything but this! "What room?"

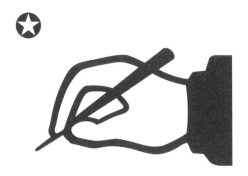

WORDS
COME FROM SOUND
SOUND COMES FROM WISDOM
WISDOM COMES FROM
EMPTINESS

EVERYTHING IS DELUSION INCLUDING WISDOM

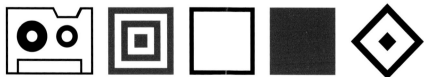

Words of Advice

When a poem works, it is a mirror held up to the audience, and they see themselves.
When you are performing a poem, you can feel it, viscerally.
You can feel them hearing the words.
When a poem really works, the audience is not seeing the words or the images,
 they are seeing themselves.
The poem is a mirror in which each person sees their own mind.
Each is seeing his or her true nature of mind.
This is a very strong moment.
The purpose of a poem is for people to see the wisdom inherent in their own mind,
 and the poem is just the vehicle.
That is what is a great poem.

Great poems in history, like Allen Ginsberg's *Howl*, Yeat's *The Second Coming*, and Walt Whitman's *Leaves of Grass*, among others, had profound effects on people when they were written, radically changed the culture, and when their job was done, they were retired to the museums of poetry, like Rembrandts and Picassos in art museums, and they became history. But great poems keep endlessly being written, and changing. You can't stop great poems from coming.

It is not so much the skills that a poet has developed, but somehow these skills make the unbelievable leap to do the miraculous, to mirror the wisdom and emptiness in a person's mind.

In March 1963, Ted Berrigan published my poems in "C Magazine." He organized a poetry reading in an old Union Hall on East 14th Street, New York, and I went because I liked all the poets. I was a young poet, had never read my work in public, Ted hadn't asked, and it never occurred to me that I would be asked to read. In the middle of the reading, Ted said, "The next poet is John Giorno."

"What!"

Ted handed me the magazine and the mic. In a state of shock from fright and the adrenalin rush, I had struggled to open my mouth, because everything was constricted, and read my poems. My hands were trembling, my body was shaking, and my legs were rattling like soft taffy. Sweat poured from me, and my lungs gasped for air, and my voice, which surprised me, was loud and full, and booming, and the gasping created a rhythm, like epilepsy, and phrases came out in big bursts of breath. I read the two poems, and with a loud applause, sat down in a state of shock. What happened?

Poets get asked to read their poems; it is part of the job. The sound of the words and their musical qualities are a part of the poem. Over the years, I learned how to perform. I was not trained as a musician, nor an actor, and not many poets were doing it, so I had it invent it myself, how I worked with breath and pitch, and rehearsed it endlessly to perfection. From 1963 to the present, 2011, almost fifty years later, I am still learning how to perform.

It's all in the breath

Breath creates the heat and energy making the sound happen. I developed skills performing over the years, which naturally arise when you do something over and over again. I invented a technique of breathing deeply, inhaling as much air into the lower part of my lungs, and released slowly with great force in the repetitions and musical qualities of the words. I had no voice or musical training, and had to make it up as I went along.

Since the 1960s, I have been a meditation practitioner in the *Nyingma* tradition of Tibetan Buddhism, and my teacher is H. H. Dudjom Rinpoche. A person training the mind and doing meditation is guided through many sequential, developing stages. An advance practice is called *Tumo*, the generation of inner heat. It is depicted in *Thankha* paintings, as a naked yogi sitting in the snow, with only a light cotton shawl, and sweating profusely. *Tumo* is a meditation practice using breath in the upper, middle, and lower parts of the lungs, creating a vase shape, and with visualizations and mantras, and pressing the air down into the lower part and holding it for long periods, and moving it around, generates enormous heat. I did the practice in retreat, and afterwards, was able to use my breath much better in performance.

I memorize all my poems. Not trained as an actor, I had to figure out by myself how to memorize. I do it by remembering the sound and music inherent in the words, without meaning, through rote. The way the mind remembers a pop song. When I perform it, the meaning and content comes back with the heat and sound. I begin the process of memorizing when I am writing a poem. Performing from memory, somehow, magically, the sound of the words go directly to the audience's heart and mind.

Being a poet, you take a vow of poverty. Poets never get paid. It's part of the job, not bad or good, but the way it is. The strange phenomenon is that poets have never been paid in every culture in every civilization in history from the beginning of time. It's curious! I have investigated: ancient India and China, Egypt, and in Western Europe, the poet was an outsider, the fool, and said what nobody else dared to say. In our time, even William Burroughs and Allen Ginsberg earned a very modest amount of money considering how enormously famous they were. Poems are not commodities, like Art is. Once you know the rules of the game, it's a joy to be a poet. Since there's nothing to lose, you can take all the risks you want. ✪

Louise B. Halfe

Louise Bernice Halfe—Sky Dancer—was raised on the reserve, Saddle Lake, although not exclusively, and was taken, along with her siblings, from her home and sent to residential school. Louise is married and has two adult children and two grandsons. She graduated with a Bachelor of Social Work and has a sub-specialty in addictions counselling. She is also a facilitator. Sky Dancer enriches her writing career with these skills, using them to move people from the perceived "writer's block." She served as Saskatchewan's Poet Laureate for two years and has travelled extensively throughout Canada, including the North, and abroad. She has served as a keynote speaker at numerous conferences. She made her writing debut as a poet in *Writing the Circle: Native Women of Western Canada, an anthology*. Her other books, *Bear Bones and Feathers*, *Blue Marrow,* and *The Crooked Good*, published by Coteau Publishers, have all received numerous nominations and awards, including: Governor General's Award for Poetry, Spirit of Saskatchewan Award, Saskatchewan First Book Award, Gerald Lambert Award, and the Pat Lowther First Book Award. ✪

To be Deaf

You no longer hear the wind,
the thunder, rain
the approach of a car
bluegrass, jazz, hip-rock playing.

You study the clouds
through your own hazy eyes
watch the slow sun
the movement of trees, grass
you tell me what the weather is saying.

pasted lovers, writhing like snakes
those dirty people, you say
fingers switching the remote
control.

the characters blaze guns
blasting one another
knives butchering spleens
this violence captures you
whole and hold.

Deer stew, rabbit, bore you
duck and fish you tolerate
even lobster you've ordered so often
while the rest of us watch,
becomes a bored delicacy.

day, night, year after year
this long hallway
separates you and I
day, night, year after year
you wait, season after season
you wait
I wait season after season
even though
residential school is a distant memory.

—Louise B. Halfe ✪

HISTORICAL

Do the following exercise in longhand and visit places as *if* you are the landscape, the year, the century, the season, and the weather.

Let a paragraph be a paragraph. Do not worry about structure, punctuation or spelling at this point. **DO NOT THINK OF AN AUDIENCE**, just write.

When you've followed these steps, return to your original writing several days, if not weeks, after you've written it. There is often a tendency to read the first draft and fall head-over-heels in love with it, thinking it's the finest piece of work you've achieved. However, upon review, after you've divorced yourself from the text, you can respond to it with a more critical eye (with an enriched approach). Always go back and review.

♥ 1. Choose the (a) year, (b) century, (c) geography, (d) season, (e) foliage, (f) dialect.

♥ 2. Define what purpose you are aiming for, for example, the famine in Ireland or the arrival of the first settlers on the North American continent.

♥ 3. Describe the weather, the winds, and how they shapes the landscape. Become the elements.

♥ 4. Describe how individuals respond to these conditions. Go into the psyche of the people involved, or the psyche of the landscape. You may wish to explore the desperation, the laughter, the tears, the survival or the failure to thrive. You may wish to use the cragginess, the ruggedness of both the land and the people. Or you can personify the mixed beauty and ugliness of a plant or animal. Give these the chosen theme's voice.

♥ 5. After you've been divorced from these observations or visions for some time, return and examine how much "telling" you've written. Underline the "telling" and rethink the text to "show" and lead readers into their own imagination. Leaving these blanks allows readers to fill in the space with their own impressions. Respect readers, for they have their own perceptions and intelligence, which they can exercise.

I am a poet. Poetry is my gift and hence I like to condense and allow the words and the thoughts some ambiguity. I even allow the words to have double meanings. I don't like to give it all away, telling the reader what it is I'm thinking or drawing. Rather than explaining my experience to the reader, I'd rather have the "painting" and the "actress" within the poem discover their own ways of "showing" or "telling." ✿

CREATION & WRITING

In the previous section you have been allowed to explore some of my process. I don't like the term "writer's block"; it is too visual and impenetrable for me. I'd rather replace the words "writer's block" with "refilling my artisan well with all kinds of debris." And then, I would let that new perspective compost. Eventually, a seed sprouts.

Sometimes I will journal at whatever place I happen to be sitting. Whether I am listening to music, listening to the voices around me (eavesdropping is great; occasionally a phrase, a figure of speech or a sentence will give me a lead down some other path), observing characters in these settings, leafing through photographs, or perusing a book. I will describe the setting in miniscule detail. What I find delightful with this practice of observation is that sometimes it produces a big piece for my manuscript, and at other times a piece of poetry is flushed out.

I also *love* the thesaurus. The word even sounds like a prehistoric animal. It holds a lot of gems. Because I love the original "source" and "meaning" of a word, I will explore Latin text and have discussions with others who share these same passions and curiosities.

And of course, I love my language, which is Cree. Algonquin tongues are the most unlike English or any other language I have explored. I am often surprised and delighted by the depth of the psychology, the philosophy, and spirituality of a word. One word in Cree can hold several concepts that lead to other concepts. My writing is, at times, based on these ways-of-seeing/being. Again, I will ask several well-versed and open Cree individuals to examine the *depth* and meaning of a word. Sometimes Cree is simply too difficult to translate because there is no English concept or word that can capture the conveyed thought.

I read everything of interest. Some things hold and captivate my attention more than others. I will highlight them and go back and study them until they are ingrained in my soul. Sometimes these jewels will jump out of a novel, perhaps just a short description of a landscape, or a character. For example, "the guy's nose was the size of a jolly green giant," or, "his left eye leaked, the flow followed the rugged curve of his cheek into his nose." Or whatever, something like that. I find it very visual. I like that it arouses my disgust; snorting through the nose, wiping the cheek and leaving grease or stains across the face. These latter thoughts are not written, however, they stimulate these other images, and sense and emotions.

So if you think you have writer's block work at these other ways to approaching creative writing. If that doesn't work find a muse (having a muse is very rich and challenging), or write a letter or postcard to a friend. Keep a copy of what you've written. It is sooo helpful. Write about what movie you saw last night and how it entered your dreams. Write about the dream landscape. These latter places are fantastic for otherworldly experiences and they are thought–provoking.

When I have finished a poem and I'm no longer in love with it, I will pace the floor with my paper and read aloud.

If my feet or steps stumble or sway uncomfortably on a particular word, it's like my feet are telling me the places in the text that are not working. Walking is important.

Prompt

Walk NATURALLY and leisurely. Listen to your breath.

Make LOVE

I follow the simple rule of KISS (Keep It Simple Stupid). I don't like unnecessary jargon. It doesn't add anything to the work, except maybe, to make you feel important and smart. The work will speak for itself and it will demonstrate in a "non-braggatory" manner, the brilliance you wish to show and share.

I will also try reading the poem or text to my most respected friends, who are not afraid to criticize and give me feed back, if it's not working or I need to examine the placement of a word. I don't particularly respect people who patronize my work. It doesn't enrich anyone. I am a critical reader and I want my text to inspire intellectual conversation and thought.

Prompt

Impersonate. When it comes to voice, I imagine what the voice of the character would sound like. I also differentiate voices by using different tones of voice.

Public Reading Note

I refuse to explain the poems beforehand other than perhaps giving a short heads-up about a storyline if it is an epic piece. Explaining takes away from the poem and doesn't allow listeners to come to their own perception. I like to have a question and answer period after a reading. Having said that, I love that other people see the work in a very different way and in the end, I often learn something. It gives me a deeper sense of who I am, and what my work is perhaps doing. It's very rewarding.

On Gesture

I may also use body language and become whatever it is I am presenting so long as I can carry voice and posture in a natural unpretentious manner. If it's pretentious, then I have failed my own work.

Bob Holman, founder and proprietor of the Bowery Poetry Club, is a poet most often connected with spoken word, performance, hip-hop and slam. He has published nine books of poetry and released two CDs. His latest collection of poems, a collaboration with Chuck Close, is *A Couple of Ways of Doing Something* (Aperture); his most recent CD, *The Awesome Whatever* (Bowery Books). The TV series he produced for PBS, *The United States of Poetry*, won the INPUT (International Public Television) Award; the series of intersticials he did for WNYC-TV won three Emmys; he founded Mouth Almighty/ Mercury Records, the first ever major spoken word label; and founded and ran the infamous poetry slams at the Nuyorican Poets Café, where he also co-edited the American Book Award-winning anthology, *Aloud!*. His globe-trotting reading tours have taken him to Medellin, Timbuktu, Vilnius, and Banff; he also performs in the touring companies of Spalding Gray's *Stories Left Untold* and David Thomas' *Mirror Man*. He is co-director of the Endangered Language Alliance, with his focus these days being on a documentary series on the Poetry of Endangered Languages. He teaches at NYU at the Art & Public Policy Department of the Tisch School of the Arts, at Columbia in the Graduate Writing Division of the School of the Arts, and at Naropa's Jack Kerouac School of Disembodied Poetics. ✪

I hate it, being labelled a "performance poet"! It's what my teacher, Walter Ong, called a retronym—renaming the original because the new model has become the standard. The example Ong uses is "a horse is an automobile without wheels," and what draws his ire is "Oral Literature" (why not "Written Orature"?). But there you have it; it doesn't "sound" right (don't you love the sound of "sound"?). And besides, Every poem must contain its opposite! So I took this epithet as a challenge, and here's my poem,

Performance Poem

which starts off with an epigraph (for the vocabularians: epigraph: quote at beginning of poem; epigram: pithy, witty "saying"; epitaph: words on tombstone; epithet: curse) (this is where the intro may seem to swamp the poem, but remember that in the Oral Tradition, the poem is the entire event. So, by that definition, this is all part of the poem!), starts off with an epigraph, as I was saying, by that great Performance Poet, Rainer Maria Rilke:

Voices. Voices. Listen, my heart, as only
saints have listened; until the gigantic call lifted them
off the ground; yet they kept on, impossibly,
kneeling and didn't notice at all:
so complete was their listening.
                                        —Rilke

He's diving off the front of the stage!
You better bring the house lights up some,
The audience can't see him.
He's still screaming,
Screaming and dancing
And he's twirling the mic—
I dunno, should we turn off the mic?
I dunno, turn it up?
He's running around, he's twirling and
He's still like reading.
The book is in his hands, sort of, the people
Seem to like it, they're into it—
Maybe it's part of the act.

If it's part of the act he shoulda told us!
Now he's in the back of the house—he's
Still going strong. This is pretty
Amazing. I've never seen anything
Like this! He's running out
Of the theatre—I can still hear him screaming
In the lobby. He's back in the house!
(What's he saying?—It's something about
It sounds like "lake snore freedom"...
I dunno. "Breaking down reason"?)

Oh shit! Oh shit oh shit—he's got a gun!

Christ! wait—awww, it's just one of those pop guns.
Shoots like firecrackers or popcorn or—
What about the hat? Still wearing the hat.
Holy—he's dying now, I mean he's acting like that,
Like he's dying. This is it for poetry in this house man,
I've had it.

He's just lying there.
The audience is wailing, they're keening
You know, like at a wake. No, I do not think
He's really dead. He's getting back up, see, I told
You—it's all part of the act!

It's all part of the end of the world.
What am I, the guy's father?
Come here! Look at the monitor yourself
He's ditched the mic somewhere,
Should I go get the mic?
Look! oh my God—he's, what's it called,
He's going up, he's levitating!
Holy shit! The roof, the roof is going up
Music is coming in
The crowd's up outta the chairs, man this is it
This is it I'm telling you—
Raising the fucking roof is what he's doing!
Now he's back on the stage with his poetry stuff
Yeah heh heh yeah,

He never left the stage
It's what his poem was about
I'm just saying what he's saying
Through the headset
Yeah, he's good
He's pretty good alright
But I could write something like that.
Anybody could write something like that.

—Bob Holman ✪

HOW TO HOWL

I f you don't think HOWL is the greatest poem of USA 20th Century then what is?

No poem has had more effect on society, no poem still reads so fresh and boppy, what other poem has been taken to court, now it's a Hollywood film....

HOWL did it. Busted up US and European poetry traditions, made the outsider poet visible. Revived the tradition of the poetry reading. Put on trial as pornographic. Made poetry synonymous with liberation politics, sex, homosexuality, drug use. Anti-government, antimilitary, anti-corporatism.

Superlatives don't sit well with poetry—the very idea that a poem might be considered "better" let alone "the best" seems gauche to many. Which is why poetry slams were born, to satirize this utopian vision of pure poetry—in slams, judges with no qualifications rate poems like at the Olympics, 1-10 with decimals.

Intimacy is the rule and role for how most contemporary poetry is taught: a poem being the meeting point of poet and reader, that quiet still-point of mind where you "read to yourself," a notion which itself only evolved slowly after writing was invented: the first books were an excuse to party, with whoever could read (Noble? Scribe?) standing in for the (usually illiterate) wandering Bard.

But superlatives are natural for Orality, where the Praise Poem is a common poetic form: a string of hyperboles for the visiting dignitary, with his or her name dropped into the poem as often as possible. In West Africa, the Praise Poem continues until the money stops dropping into the griot's kora's resonator hole. Sometimes, if the cash isn't enough, the Praise Poem becomes downright hostile!

Allen Ginsberg wrote HOWL to contradict the blandess of USA 1950s, as an indictment of the military-industrial complex, as a howl of joy for the liberation of the soul. He was 29 when he wrote the poem in 1955. Its first performance was on Friday, October 7, 1955 at the Six Gallery, 3119 Fillmore Street in San Francisco, now a rug store. It was a historic Saskatchewan, immortalized in Kerouac's *Dharma Bums*. The day after the reading, Lawrence Ferlinghetti telegrammed Ginsberg offering to publish the work, which would lead to his standing trial to do so.

This storied work has the glow of history about it, and offers the opportunity to research on many levels. The poem makes many allusions to literary and historical sources but mainly to Ginsberg's friends and the early history of those who would become the Beats. You can explore the whole Beat mythology with HOWL as the basis; find your way into Buddhism, jazz, and a wide variety of literature, from the Bible, Torah, and Koran to the underground writers of the 50s. There are numerous books written on the subject:

☆Morgan, Bill and Joyce Peters, *Howl on Trial*.
☆Jonah Raskin, *American Scream: Allen Ginsberg's "Howl" and the Making of the Beat Generation*.
☆Lewis Hyde, *On the Poetry of Allen Ginsberg*.
☆Jason Shinder, *The Poem That Changed America: "Howl" Fifty Years Later*.

There are numerous versions of Ginsberg reading the poem. Composer Lee Hyla set it to music. Eric Drooker's *Illustrated: Howl: A Graphic Novel*, was published in 2010 and was the basis for the animations in the James Franco-starring movie *HOWL* of that same year. There is an annual

HOWL! Festival in New York City's East Village, and a HOWL HELP Fund for artists that that Festival supports. You can also watch *Pull My Daisy,* made by Robert Frank and Alfred Leslie in 1959, in which Ginsberg and Corso and Orlovsky and Amram and others cavort to an improvised "spontaneous bop prosody" narration by Jack Kerouac. The Beat goes on. And of course you can HOWL yourself.

Write Your Own

Students can write their own HOWL. It can follow the HOWL form like this by Oyl Miller.

TWEET.

BY OYL MILLER
I saw the best minds of my generation destroyed by brevity, over-connectedness, emotionally starving for attention, dragging themselves through virtual communities at 3 am, surrounded by stale pizza and neglected dreams, looking for angry meaning, any meaning, same hat wearing hipsters burning for shared and skeptical approval from the holographic projected dynamo in the technology of the era, who weak connections and recession wounded and directionless, sat up, micro-conversing in the supernatural darkness of Wi-Fi-enabled cafés, floating across the tops of cities, contemplating techno, who bared their brains to the black void of new media and the thought leaders and so called experts who passed through community colleges with radiant, prank playing eyes, hallucinating Seattle- and Tarantino-like settings among pop scholars of war and change, who dropped out in favour of following a creative muse, publishing zines and obscene artworks on the windows of the internet, who cowered in unshaven rooms, in ironic superman underwear burning their money in wastebaskets from the 1980s and listening to Nirvana through paper thin walls, who got busted in their grungy beards riding the Metro through Shinjuku station, who ate digital in painted hotels or drank Elmer's glue in secret alleyways, death or purgatoried their torsos with tattoos taking the place of dreams, that turned into nightmares, because there are no dreams in the New Immediacy, incomparably blind to reality, inventing the new reality, through hollow creations fed through illuminated screens. Screens of shuttering tag clouds and image thumbnails lightning in the mind surfing towards Boards of Canada and Guevara, illuminating all the frozen matrices of time between, megabyted solidities of borders and yesterday's backyard wiffleball dawns, downloaded drunkenness over rooftops, digital storefronts of flickering flash, a sun and moon of programming joyrides sending vibrations to mobile devices set on manner mode during twittering wintering dusks of Peduca, ashtray rantings and coffee stains that hid the mind, who bound themselves to wireless devices for an endless ride of opiated information from CNN.com and Google on sugary highs until the

noise of modems and fax machines
brought them down shuddering,
with limited and vulgar verbiage
to comment threads, battered bleak
of shared brain devoid of brilliance in the drear light of a
monitor, who sank all night in in-
terface's light of Pabst floated
out and sat through the stale sake
afternoon in desolate pizza par-
lours, listening to the crack of
doom on separate nuclear iPods,
who texted continuously 140 characters at a time from park to pond
to bar to MOMA to Brooklyn Bridge
lost battalion of platonic laconic
self proclaimed journalists committed to a revolution of information, jumping down the stoops off
of R&B album covers out of the
late 1980s, tweeting their screaming vomiting whispering facts and
advices and anecdotes of lunchtime
sandwiches and cat antics on
couches with eyeballs following
and shockwaves of analytics and of
authority and finding your passion and other jargon, whole in-
tellects underscored and wiped
clean in the total recall 24/7 365
assault all under the gaze of once
brilliant eyes.

Or you may like to read some of the other and
more obvious great manifestos and make your
own: *Projective Verse* by Charles Olson, *Personism*
by Frank O'Hara, *Dada Manifesto* by Tristan
Tzara, *The Futurist Manifesto*, F.T. Marinetti, *A
Slap in the Face of Public Taste* by Mayakovsky,
and others.

Look on the writing of HOWL as breathing—
here Ginsberg took to heart his great alignment
with Whitman, that the line follows the breath,
not a form. Then try some formal experiments

with HOWL. Cut out all the unnecessary words.
Whoops, there aren't any! Ginsberg was experimenting with dropping articles and other words,
making the line gallop and drive by condensing,
pushing words together. Well, maybe you can
find some.

Researching HOWL is to learn about the US in
the 50s, a very conservative time, the time of
HUAC, the House Un-American Activities Com-
mittee. You can research the trial that declared
HOWL not obscene, but a work of art. And you
can discover whether HOWL can be read on
radio/TV now—what would happen if this happened? With HOWL you are always close to the
edge.

Who were the Beats? Try drawing a chart of their
connections to each other. Who slept with
whom? HOWL foretells many of the Liberation
Movements that would come in the 60s and 70s.
Buddhism is another angle.

The Gallery Six reading, where HOWL was first
read publicly, was an astonishing event. Kenneth
Rexroth was the MC. Kerouac was in the audience. Research this event, write about it, perform
it—what poems did Philip Whalen read? What
was unusual about Michael McClure's reading
that night? What was the San Francisco Poetry
Renaissance? Who was John Hoffman—can you
find his poems? Do a recreation of this reading.
HOWL. You and Jack 'GO! GO! GO' Allen's
words—and listening to versions of Allen's reading you'll note how he grew into himself, how
the poem goes into larger and larger orbits as it
unfolds over the years. Now it's your turn....

The Fugs were a great poets' rock'n'roll band
whose lead warbler was the poet Ed Sanders.
They are totally inspired by HOWL and the
Beats, and are another link between the Beats
and Hippies. Who are they? Listen to their music
and write a paper on a a 120-foot scroll, the way
Kerouac wrote *On the Road*. How did Tuli
Kupferberg figure in HOWL? Make your own
performance of Fugs material part of a HOWL
reading: *Ah Sunflower, Slum Goddess from the
Lower East Side, Nothing, We're Both Dead
Now, Alice.*

Performing HOWL

is an honour and a treat.

Group HOWL

For years I've conducted an annual Group HOWL of 15 to 20 poets. Held in historic Tompkins Square Park, the Group HOWL is the conclusion of the Allen Ginsberg Poetry Reading, which itself is the kickoff of the HOWL Festival of Lower East Side Arts. The ensemble is comprised of poets from the downtown NYC poetry scenes: St. Marks Poetry Project, Nuyorican Poets Café, Steve Cannon's Gathering of the Tribes, Cave Canem, the Bowery Poetry Club. Each group selects three to four poets. The AGPR runs like this: a famey Loisaida (Lower East Side) poet reads—John Giorno, say, or Anne Waldman, Hettie Jones, David Henderson; then the processional—each poet reads a single poem, usually about three minutes. What a beautiful way to colour the air at this gorgeous gritty urban site! And then, baton aloft, all poets on stage, we begin. "I saw the best...".

We've begun in French, with D. Kimm and Alexis O'Hara, we've begun with Anne Waldman soloing. After that, madness, chaos, beauty ensues. There are solo, duets, repetitions ("Boxcars boxcars boxcars boxcars..."). I use the "conduction" techniques developed by jazz genius Butch Morris, and used by Edwin Torres. These hand signals can be learned by the conductor (if you have one), or you can develop your own. See the film about Butch, *Black February*, as a way in. Maybe you want a strict and formal concert. Maybe you want total improv. At the HOWL Festival, poets jump off the stage and read to people in the audience, musical instruments suddenly appear, multilinguality, polyphony, and anarchy rein.

A great way to start building your Group HOWL is to have the poets (now, I use the word poets to describe the performers, but you can use whatever word you like, such as, "persons") select their own line. This will be their solo. What if two (or more) choose the same line? Hallelujah! A "mistake"! Because in group creation, these mistakes are signs that show the way.

You can rehearse. You can designate the sections by falling down or falling asleep or spinning on your toes. Rollerskate. Tapdance. The possibilities are forever.

Mainly what you want to do is capture the spirit of this extraordinary poem. Which you can never do. Because like all great art it cannot be captured or boxed or sold. HOWL is a living thing, and it can be part of your life. It's no secret—pass it on. Somehow you should get Allen into the show. After all, he started it. One human.

Kaie
Kellough
kaie.ca

N é in the way out West, Kaie Kellough has been based in Montréal since 1998. He is a bilingual author, editor, educator, and general word sound systemizer. His bop-inflected vox and text syncopate Canada's solitudes. Kaie has performed and published across Canada and in the United States. His poetry has recently appeared in *Shelf* magazine (Houston, TX, 2010), and *580 Split*, a journal of arts and letters (Oakland, 2010).

Kaie is the author of two poetry books, *Lettricity* (Cumulus Press, 2004), and, his latest book, *Maple Leaf Rag* (Arbeiter Ring Publishing, April 2010). Kaie and his work have been featured on CBC radio, Zed TV, and Bravo. He recently completed a sound recording, *Vox Versus*, that will be released on the Wired on Words imprint in 2011. Since 2005, Kaie has conducted language workshops as part of Blue Metropolis, Montréal's premier literary festival. Since 2007 he has received annual invitations to discuss language and poetry with undergraduate students in McGill University's Faculty of Education. He has given educational, language-centred presentations throughout Montréal at the high school, CÉGEP, and university levels, and he has twice been commissioned to create themed performance poems by the Quebec Ministry of Education. His commissioned works have been taught throughout the province of Quebec. ✪

Photo credit, Elsa Marie Jabre

goodbye hip hop

goodbye nigger & all that chimes with you, middle fingers & triggers, biggers &
figures, gold diggers. goodbye
end rhyme. goodbye gangster minstrels, b.e.t. shuck & jive, cornrows pinching
teen minds

goodbye slang memes: willy, front, bling, kicks, floss. goodbye arch type, lip
synch stereo trope, whole ghetto
hefted on shoulder hype

goodbye hip hope, club shot up, hole in heart, diamond copped, spade dropped by
a hot steel tip, afterlife shades
who flip rocks into royce rolls & stack stocks cold & spit golden stools, who
hire white chauffeurs to spirit fools
across the cross, fader, over the main seam

goodbye detritus of american dramas, one hit wanderers turned cab drivers, rap
raconteurs in obscure hoods, lyrics
falling on deaf ears, cipher at your ear's epic enter

goodbye representation & your insane demeans, have not rental dreams, benz lexus
& fabulous beams, goodbye 5%
notion, afro asiatic slack men, jingling booty vixens, supermasculine menial
gender prescriptions

goodbye head nod, blunt thought, ebonic champ rhyme chops, subwoofer hard knocks
& b movie barber shops.
your moment is moot. if you be table turning revelation, looping reincarnation,
if movement you be, mutate

—Kaie Kellough ✪

First appeared in *580 Split, A Journal of the Arts and Letters*
2010, E-zine; a *Canada Speaks commission*

HISTORY EXERCISE

OBJECTIVES

To introduce students to several important modern branches of the oral tradition; to give students a sense of inhabiting the history of the oral tradition; to engage students with a live example of story-telling as oral history.

INTRODUCTION

This workshop confines itself to English oral traditions of the 20th century. It focuses on traditions from the Caribbean and North America. The workshop is bracketed by a story that links personal history with spoken word history.

REQUIRED SUPPORT MATERIAL

All of the poets mentioned herein can be located online. Their work can be purchased or accessed for free. Individual tracks can be purchased from online music stores.

INSTRUCTIONS

The following narrative should be passed out to the students. It should be read aloud, either collectively or by the instructor. The reading should be interspersed with examples of material from the artists and art forms mentioned. All are included in **bold**. The instructor can decide which artists to include based on student needs and the suitability of available material. Ideal places to insert material are after paragraphs 2, 4, 5, 6, 7, 8, 10, 11. These places are also noted in the text.

Discussion can then ensue about what the students heard and how they heard it.

Examples of guiding questions:

➥ **1.** When you listen to this artist, how does his/her vocal delivery differ from regular speech?

➥ **2.** Do you notice anything unique about the language the poet uses?

➥ **3.** How does the poem interact with the music? Is it a song form? If not, what do you think is happening between the musicians and the poet?

TIME

This exercise should take 50 minutes, but can be extended based on the number of audio/film samples the instructor wishes to include, and the amount of discussion about these samples.

AN AUDIENCE WITH SCRIBE WILLIAMS

By Kaie Kellough

Growing up I was always interested in the spoken word and the human voice. I loved radio, and so I became a radio programmer. My station was CKUT 90.3 FM, radio McGill, Montreal, and I interviewed many people, from politicians to athletes, but one of my most interesting guests was the spoken word poet Scribe Williams. When I asked Scribe about his poetic influences and about how he became interested in spoken word, he provided the following biographical sketch:

"My father came of age in Jamaica in the 1970s, when reggae was becoming the musical voice of the island. That time also saw the rise of a unique form of poetry, **dub poetry**, which was spoken in the Jamaican patois. Dub engaged with people's everyday experiences, explored the island's history and politics, and examined international affairs. In our home, when I was much younger, my father played records by the British dub poet **Linton Kwesi Johnson**. Linton was the first poet I ever heard speaking his work aloud, to music.

"My mother grew up in San Francisco. She tells me she was always a reader, and her family is a family of readers. We could all be together in the same room without speaking a word. My grandparents might be obscured behind the *New York Times*. My aunts and uncles would be bent over **Jack Kerouac** novels or *Time* magazines. I'd have my **Dr. Seuss** books—by the way, I consider Dr. Seuss an excellent children's poet whose work is best read aloud—and we would read together for hours.

"In college my mom attended poetry readings at **City Lights** bookstore. City Lights was a hub of **beat-generation** culture, out of which grew some of the artists that were very important to spoken word. **Lawrence Ferlinghetti** founded the bookstore, and he produced several recordings of his poetry recited with jazz accompaniment. **Allen Ginsberg**, one of my favourites, was published by City Lights, and has been recorded many times,

with and without instrumental accompaniment. I discovered books by these artists on my mother's shelves, and when she found me reading them, she told me: "If you want to hear what their voices sound like, I can play some of their poems for you." So I was introduced to the beat generation in both literary and oral form.

"My parents met in New York in the 1970s. They were both attending graduate school. As the story goes, they met in Greenwich Village at a loft performance that featured the poets **Jayne Cortez**, **Sonia Sanchez**, and **Amiri Baraka**. My parents still have the poster advertising the poetry reading. It's framed and it hangs in their hallway. These artists formed part of **BAM**, or the **Black Arts Movement**. One of the important features of BAM was, again, the use of voice and body to deliver poetry. When poetry was combined with music, as it often was, the music was blues- and jazz-related.

"My dad also had a record called *Anthology of Negro Poets*, which featured the ancestors of the BAM poets. All of the recordings were a capella, that is, without musical accompaniment. The record was badly scratched, so not all of the voices came through clearly, but it included **Langston Hughes**, **Gwendolyn Brooks**, and **Sterling A. Brown**. Their performances have an easy swing that recalls the blues.

"One of the things you've probably noticed is that all of these different groups of poets cultivated a relationship to music – to jazz, blues, and reggae. My dad, being West-Indian, also listened to a form of music that comes from Trinidad, called **calypso**, and calypso has a parallel poetic tradition called **rapso**, which is basically poetry 'rapped' to the form and structure of a calypso song. The early calypsonians, for instance **Mighty Sparrow**, composed satirical lyrics that, like those of the ancient Roman poets **Juvenal** and **Martial**, commented directly on the people and the society about them.

"My father had a lot of family in Toronto, and after my parents married, they decided to migrate north. Toronto wasn't yet the largest city in Canada, but it was growing and it seemed to provide my parents with a new beginning. To my father's delight, Toronto had a vibrant dub poetry community, one of the most important ones in the world. Poets like **Lillian Allen** and **Clifton Joseph** were actively performing, writing, publishing, teaching, and recording, and today they are still active. My mother discovered Toronto's **sound poetry** community, which included **The Four Horsemen**, a quartet whose pieces often dispensed with words in order to more fully experiment with voice and sound.

"I'm giving you all of this background to make the point that I can trace the 20th century history of my art form through my personal history. I may be leaving some things out, but I have to repeat that this is personal history, so it only includes the artists whose work directly affected my own. Since we often discover the arts through some personal connection—books on our parents' shelves, or records in their collections, the history of spoken word can be understood by looking into our backgrounds, and that way we can construct our poetic lineage.

"My own performance also has a strong relationship to music. I was born in 1980, a child of the **hip hop** generation. Toronto boasts a large concentration of black Canadians, Caribbean Canadians, and African Canadians. Toronto is the centre of black Canada's culture, home to our major hip hop acts, reggae acts, dub poets, jazz outfits, and to a large spoken word and slam scene. In my early twenties I saw **Ursula Rucker** perform. Ursula is a spoken word poet whose voice and delivery resemble Sonia Sanchez', whom I mentioned earlier as part of **BAM**. But Ursula has performed with the hip hop group **The Roots**, and has released solo albums that fuse her words with electronic music.

"When I was younger I competed in **poetry slams**, and that was how I first got into performing poetry. My verses were informed by the cadences of hip hop. I slammed for several years at the national level, and eventually outgrew the slam's competitive format. I am now trying to work with a more diverse set of influences: calypso, jazz, sound poetry, blues. I've once again taken to studying the poets from all of the movements that I've mentioned so far."

Scribe Williams and I talked further about his art and his family, and he admitted that he wouldn't have become a poet if he hadn't explored his family background. Even though neither of his parents are poets, he said that: "...poetry accompanied them from city to city, country to country. It bridged different places and different decades. It also gave each place a distinct voice, and those voices have blended into my own." The last time we spoke, Scribe was moving to Kingston, Jamaica after having spent two years travelling between San Francisco and New York.

INDEPENDENT STUDY EXERCISE

Write out your personal and immediate family history, and this should include: place of birth and the places you have lived; places your parents were born and have lived; grandparents' birthplaces and places of residence. If you do not know or are not aware of some of this information, that is fine. Work with what you know. From here, you can research poetry and spoken-word connections to all of the places you and your immediate family members have lived. This helps to develop a personal connection to the art form and to situate yourself within it. ✪

WRITING EXERCISE

OBJECTIVES

To explore the elasticity of language; to engage students' language capabilities, for instance their ability to manipulate meaning; to engage in problem-solving.

INTRODUCTION

The activity presented in this exercise is an ANAGRAM. In an anagram, the letters of a particular word are permuted to form other words, for example: bard = drab, brad. With all of the new word formations, a coherent piece of writing is assembled.

REQUIRED MATERIALS

The students will need paper and pens, and the room will need to be equipped with a chalkboard or impermanent marker board.

DIRECT INSTRUCTION

Ask students if they know what an anagram is. Give the above definition, including the example. Explain to students that they will be composing an anagram.

Step 1 ♥ Danger (10 minutes). Instruct students to write the word DANGER at the top, centre of their page. Also write the word on the board. Explain the following rules of anagram composition:

Only the letters of our subject word, D-A-N-G-E-R can be used.

Letters can be repeated, for instance: Arrear.

All of the letters of DANGER do not need to be used each time; for instance we can create words using only some of the letters: Egg, Dad.

Abbreviations and acronyms are acceptable, for example: G.E. and A.D.D.

Vernacular terms are acceptable, so long as the students can prove that the terms are, in fact, used.

Instruct students to begin creating their own individual word lists, coming up with as many permutations and combinations of D-A-N-G-E-R as they can.

Step 2 ♥ Collective word list (30 minutes). Once students have their individual word lists, begin to cull a collective list of all the words that can be made using D-A-N-G-E-R. It is best to begin methodically, with the letter D, and so forth.

Print a D in the top left corner of the board, and ask students one by one to provide words that begin with that letter. Proceed to the next letter, until DANGER's letters have been exhausted, and a comprehensive list has been collected. Students should follow suit and take down the list as it is compiled on the board.

☛ The role of the instructor is to move the process along efficiently, and to point out words that the students may not be aware of.

☛ Draw student attention to the following: Words that can produce multiple meanings, for instance: Darn, Dear, Gander.

⇢ Draw student attention to the following: For each letter ask them if they are aware of any acronyms or abbreviations that begin with that letter, for instance: D.E.A. (Drug Enforcement Agency), A.D.D. (Attention Deficit Disorder), N.D. (North Dakota), G.A. (Georgia), e.g. (for example), R.N.A. (Ribonucleic Acid).

☛ Draw student attention to the following: words that can be repeated by adding the prefix EN-, RE-, the suffix -ED, -ER, or a combination, for example: Read, Reread, Reader. Danger, Endanger, Endangered.

Once all of the possible combinations have been discovered, halt the process and count the words that have been generated. Let the students know how many words have been generated by permuting the letters D-A-N-G-E-R. Explain that R and N are consonants that appear in a high number of words, and that the vowels E (in particular) and A are the two vowels that appear most frequently in the English language.

Step 3 ♥ Composition (30 minutes). Divide students into groups. As this exercise can prove challenging, it helps students to be able to negotiate the anagram with their peers. This allows for multiple solutions to present themselves, and it helps students to avoid feeling alone or defeated if they become stumped. Encourage students to ask questions, and circulate among them as they compose.

Step 4 ♥ Presentation (15 minutes). Once the anagram has been composed, the individual groups share their works with the group at large. Though this workshop is focused on written language and not on orality, students should be instructed to think about the presentation of their work, to stand up, and to deliver the work in a clear voice without rushing, so that others can hear the creation. It would be prudent to give students five minutes to prepare their delivery.

FINAL QUESTIONS

Questions should be asked of each group as they finish presenting their work: Where did the idea come from? What were the difficulties you encountered? Which words or letters did you most want to use (but couldn't)?

The instructor should also listen for interesting passages, and ask students to repeat and explain those passages.

DANGER

Instructor's list—This list comprises 100 words generated by permuting the letters DANGER. The list is not exhaustive. For instance, past tenses like Deranged or Gangrened are not included, and neither are all possible slang terms, abbreviations, and acronyms. Nonetheless, the list does include some archaic constructions like E'en, Ere, some onomatopoeic words like Grr, acronyms like N.R.A., and proper names like Reagan.

D

Dad, Dade, Dan, Dane, Darn, Dean, Drear, Dear, Deer, Derange, Dander, Danger, Dagger, Drag, Dreg, Dread, D.N.A., D.A., D.E.A., Dr., Dang, Dead, Deaden

A

A, An, Add, Are, Area, Arrear, Adder, Age, Aged, Adage, Agenda, Anger, Arrange, A.D.D.

N

Nag, Near, Need, Ned, Nerd, N.R.A., N.D.

G

Gander, G.E., G.E.D., Grand, Garden, Gardener, Green, Greed, Gear, Gender, Gad, Gaga, Grade, Gangrene, Grr, Gee, Grenade, Grenada, Gene

E

Ear, Earn, End, Endear, Engender, Ere, Err, Errand, Egad, Eden, E.G., Egg, Eager, E'en

R

Ra, Ran, Rang, Rage, Rag, Ragged, Radar, Range, Ranger, Render, Rear, Reared, Read, Reader, Renege, Reagan, Rearrange, Regard, R.N.A., R.N., Rad, Red, Redden ☺

PERFORMANCE EXERCISE *With special thanks to Chris Masson*

OBJECTIVES

To explore our voices; to introduce the ways voice and movement interact when in performance; to explore vocabulary; to engage collaborative working practices; to think about voice and expression.

INTRODUCTION

Our voice is our intimate companion. As breath, it swells in our belly, builds in our chest, surges through our throat. As sound it vibrates our vocal chords, and resonates in our cranium. It is shaped by our teeth, tongue, and lips, and it projects out of our mouth. We use our voice every day, and at moments we are conscious of how we sound, but at other moments we are not. This workshop will help us to engage with our voices and with our personal sound.

INSTRUCTION

This workshop can be contracted to one hour and it can be extended further, depending on how much time the instructor allows for each step.

Step 1 ♥ Questioning our voices (five minutes). Ask students to think about their voices, to hum quietly in the middle of their vocal range, and to hear their voice in their head.

Ask students to take out a pad of paper and a pen. Ask them the following questions and give them time to jot down answers to each question.

+ **1.** Think about your voice. Where does it come from?
+ **2.** Do you know your voice? Is your voice your friend?
+ **3.** Do you know how you sound? Please describe how you sound in one short phrase.
+ **4.** Do you have any control over how you sound?
+ **5.** Do you sound how you would like to sound? Please describe how you would like to sound in one short phrase.

Step 2 ♥ Introducing the alphabet (10 minutes). Ask students to read out their answers to the above questions.

The workshop will now use the alphabet as tool to help explore voices. Ask students to call to mind the alphabet, A-to-Z. If they were to recite the alphabet in their natural speaking voice, how would it sound? Instruct students to take a deep breath and recite the alphabet aloud. While reciting, consider how their voice feels and sounds in their throat, in their mouths, in their heads. *(recite)*

If students were to recite the alphabet in the voice that sounds as they wish it would sound, how would they recite the alphabet? Instruct students to take another deep breath and to recite the alphabet again, in their perceived voices, listening and feeling attentively. *(recite)*

Question—Ask students what the differences were between the two voices they presented, and discuss.

Step 3 ♥ Abecedary (10 minutes). This step involves the students in the construction of a type of poem called an abecedary.

Write the alphabet on the board in front of the class. Explain the abecedary: It is a simple language game, and it is a composition in the sequence of the alphabet. Each word begins with the next letter of the alphabet, for instance:

"Andrew Broke Charlie's Digits. Each Finger Got Hammered. Injured Joints Killed… etc."

The abecedary must run from the beginning to the end of the alphabet, using all letters, without inserting any words that might disrupt the alphabetical sequence. The poem should contain 26 words. The poem can be divided into sentences and punctuated, if that suits students and helps them to create a coherent work.

If the group is small enough, the abecedary can be constructed collectively. But if the group is large, it may help to divide students into smaller groups. Each student should write the abecedary down.

Question—Once the abecedary is constructed, seek out a volunteer to read it to the group. Ask students what they think of their construction.

Step 4 ♥ Performing the abecedary (15 minutes). Break students into groups of two to rehearse how they would deliver the abecedary to an audience. However, there is a twist to this rehearsal. From the following list, students must choose one way of performing the poem:

✦ **1.** With slow-burning rage
✦ **2.** With despair
✦ **3.** With impatience
✦ **4.** With bliss
✦ **5.** With terror
✦ **6.** With hilarity

While the students prepare their performances, the instructor should circulate and answer questions. Have the students who are willing present for the group.

Step 5 ♥ Movement, expression, and body (15 minutes). This final step is about how silent devices like gesture, movement, and facial expression complement our voices, and how these devices can have their own silent voice.

Students should return to their groups to silently revisit the abecedary, and then to consider the way they delivered it. In this stage, students are to re-present the abecedary in the same way, but without any sound. They can mouth the words, but they are not to utter a sound. They are to use facial expression, gesture, and movement to emphasize the piece. Once they are comfortable with their delivery, those who wish to do so should present their silent expressions to the group at large, and the group at large should try to guess which state of being they are trying to emphasize.

Final question/Independent Study Exercise: Ask students to ponder the questions asked at the beginning of the workshop:

✦ **1.** Think about your voice. Where does it come from?
✦ **2.** Do you know your voice? Is your voice your friend?
✦ **3.** Do you know how you sound? Please describe how you sound in one short phrase.
✦ **4.** Do you have any control over how you sound?
✦ **5.** Do you sound how you would like to sound? Please describe how you would like to sound in one short phrase.

Would they answer these questions differently? Ask students to independently consider and write out new, detailed answers to these questions. ✪

Shane Koyczan

Born and raised in Yellowknife, North West Territories, Shane Koyczan was the first poet from outside the USA to win the prestigious USA National Individual Poetry Slam. Koyczan has published two books, a poetry collection *Visiting Hours*, and a novel in verse, *Stickboy*. *Visiting Hours* was selected by both the *Guardian* and *Globe and Mail* for their 2005 Best Books of the Year lists. Shane was featured in *Quill & Quire* magazine in May 2006. He has performed to full houses around the world. Koyczan has rocked the stage at the Edinburgh Book Festival, the Vancouver International Writers Festival, the Winnipeg Folk Festival, and was named the highlight of The Hillside Festival in Guelph in 2009. He performed at the 2007 Canada Day Celebrations in Ottawa, where he opened for Feist. His recent performance at the 2010 Olympic Opening Ceremonies brought the 55,000+ seat house to their feet with his homage to Canada *We Are More*. ✪

Pre–History

I had an ancestor
(I must have)
who lived through the ice age

and before him or her
was another ancestor
who didn't get to see any dinosaurs
but witnessed fire for the first time
with all of the wonder we must have had
when they unveiled the iphone

and before him or her
another ancestor who lived
back when moths
the size of department stores
roamed the earth

don't look for their bones
being attracted to the light
they left one night a long time ago

why do you think there are all those craters in the moon?

and on and on through the ages

there is someone in my family
who was the first one of us
to ever use a toilet
and being an ancestor of mine
no doubt thought
"this is heaven… but something to read would be divine"

and while I do often wonder about my ancestors
and the wars
my family
and the plagues

often
my mind floods back to bone daggers
                    to unsuccessful hunting trips
when the cost of food
could take in return
not only a life
but perhaps an entire lineage
"we're sorry Ug… we regret to inform you that Ga was heroically stepped on in
battle… here is your share of the meat… you have two moons to vacate the cave"

I think of how unibrows
were the first sideburns
        of how I am most likely the product of a rape
that occurred before anyone invented a series of grunts
that meant "I like you… do you like me?"
        of how that may have been
the world's first love poem

and then I think of you
and want so desperately to ask
"do you have any idea what I've been through to get to you?"

but I don't

knowing full well
that you had ancestors too
(you must have).

—Shane Koyczan ✪

SHERI-D WILSON INTERVIEWS SHANE KOYCZAN DECEMBER 12, 2010

HISTORY

What is history to you, as it relates to writing?
As it relates to writing, I think all of us started off in school with those books on poetry and poetics, and we all had the same notebooks. It was all, you know, very William Blake, or T.S. Eliot's "The Love Song of J. Alfred Prufrock" — work that, while it was very well written, I didn't understand all of it at the time because it didn't really relate to me and I had no way to relate to it. Because I didn't know the history involved.

Umm… then over time, being exposed to more contemporary writers like Al Purdy, Tom Wayman, Leonard Cohen, and Tess Gallagher, and relating more to that kind of expression, I started to see the value in poetry. Umm… and it allowed me to express what I was going through at certain times of my life…

What history has most influenced your life and your writing?
I think my personal history… a lot of what I write is based on personal experiences, whether or not they were stories told to me or events I lived through. A lot of my writing comes from a personal place and I think that's the landscape that a lot of other writers attempt to traverse when they are writing… I guess personal history would mean the most.

What prompt would you give to students to shift them into their own personal history, what would you say to them?
I would say: "Take the first memory that pops into your mind and then think: Why did that one pop into my mind? Why is that memory the most relevant for me at this moment? And go from there."

Speak to me about your own history.
I had a pretty hard childhood growing up… my mom wasn't there, my dad wasn't there… I was raised by my grandparents, so my grandparents have had a big influence on my life and I probably wouldn't have been afforded the educational opportunities that I was had I not been with them. So that played a large part… in terms of writing, I didn't really break through, I didn't really start seeking out poetry until university rolled around and I started reading writers like Al Purdy, Tom Wayman, and Leonard Cohen. Of course, musically, artists like Ani Difranco, who from time to time, will do a spoken word piece that's pretty influential.

Great. I love you, Shane Koyczan. Personal history is such an important part of all of our work when we do spoken word, while getting to personal history is sometimes very difficult. You know, in the sense of what to do when you traverse those more difficult areas. Do you have any prompts for students as to what to do if they hit a difficult patch?
The first thing you have to do, I think, is truly process your experiences. You know, you can't just say, "Oh this is something that happened in my life, so I'm going to write about it." You really have to go through the process and come out the other side first. And then, you know, try and live through the experience, as painful as that might be, when you are ready to write about it — and believe me, you will know. In some cases, that is probably the best jumping-off point and to have a full idea of what it is and what it has meant to you this far in your life, because over time, the experience will change in your mind. I don't think it's either positive or negative, but it changes. I can't describe what I'm talking about.

I think to process things before you get into writing them down and then putting them out into the world is a really important aspect, and I think you did a great job of expressing that. You mentioned three Canadian male poets that have influenced you… is there any movement, like the Beats, the Black Mountain poets, or the Four Horsemen, who have influenced you?
You know, the Beats definitely had an influence, even people like Lillian Allen and yourself and

Ivan Coyote. In terms of storytelling, there are so many influences. Musically, too—a lot of people ask me all the time, are you into hip hop? I'm not really into hip hop. I realize my style is definitely derived from influences of hip hop, but I don't emulate hip hop. I take it more from the story-telling angle. But I think for me, growing up, and listening to music when I was a kid, did have a lasting effect. You know, you get the little liner notes for the songs so you can read along with the lyrics, and for a lot of songs, they were really short. Like one of those tiny pages on a cassette book. And then hip hop came along, and people read the liner notes and each one was three or four pages long. That definitely influenced me, in terms of what you can have, and how you can create it. More lyrical content can be as important as the music that's driving it.

Nice… let's move on to "Writing."

WRITING & COMPOSITION

Advance Questions:

❧ Why do you write?

❧ Do you collect images and then put them into the work?

❧ Or do you write from the top to the bottom?

❧ What do you look for?

❧ What do you listen for?

❧ How many times do you write a piece?

❧ Do you have a notebook?

❧ Do you take notes and write things down?

❧ What would you say about writing, to someone who wants to write?

All right, so we'll start from the top. Shane Koyczan, why do you write?

I think it gives me a level of personal relief. A lot of writers say it's cheaper than therapy. I don't know if that's true, but I think at the base, it's just something I really enjoy. I enjoy expressing the creative aspect of myself and the fact that I'm able to create something from scratch or from a memory and transcribe it to something that someone else may connect to. I think it's really…

I really enjoy the aspect of bridging a connection between strangers… and that's what I love about writing.

Communication, that's true. You collect images. I ask you this because of the strength of the images in your writing and your remarkable metaphors. Do you collect images and then put them into the work or do you write from the top to the bottom?

Well, when I write a piece, I try to write it backwards. I start at the end and work towards the beginning. That way, by the time I reach the end, I know it's the end and the audience should also know it's the end. I have been at a number of poetry readings where I can't tell if the poet is finished his/her poem or not. People start clapping half-way through the poem and the poet keeps going and then the audience feels unintelligent. So when I write, one of the things I want to do is drive the poem straight through to the end.

In terms of collecting images, I tend to write every day, and not everything that I write is useful in the moment. So a lot of the time, I'll take what I've written for the day and maybe if I can't use it yet, I'll put it into a file on my computer called "purgatory." That way if I get stuck for an idea or an image down the road, I can open my "purgatory" file, and look up something that may get me writing or inspire me into something completely different. That's just one of the tricks I've picked up… but everyone has their own method.

You say you write every day… does it just come to you, as it comes to you?

It comes to me, as it comes to me. I enjoy writing most when I'm tired. That way I feel I'm more in touch with my subconscious. It's crazy because I really want to go to sleep and in that way my subconscious is keeping it true. Being tired tends to lend itself to more vivid imagery. So I like writing when I'm tired even though I hate writing when I'm tired.

That's quite a dichotomy! And I totally understand what you are saying. I think it's a relevant idea for students and like you say, everybody has their own

method. Tiredness is one of them.
Meditation. Hunger…

I'm an insomniac, so a lot of the times, that's where it's coming from.

And is there a particular thing you look for and/or listen for?
In writing?

In finding the subconscious…
Not really. I think the best moments are when you shut off the computer or typewriter, walk away for a little bit, and then come back to it and realize, "Oh geez, I don't even really remember writing that." I enjoy that moment of being surprised by it all over again. I'll write something but I can't go back and process it right at that moment. I have to let it sit for a little bit; a lot of the time, the best part for me is rediscovering, "Oh wow, I can't believe I made that connection, or metaphor, or these parallels in this piece."

Très bien! Do you write in a notebook, by hand, with a pen or…?
I do both ways. I always have my handy Moleskin notebook that I take everywhere, because you never know when inspiration is going to hit you. So I always have my pen and pad on hand. I definitely keep one on the side of the bed, because I may wake up in the middle of the night and think of something amazing.

It's true. Like last night, in the middle of dream, I thought of the title for my new book.
There you go. You see the same thing as me. Every now and then, I'll wake up in the middle of the night and write it down.

And I think it's good to get up in the middle of the night, even though sometimes it's hard, but you have to force yourself otherwise you'll forget your ideas and you'll walk around the next day feeling like you're in Bardo—creative coitus interruptus!

Maybe it's a good time to move into performance.

PERFORMANCE

Advance Questions:

❧ What are the first things that you do when you go into performance?

❧ Do you change? Like I change shoes, as one of the things I do.

❧ How do you choose your music?

❧ Does the music follow you? Do you follow the music?

❧ Does a piece change with music?

❧ When do you go into the performance phase, what are the first things you think about?

❧ Do you have any exercises that you do with the text, in order to bring it to performance?

❧ If so, what are they?

❧ You collaborate a lot. What guidance can you share with someone who is beginning this process?

What is the first thing you do when you go into performance mode with a text?
I think the first thing I do is stretch. Stretching is really important. Also I like vocal acrobatics, tongue-twisters, because it's really easy to get mixed up and flustered when you have an audience in front of you, which is always nerve-wracking. So I think one of the most important preparations is warm yourself up.

What kind of stretching do you do?
Oh, basic stretches like arm stretches, opening up your lungs, back, and shoulders. I don't worry about legs too much because for the most part, I'm pretty stationary. But I definitely work the upper body, neck, and I open up the throat. A lot of times, people have remarked that I'm constantly yawning backstage, that I look so calm because I'm always yawning. The truth is it's a nervous reaction—I tend to yawn because I'm not getting enough oxygen; I'm not breathing properly so I really have to be conscious of that. So while I may look calm or un-worried, I'm actually freaking out.

Well, you also play for audiences from 200-20,000; is there a difference?

I think that whether you are performing for two or 2,000 people it's really the same show. I remember when I first started off, playing coffee houses with three people in the audience, I was just as nervous as I would be performing for 2,000 today. In a way, it was even more nerve-wracking because the smaller the audience is, the more intensely focused they are on the performer. When you have a bigger audience, it's nerve-wracking as well, but there are different people to look to, there are different areas you can go. When there are three people, you're really limited in terms of who you can connect to.

My grand-dad always said, "Say you have an audience of 100 people, that's a 200–eyed–monster that you're trying not to piss off." That's his advice for public speaking!

And what are your vocal tongue-twisters?

There's a number of them, there's the old standards, "Peter Piper picked a peck of pickled peppers"—you know. CR Avery's got the… sort of rhyme-y, tongue twister-type ones. I don't have any favourites. There are ones I do over and over again. There's one that's really simple: "peachy, peachy, peachy, peachy…"—you know. It warms up your mouth.

I do red leather, yellow leather, red leather, yellow leather, red leather, yellow leather. How do you choose your music?

Do you mean in terms of The Short Story Long?

Yes, a great group! You must have a lot of advice, so I thought it might be a good area to step into.

To me, it's always a collaborative effort. Sometimes, one of my band-mates will come in with a new song they wrote and we'll play it out and see, "Do I have something that fits? Can I write something to this?" The main thing with picking music to go with poetry is the music has to be pretty simple… if the music is too complex, the music can overpower the words. I think that's one of the mistakes that a lot of people make when they put music to poetry; they have this really intricate music going-on behind the words, and the listener ends up being distracted by that—they'll just start listening to the music and lose the words. So I think you have to start off with a pretty simple line and develop it from there. But all the music should go towards driving the words and it shouldn't be the other way around.

What do you think about when you go to performance of text with music?

The important thing going into any performance, with any piece that I do, whether it's with music or without is: I really have to step into the emotional place that prompted me to write the piece in the first place. I have to remember why I wrote the piece, and why it was important to me. I have to be able to connect with it; otherwise, what's the point? I'm just standing there reciting. That's one of the things people tend to forget: performance versus recitation. In performance you really have to have an emotional connection with what you are saying; otherwise, you might as well just be reading off a page.

Do you choreograph gestures when you first memorize the text?

You know, I don't really. I have a couple of movements that I'll do throughout. I realize that muscle memory is pretty important to help people with memorization. For the most part, I just let my arms go and create a picture for someone. If not, it just looks like I'm just standing there, doing the hip hop thing—pushing to drive a rhythm is what I'm really doing.

Do you have any exercises that you do with the actual text to bring the images to life?

In terms of performance, I do a lot of "Italians." It was a term introduced to me when I was in high school drama. "Italians" are just a really quick run-through of the text. We'd be rehearsing a play for three weeks and then the last two days, we'd just do "Italians" of the play, which were really quick. We'd try to get through as many lines as possible!

So in terms of doing a poem, to get it cemented into my mind, I'll do an Italian, just to make sure I've got the memorization down. That way,

when I'm performing, I can forget that it's memorized and just be in the moment.

When beginning a collaboration, what are the first steps you need to take so that you have a strong collaboration?
Musically or with words?

I think both.
In terms of words, if you're collaborating on a poem, you have to make sure you're on the same page. While you may have different takes on the same subject, you should have the same theme working in your head. And I think the collaborations that work best are the ones where people have different takes on the same situation as long as the theme is there. The theme is what will tie it all together.

Anything else you would like to say to people who are writing poetry?
Keep writing, as clichéd as that sounds. Don't let anyone tell you that you can't use the word "unicorn" in a poem. That's bullshit.

Thanks sweetie.
Darling.

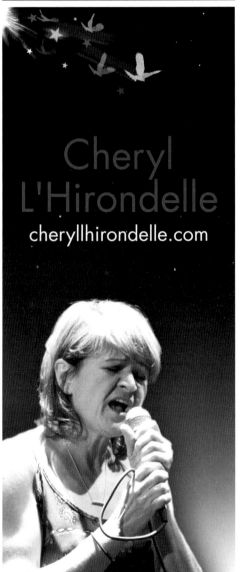

Cheryl
L'Hirondelle
cheryllhirondelle.com

Cheryl L'Hirondelle is an award-winning interdisciplinary artist, musician, and curator, from the land now known as Canada. A nomadic mixed-blood Indigenous woman originally from Alberta, L'Hirondelle investigates the junction of a Cree worldview in contemporary time and space. Her creative projects span a wide array of disciplines including music, performance art, spoken word, storytelling, audio art, public activism, and new media. ✪

Photo credit, Jason Jenkins

NDNSPAM Song

Our mama always said "you'll shit if you're well fed"
but that was just her way of saying "don't waste food"
"quit your belly-aching" and "clean your plate up"
"don't go to bed on an empty stomach"
"if it doesn't kill you, it'll make you stronger"
and "as long as we got water we got soup"

Some people like to gossip, and others lurk and hide,
And some were born to share their truths, broadcast them far and wide
still others well, they're into jokes, the kind from bathroom stalls
There's high tech and exclusive forts, passwords and firewalls
And who doesn't want five thousand "friends" to cc with spam mail?
"you're either hanging on the cross or banging in the nails."[i]

Our mama always said "you'll shit if you're well fed"
but that was just her way of saying "don't waste food"
"quit your belly-aching" and "clean your plate up"
"don't go to bed on an empty stomach"
"if it doesn't kill you, it'll make you stronger"
and "as long as we got water we got soup"

so come and have some:
pork n beans, rubaboo, bullet soup, smoked salmon too
ndn frybread or moose nose, la gallette or ndn tacos,
ndn steak, Klik – Prem – Kam, fried baloney – its all ndn spam,
maskehk-apoy, kahkiyawak, minisapoy, sash-ga-nuck,
ndn ice cream and fish cheeks, baked bannock-n-scratch with bear grease,
ndn popcorn and neck bones, come taste why "there's no place like home!"[ii]

now all this talkin' about food is making me remember things like…

"A good man is hard to find, but a hard man is good to find."
"Beauty is skin deep, but ugly goes right to the bone."
"Don't ever forget what colour your feathers are."
"Remember that a woman can run faster with her skirt up,
than a man can run with his pants down."
Note: these are all things our mama actually used to say to us!
And here's my personal favourite—"If you're looking for sympathy,
get a dictionary—you'll find it there—somewhere between shit and syphilis."

Our mama always said "you'll shit if you're well fed"
but that was just her way of saying "don't waste food"
"quit your belly-aching" and "clean your plate up"
"don't go to bed on an empty stomach"
"if it doesn't kill you, it'll make you stronger"
and "as long as we got water we got soup"

"I got something to say, and then I ain't gonna say no more."[iii]

"As long as we got water we got soup!"

[i] from the movie *Heart of Darkness*
[ii] from the movie *The Wizard of Oz*
[iii] from the movie *To Kill a Mockingbird*

—Cheryl L'Hirondelle ✪

First appeared on *AND Aurealities (CD)*
2005, Ambiuances Magnetiques,
© miyohtakwan music

The Personal

I am a mixed blood (Cree/Métis/French/German/Polish) singer/songwriter, storyteller and performance artist who's from a family who knows how to make a short story long. Though you may think this a funny introduction, in reality it has become a way of life and how I make a living, as I travel around the world and have the opportunity to experience the world around me. I try to do everything creative from a Cree worldview [nêhiyawin — pronounced: nay-HE-ya-win]. Regardless of the artistic discipline I'm working in, I have this enduring meta-image of myself — I am a bird singing my uniqueness hopping around from branch to branch of a large tree and I am singing in every direction — north, south, east, west, above, below, and deep inside too.

Exercise Do you have an image of yourself or is there an animal you dream of, that you think might be you? If you do, try writing a poem or a song about it. If you haven't, shut your eyes and see if anything pops into your imagination — then write about it.

I hope that none of you reading this grew up in a troubled home like I did. My parents rarely got along and my dad spent most of his time travelling for work. Although we lived in this land now known as Canada, neither of my parents had English (or French) as a first language (or their "mother tongue"), so communication was skewed and their cultures rarely were on the same page, and they were always at odds with the dominant culture of this land. My mother is from the Cree/Métis of the northern Alberta bush, and my German/Polish father emigrated from Europe to work in a lumber mill at Imperial Mills, Alberta, shortly after he was released from prisoner-of-war camp following World War II. Luckily my mom's family always dropped in for visits — so I had aunties, uncles, and cousins around and we were privy to hearing all the family stories, as we strained to listen to our parents sitting in the kitchen late into the night. Over the years, I have spent much time rethinking my personal history and researching my large family tree. It has been of much consequence, informing a lot of artistic projects when I was younger. I heard it said once, that if you don't know where you're from, how can you know where you're going?

Exercise Can you say the names of your grandmothers and grandfathers on both sides of your family? How many generations can you go back?

The Tradition of Orality

Native people have been referred to as belonging to oral-centric cultures. Cree people had camp chroniclers whose responsibility it was to move through the camp and announce to everyone what was going on — if a hunt or a skirmish had been successful, if there was a new couple, a birth, an illness or a death. These criers also woke up the camp in the mornings by singing a wake-up song as the sun was rising, and would sometimes settle disagreements, because they knew the dynamics of the camp so thoroughly.

While I agree with this idea of how oral our worldviews are, I have found that we also had objects and structures that were equally central. Since these "things" were made out materials that were biodegradable and/or mobile, they either ended up appropriated, catalogued and maybe forgotten in museum cases, or discarded when worn out, and gently covered over, and recycled by mother earth. We also had written languages that were systems of glyphs and imagistic signs—think about syllabics, petroglyphs, pictographs, and even the designs on our clothing. The Chippewa writer Louise Erdrich referred to the islands around the Lake of the Woods as books, because of the frequency of pictographs and what kind of messages and information these images were conveying.

Exercise
Have you ever seen them? Try to "read" a pictograph or a petroglyph out loud.

There is a strong relationship between the oral and the object. For instance, think about a talking stick. A talking stick is used to pass around a circle. When a person is in possession of the stick it is their turn to speak. The circle collectively imbues it with its authority as they take their turns holding it, as they rub their fingers over its surface or grip tightly while they speak.

We don't think about it much, but what if the same concentration we give to holding and touching the talking stick is the same concentration we use on an internal level as we commit to speaking our truth in public. We can then allow the words to caress the inside of our throats and roll around in our mouth to be uttered or come out firm with authority.

Also, the very act of speaking becomes an object because speaking becomes an event that everyone who witnesses it, sees and remembers it from a slightly different angle—almost like a sculpture. Perhaps this is why in this visually-centric world, we say "I saw a great show," where the "show" might have been a spoken word artist performing, a theatre piece, or your favourite band.

Indigenous worldviews are also considered land-based, and our languages are verb-oriented. So, when I think about the "oral tradition," I also like to combine it with this connection to the land by being involved with it. Native people always have had large territories that they would spend different times of the year hunting and gathering on, or having ceremonies and in the winter where we told stories, sacred stories about how the land and her creatures were created; winter recounts of a camp's history; stories of strength, bravery and courage; and personal recollections that would engage the young and old during long dark winters.

Exercise
Do you know what one of the earliest forms of storytelling was? If you guessed dance, you'd be correct. Think about the relationship between movement, land, and language. What does it make you think about—can you see an image or hear some words or sounds or perhaps a melody?

Residential schools forced Aboriginal children to speak only English or French, so in contemporary times some of our most effective orators have been chiefs, leaders, and political activists who have learned a great command of the two "official" languages, its pluralistic meanings, cadences and structures. Many secretly retained their language and many more are now relearning our Indigenous languages, though sadly there remain only about 150 Indigenous languages in this land now known as Canada.

Exercise
Please research languages that are becoming extinct. Think about the other related aspects which are also being lost, like cultures and therefore ways of seeing. Integrate these ideas into your being. When you write—

write from this place ♥

The Spoken Word

As the restrictions of the reserve system began to slacken and native students finished their residential school education, Native people once again began to travel—this time migrating into towns and cities. It was urban Native clubs/socials, and music and dance troupes where performing and playing Indian was regularly practiced. Later, poets and singers in cities became connected to jazz, hipster and underground scenes; several eventually reached mainstream audiences to achieve worldwide renown. Still later, Indigenous writers transformed theatres as they began to re-tell personal, sacred, and historical stories for the stage. More recently, younger wordsmiths have taken the slam poetry, rap and hip hop forms to express themselves. Throughout all this both intertwined with these forms and alone, storytelling remained an important part of how Indigenous people related cultural values and worldviews to each other and the rest of the world. ✪

Inspiration

It is no surprise that many of our best Indigenous writers, songwriters, poets, orators, storytellers, and artists have continued to use these "official" languages creatively. It may be because artists are always turning adversity into art. A will to succeed and its many challenges is part of the fuel and reward that keeps my creative spirit engaged to continue to express myself. What may be tension, whether personal, political and/or historical can usually become great artistic fodder. Depending on one's artistic practice, this tension can be useful in myriad ways: symbolizing the dynamic relationship between ideas, divergent material usage, and even creative disciplines, and it can be perfect when using irony to express oneself.

When I was young, I had many poems, stories, songs and most notably a favourite scene from a movie that was like an anthem expressing so many deep emotions. As I grew up my understanding of the scene changed in meaning but never lost its poignancy or impact. In part I also knew it was the delivery of the text based on the acting ability of the actor and the director of the film. But just thinking about it helped me assess my own words based on how close it made me feel when I heard the actor in *To Kill a Mockingbird* say "I got something to say, then I ain't gonna say no more."

What is your all-time favourite line from a poem, song, movie or TV show? Why? Now write about something that evokes the same feeling and try to hear the imperative, the rhythm, the melody or the tone of that voice in what you are writing. Does it have the same impact?

My own troubled childhood and home life provided me with plenty of insight into communication breakdowns and people not knowing how to read signs, and with that I cultivated a desire to decode and play around with the English language. As I learned more about myself via learning the history of how imperialism affected people all around the world, it also gave me a sense of duty to relearn both of my parents' languages. While I stumbled, mixing up sounds and saying things wrong or out of context, I experimented even more using my own body to create sound. And as I learned to hear myself, I also became more and more aware of how uniquely I could see and hear the world around me – leading to more inspiration.

Take a few moments to listen to what is going on around you. Write down what you hear. It may be something in your mind wanting to be released, it may be your heart beating, your neighbour shifting in their seat or it may be another sound. Sometimes these sounds remind us of melodies, rhythms, words or evoke feelings—can you say what it is in words, letters, or perhaps in a melody? The words don't have to be spelled correctly and can just be sounds effects, but they should be meaningful to you and have a connection to what you have heard or witnessed.

There's also a lot of things on a daily basis that trigger me to return to some of those early childhood aches and pains. Instead of thinking that the comment is personal, I have creatively responded with a commentary to things that irk me or rub me the wrong way. In this way, I am also teaching myself about how to be able to respond in the moment and not freeze up or seethe silently with rage. Also, the need to have a deadline or time limit in place is an interesting way to be forced to create. It causes adrenaline to be secreted and if we rise to the challenge we are rewarded with some wonderful chemicals our bodies produce because we not only did the work but also because in the end we found some joy in the expression and creative output.

Think about and write down in a sentence the last thing that really got you upset. It could be anything from a statement by the Prime Minister to something your teacher asked of you, your best friend, or a complete stranger you had to stand next to at a bus stop, said. Now, set an alarm clock for three minutes and write at length about what you should have said in response, to make your point and/or defend your point of view. It could be the beginning of a great protest piece.

When I've got a basic idea of what my concept or interest is, I find the easiest way to extract other important bits of associated information is to make a list. I'll use a variety of tools for this—after I've of course exhausted my own brain. These tools will include a rhyming dictionary, as a list could be words that rhyme with "idea" or it could be a thesaurus to list words that are "like," or maybe I'll use a browser's search engine or an actual encyclopedia. What I am trying to do is just leave no stone unturned and generate raw data. If you have ever made a mold you know there is much structural support that needs to be created and then stripped away only to support the eventual object you desire.

So, go for it—get your tools handy and for the next 10 minutes gather anything you like. Write it down—make a list or make several lists. Don't be precious or exclusive—everything at this point could be valid, interesting, and of use.

WHY should the easiest thing—being authentically one's self—sometimes become the most difficult thing to be? Well, just judging from my various modes of inspiration (above) they are all based on some kind of response to the external world. We're always being bombarded with so many influences and sensations that we think would be cooler, more popular, and of more worth. As I matured I realized that listening to my intuition, looking for signs in the environment around me, and paying attention to my dreams, was my own personal source for inspiration. No one else was going to understand or sense anything exactly the way I was. What will emerge may be scary at first because what you will record or write is not like anyone else, and many times breaks your own notion of what you think is your voice.

PERFORMANCE

Rehearsing

The rehearsal process is always actively part of the creation, and because of the variances of audiences, physical spaces, and technical capabilities available, so too are the public performances. A rehearsal itself may in fact be a performance—especially if you have it documented or have a director or some other feedback support in the room.

If you're lucky enough to be in a classroom setting or are part of a collective, this can be an excellent workshop space for developing your work further. If you are not, but want feedback on the kernel of a new idea, there's an exercise I like to use that is effective in shaping the new work before it gets to the polishing stage. It can, though, also be used further along in the process for the more seasoned performer as I'll describe a little later.

Whenever we witness something, we're always "reading" meaning into it. I alluded to this and have asked you to do this with a couple of the previous prompts ("performing a petroglyph" & "surveying your environment for inspiration"). Your audience will "read" your piece and your performance as well, and sometimes they get wildly varied messages. This is in part because a performance or an event is actually an object—like a sculpture with many facets. Everyone witnessing your performance sees it from slightly a different point of view and brings with them their own history that informs how they understand the world and this particular nexus of time and space.

♥ **Part 1**—Broken Telephone: Write down in two to three short sentences the central idea of what your performance/spoken word poem is. Sitting in a circle, whisper this into the ear of someone seated on either side of you. Tell them basically what your performance piece is about in three short sentences or less. Let their versions of your project go around the circle until it gets back to you. State out loud what the final result is then let people know what your original statement was. Take a few minutes to go around the room to find out where it started to change drastically. Write down as many of the derivations as possible.

♥ **Part 2**—Word Association: After everyone has had a chance to do the same with their project, now go back to your original statement and, quickly moving around the circle, ask each person to give you a word or a phrase that they associate with what you've told them. Write as much down as you can and don't dispute anyone's response. Also, if anyone is taking too long to respond, move on to the next person.

What you now have is a lot of information about how your potential audience could "read" your performance of your piece. Maybe someone has given you clarity into what your work really is about, maybe another person is so far off base that you think they don't get it. Really, though, what has been shared with you is, in total, extremely useful information, because now you can figure out how to shape your piece to elicit the kind of meaning and understanding you're aiming for. This will come in handy when you're in front of people you want to reach through your work.

From a Cree worldview there are many things that are considered animate or alive that much of the western world considers lifeless. So from this point of view, there may be many things in a room witnessing your rehearsal that you'll be bouncing ideas off of—literally and figuratively. When rehearsing in a room without other humans providing feedback, I become aware of many things that are going on within myself that will have an effect on my ability to perform.

Here's an inventory of some things I usually take note of:

◈ Are you breathing?

Have you figured out when best to breathe during your piece to add punctuation, dramatic effect, and/or meaning? Trained singers generally take breaths on commas and periods so that they doesn't detract from the melodic line or phrasing, but perhaps you're performing text that is about anxiety or rage—then you might want to breath in all the "wrong" places to make your audience feel the sentiments in the text more acutely. The key thing is to keep breathing—holding one's breath is *never* useful in performance—(unless you're performing underwater).

◈ Are you aware of your voice?

Can you hear your voice bouncing against the walls and echoing back? Can you feel the reverberation of some of the text in other parts of your body? How do the words feel in your mouth—are they rolling around like dice in your hand or are they getting knotted up in your tongue? You probably need to warm up your mouth and make sure you're not holding your breath.

Here's my favourite backstage warm-up: lip buzzing. Take a deep breath in and, as you exhale, hum the melody to your favourite song, but instead of pursing your lips, allow them to be loose and slack so they start making a sound like blades on a boat propeller. If you're doing it properly, you'll be amazed that you can hum (or buzz) the whole song in one breath and that your nose may be getting tickled from the activity. If you're holding your breath or you are clenching your jaw, you'll have trouble with this.

◈ Are you feeling physical tension?

It's really important to get a good night's sleep, exercise, and to drink plenty of water and eat well. I'm not trying to be your mother or sound like a doctor, but if you think in your life you're going to need to know how to be in front of people, you need to understand that there is an energy exchange going on, and since there is only one of you, you'll need strength and stamina to be able to be grounded and deliver the goods. Okay, failing all that—the quickest backstage warm-up is a large glass of room temperature water and a few deep knee bends and shoulder stretches.

Reading your audience

Just as you can learn to read or listen to a landscape can you cultivate insight and read an audience. Previously I've mentioned and asked you to read the landscape like a book and listen to it for clues as to tone, rhythm, and melody. During your rehearsal process besides the internal exploration described above, you should also be reading the people in the room. Are there people who don't want to make eye contact? They may be deep listeners—can you purposely deliver phrases to them that you know will have an impact? These types of people, by their very focus, will help you get your message to everyone within earshot. Are there people who want eye contact? Can you look at them from time to time during your performance without getting lost there? These types of people want to give you their energy and will help keep you grounded and in the room. Are there a few in the room who you think want you to fail and stumble or make a fool out of yourself? These types of people really want to you reach higher and dig deeper. They want you to act on impulses you may have felt all along but were unsure of or edited out. They may not be there to catch you—for that you'll need to use the listeners and the eye contact people, but they'll be there psychically heckling you. These are just three types of audience members —there are many more and as you get more accustomed to being in front of people you could learn to connect with everyone on deep and profound levels and in doing so reach more and more with your original and unique

e x p r e s s i o n .

H a v e   f u n !

Billeh Nickerson is the author of *The Asthmatic Glass-blower*, which was nominated for the Publishing Triangle Award. Other books include *Let Me Kiss It Better: Elixirs for the Not So Straight and Narrow,* and *McPoems*. A new collection entitled *Impact: The Titanic Poems* will be published in the Spring of 2012. He is also the co-editor of *Seminal: the Anthology of Canada's Gay Male Poets* and the former editor of *Event* magazine and *PRISM International*, two of Canada's most prestigious literary journals. He currently lives in Vancouver, where he teaches Creative Writing at Kwantlen Polytechnic University. ✪

Pickle Sundae

How can you refuse to make a sundae topped off with pickles when a customer explains this is how she'll tell her husband about her pregnancy? When she walks back to their table with a hot fudge sundae for him and a pickle sundae for her, he doesn't even notice at first, just stuffs his face with spoonful after spoonful until he sees the pickles in her ice cream, then hugs her so tightly you worry about the baby.

The Chicken Truck

In retrospect you should have known that the snowflakes you saw weren't really snowflakes on a hot summer's day, but little white feathers from the chicken truck that overturned in front of the restaurant. All day long people found zonked out chickens hidden in the landscaping and, unfortunately, a few were run over by customers in the drive-thru. One man screamed that he didn't take his family out for dinner to kill something. That made you think for a long time.

Bulimia

You want to tell her you can see everything when she parks in the vacant lot across from the restaurant, how you swear the birds recognize her and wait until she sticks her head outside the door, finishes her business, then drives away. There's always a commotion when she leaves, a flock of seagulls, a murder of crows, any number of bird groupings you don't know the names for.

100 Cheeseburgers

An elderly man you recognize as someone who moves slowly and pays for everything with change scrounged from his pockets surprises you when he pulls out a wad of bills and orders 100 cheeseburgers. You get him to repeat himself a couple of times, 100 cheeseburgers, 100 cheeseburgers he says, tells you he intends to freeze them, they'll get him through the winter, no need for pesky walks on cold days, no danger of slipping and breaking a hip. 100 cheeseburgers will keep me going for a little while longer at least, I don't need much.

—Billeh Nickerson ✪

First appeared in *McPoems*
2009, Arsenal Pulp Press

HISTORY

It amazes me how many writers and performers think they live and create in a world devoid of influences. Some folks actually believe that their every thought is always original and that their every feeling has never been felt by anyone else before. This just isn't the case.

In order to become better practitioners within their chosen genres, writers and performers need to be active participants in their communities. Folks who do not understand the origins of their field often become ego driven and isolated, not to mention limited in how they develop artistically. This does not mean you need to enjoy everything that you encounter; it just means you will be better positioned to create inspired and engaging work after you consider the history and courage of the creators that came before you.

♥ 1. Consider the communities that you're a part of—even the ones you may not want to be a part of, or do not feel that close to—and how your work does or doesn't stem from their histories or traditions.

♥ 2. Talk to your mentors. Ask questions. Ask for a reading list and suggestions. Ask for advice.

♥ 3. Talk to your mentors' mentors. Ask questions. Ask for a reading list and suggestions. Ask for advice.

♥ 4. Read and listen. Soak it all up like a giant sponge. Check out archives and research papers to see what creators were doing hundreds or years ago, at turn of the century, and when you were born. Read interviews. Listen to the radio and documentaries. Watch youtube clips. Experiment.

♥ 5. Write and perform responses to what you've discovered. Perhaps you'll want to subvert, or appropriate, or reclaim. Perhaps you'll want to thank.

♥ 6. Remember that imitation and mimicry are a way of learning, not an excuse to rip-off and take as your own.

KNOWING THE ORIGINS OF A PARTICULAR STYLE WILL HELP YOU APPRECIATE A WORK MUCH MORE THAN IF YOU BELIEVE CREATION ONLY HAPPENS WITHIN THE CONFINES OF YOUR OWN ROOM. ✪

Thinking Backwards

Thinking backwards gives you permission to start over without starting over.

Some writers find their words almost sacred and so emotionally charged that they find it difficult to revise without a lot of frustration. When you can't gain some distance from your work, you won't be able tell the promising bits from the parts that need revisiting. Not every single word you write will be golden. Let me repeat: Not every single word you write will be golden. And even once you achieve golden words you will sometimes still need to cut them.

Many writers and teachers talk about the need to put their pages into a drawer for a few weeks or the need to turn off that piece of their brain they associate with their writing process. Some writers achieve distance from watching movies or rearranging their furniture or baking a whole season's worth of holiday treats. This may seem like procrastination or pure and simple avoidance, but it can serve a purpose.

While I'm fond of any excuse to bake cookies or rearrange my furniture, I've found it just takes too much of my time. For this reason and for its effectiveness, my favourite way to gain some distance and a new perspective on work is to take a fresh piece of paper and write out my piece—only starting at the end. Point form will do. This doesn't mean trying to write out your whole piece word by word backwards; rather marking down the parts of your writing you remember most. This could be actions or the emotions elicited from a particular section. It could be images, or colours, or descriptions, or dialogue. Include whatever comes to mind.

This exercise acts as a natural filter for the parts of a poem or story that really matter. It circumvents all the phrases and images that a writer wants included not because of their necessity to the finished work, but because the writer has fallen in love with them during the writing process.

Once you've finished, take a look at your original writing and compare it to the backwards version:

Do you find any sections or scenes didn't make it to the backwards rewrite?

If so, there's a good possibility that you don't need the missing bits in the original either.

Do you find more emphasis on certain images or phrases or actions?

If so, there's a good possibility that you'll want to complement these sections or forefront them more.

Do you find any new parts that don't appear in your original work?

If so, you may want to consider why you forgot to include them in the first place.

Thinking sbﾱɒwʞɔɒd gives you permission to start over without starting over. ✪

PERFORMANCE

On Professionalism

Many beginning writers think that acting like rock stars—on stage and back—will gain them fame and success. While there's something to be said for spectacle and stage presence, the truth is that the folks that book events are just as likely to curate someone who is professional and easy to work with, than someone who is popular and difficult. The goal is to be both: engaging and organized.

Festival producers and reading series coordinators talk, so do the folks that work at granting agencies, and even the tech assistants at venues around town. If a performer earns the reputation for being difficult or even, simply, unpleasant, he or she will soon find themselves on the outside looking in—and when I mean outside, I mean nose pressed up against the window looking in at the reading he or she wasn't invited to.

Here is a short list of things to achieve and to think about in regards to your performance career.

♥ 1. Show up on time and be prepared.

Nothing stresses out organizers and hosts more than late performers. Try to be on time and if you think you may be late let the organizer know. Always bring an extra up-to-date biography so that unprepared hosts have something legible to introduce you with.

♥ 2. Time out your work before hand and practise your order or a few potential orders.

Nobody likes writers that go over their allotted time. Not only can it drag the evening down, but it's unfair to the readers that come after you. I once saw a mother who had to pay for extra child care go off on a reader. Trust me, you don't want this to happen. Remember to add time for banter and for when you need to slow down or stop while the audience laughs.

♥ 3. If you have special technical requirements, make sure to discuss these with the organizers weeks (or months) in advance.

Nothing stresses out a stage manager or a performer—that's you—faster than last minute technical glitches and challenges. Be prepared to perform an unplugged set without all the bells and whistles just in case the technical requirements aren't met.

♥ 4. Respect the audience

Remember that for some people, you may be their only night out for the week or month. In many cases, people will be paying to see you and/or may have made considerable effort to reorganize their lives to be at the venue. You owe it to them to give a polished and professional presentation.

♥ 5. Respect the organizers

While some folks may believe that putting on events looks easy, it's a difficult and time-consuming task. It only looks easy as many people are passionate and experienced. Some folks have probably been organizing events for longer than some of their readers have been alive.

♥ 6. Respect the volunteers and crew

Without them you are nothing.

♥ 7. Respect the other performers

As mentioned above, time out your reading. It's more than likely you'll be reading with the same people your entire career. It's much easier to sit in the same room together when you get along or at least know how to be cordial toward each other. Make a point to slow down and listen to your peers. You're bound to learn something.

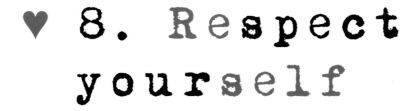

♥ 8. Respect yourself

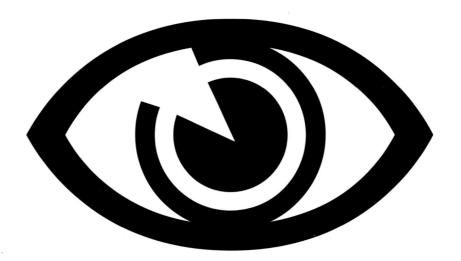

Pe

Hilary Peach

hilarypeach.com

Hilary Peach is a writer, audio poet, recording artist, arts activist, and producer. She has performed at events that include the Vancouver International Folk Music Festival, Montreal's Festival Voix d'Amériques, and the Poetry International Festival in Rotterdam. Her debut recording, an audiophile CD called *Poems Only Dogs Can Hear* (2003), suspends surreal vignettes inside a matrix of music. Peach's 2009 CD release, *Suitcase Local*, is an adaptation of her touring folk opera of the same name. This spoken word and music fusion is a spooky retelling of Peach's experiences working as a Canadian welder in the construction and maintenance of power plants in the USA. Publications include: *10 Flowered Cactus* (1996), *Love is a Small Town* (2001), and inclusions in various anthologies and magazines. Hilary Peach is the BC Yukon representative of the Canadian League of Poets and the founder and Artistic Director of the Poetry Gabriola Festival on Gabriola Island, BC. ✪

Photo credit, Penny White

May The Artists Be Forgiven

May the artists be forgiven for living ferociously
for being driven, furious, untamed and immoderate

oh my brother

it is not easy
to be born in the body that craves
burning and ice in equal measure
and without contradiction

it is not easy to want everything
when appetite is not the fashion

In a world of casual insults
I struggle daily toward measured answers
construct nothing sentences like
"In light of what you have said…" and
"I understand your concern but…"

phrases that fill me with shame
at my own insincerity
and the ease with which
they roll off my tongue

The artists are the conscience of the nation
and we live in a nation
that does not want a conscience
which is worse: to be candid
or to weep silently for 30 years?

your artists are annihilated daily
but are still expected
to make small talk at parties

must we always be polite?
YES.
you must be polite as often as possible
and when impossible
spill your drink in somebody's lap deliberately

say what you actually think

if you are small
once in your life
punch your tormentor in the face
as hard as you can

and you will be forgiven

oh brother
how I struggle against these furies

let us instead
climb and run, plunge and swing
swoop and recoil and shriek,
quicken and sweat
full of juice, ecstatic

how we all love hot weather
but the skies have to open up sometimes
and when they do
may the rain come down in cataracts
and lash us to the ground
may the storms rip through us
may the weak trees be pulled up by their roots
and the wind scare us senseless

forgive your artists their savage appetites
their barbaric temperaments and tempestuous moods
forgive them their vision, wisdom, sanctity and truth
their turbulent relationships and untidy appearance
their refusal to compromise
their gentleness
their hard-loving ways
their tangled logic and unruly opinions
their beauty
their delirium
and their disrespect
for common, tepid answers.

—Hilary Peach ✪

The Teacher's Voice

The oral tradition, in the sense of stories, rituals, rites of passage, traditions, and historical information, is arguably the most ancient art form. In many cultures oral traditions occupied second place after writing entered the scene, and societies that relied on orality have been diminished or have disappeared completely as more and more humans rely on the written word. However, all is not lost.

My art practice springs from an oral tradition that is an amalgamation of disciplines that were brought together and formalized in the 1950s, in Poland. Jerzy Grotowski's notion of "poor theatre" and the work that he spearheaded through the Teatr Laboratorium (Theatre Laboratory) revolutionized approaches to performance training and theory. Little has been recorded about the process, however, because most of it has been handed down through the oral tradition.

One of Grotowski's apprentices, Ryszard Cieslak, became a teacher of the work that has become known among initiates simply as the Work. Linda Putnam, a student of Cieslak's, became my teacher in 1990, and after many years as a student, I am beginning to teach the source and performance curriculum of the Work. In oral traditions the lineage is important because the student carries the teacher, and the teacher's teacher, and the teacher's teacher's teacher, into everything. The student has the benefit of generations of knowledge.

How is this information carried? Mainly, it is carried in the physical body. But in the work that I study the voice is a body part, so it is also carried in the voice. My teacher, Linda, talks about the teacher's voice. This is a phenomenon whereby, when you study with someone, you begin to accept that person's voice inside your artistry. After the student leaves the actual relationship with the teacher, the teacher's voice stays with the student, giving direction, asking questions, and helping the student on his or her search.

The teacher's voice occurs, in my body, somewhere in the back part of my head, above the right ear. I hear it as a kind of eidetic voice —part memory, part "mind's ear." The voice imparts different kinds of information, from direct commands, such as *change rhythm*, or *inhale* or *see the image*, to maxims. One such nugget oft repeated is:

As an artist, you can take no master. But you will have many teachers.

I feel fortunate in that this has proven to be so. I have had excellent teachers, and I still benefit from their wisdom as it is transmitted just above my right ear. Linda also has had many teachers, one of whom she calls *that bench by the river*. The notion that a particular bench by a particular river can embody or function as a teacher's voice has always interested me. Maybe the bench is the teacher, maybe the river. Certainly solitude is a great teacher of artistry, as is a peaceful place in nature, where one can quiet the mind, listen, and take instruction.

PERFORMANCE

The Outer Voice

As an audio poet/literary performance artist, I generally perform on a stage facing an audience, and employ the use of a microphone, depending on the setting and whether or not I am collaborating with musicians. My formal training is in theatre, and I have a lot of physical technique in my performance body, but the form I use most often is fairly static.

I have come to realize, however, that even though I don't walk around a lot on stage, there is an entire choreography going on inside my body. I employ different ways of breathing, different vocal resonators (head, top of skull, throat, chest, vulnerable diamond, pelvic floor), different eye focuses, sound dynamics, vowel lengths, use of body parts, and other techniques in the performance of a piece. I also create imagery, inside and outside of my body, for the length of the script.

This score, or blocking, is developed during a rehearsal process. The formula for rehearsing, roughly, is that every one minute of finished script is rehearsed for approximately one hour. So a 50-minute performance takes a minimum of 50 hours to prepare for performance. This isn't very much time to effectively incorporate all of the technique necessary for a full rendering of a completed performance score.

Fifty years ago it was closer to two to three hours per minute of finished script, but the time demands of the modern age have forced artists to trim their rehearsal times.

One way to get the most out of a limited rehearsal period is to embark on some preparatory text analysis prior to rehearsal so that the performer has a general idea of which aspects of the piece she (or he) wants to underscore or emphasize. Another way to get the most out of the rehearsal process is to find a compatible director.

THE WORST STRATEGY

I can think of for rehearsing a new piece is to emulate another person—whether it is a teacher, a peer, or another performer whom you admire. The work will sound like you are trying to sound like someone else, and are in denial of the artist's own voice.

THE BEST STRATEGY

for rehearsing a new work, in my opinion, is to listen to what the piece wants in performance. I always begin rehearsal by trying the words out loud and listening to the ways that the language itself wants to be crafted. The poem is your best mentor, and the sound of the physical voice will be your best director. It will generally give you an excellent idea of the direction of your search.

PERFORMANCE EXERCISE

The Inner Voice

i) RECORDING THE INNER VOICE
Let's investigate the idea that a bench by the river is a teacher.

Bring a notebook and pen, and find a place in nature—a park, beach, island retreat, garden, or a corner of your own back yard—where you feel that it might be possible to quiet the mind and listen (no actual bench necessary).

Sit and listen for the poem, emptying all other sounds out of your body with the breath.

The poem may come as a soft voice in your mind, as a memory, as a series of nonsense words, or as visual imagery.

Write down everything that you "hear" from the inner voicings.

BREATHE EVENLY.

Listen on the exhale.

If the voice wants to describe what you are seeing, write down the description.

Consider that the description might be the poem, or it might be code for the poem, or it might inspire language that will become the poem, or it might remind you of an image that triggers the poem.

ii) VARIATION WITH A PARTNER
After you have worked in solitude try working with a partner.

♥ **1.** Agree on a specific theme or source, such as a piece of music, a specific place, or a time of year.

♥ **2.** Think of a story from your life that ties to the theme or source. It has to be a story that you are willing to tell, and it has to be a story you can tell in three minutes or less.

♥ **3.** Tell the story to your partner. Your partner is the scribe. While you are telling the story your partner writes down everything you say as fast as she can. She (or someone else) also keeps track of the time so that you don't go over three minutes. When your time is up, stop. Your partner gives you the notes for your story.

♥ **4.** Take a minute or two to reduce the story you just told down to an essence line—one line from your story that sums up or reflects the essence of the story.

♥ **5.** Switch with your partner. She becomes the teller and you the scribe.

Both of these exercises are designed to start you off, generating some raw language directly out of your imagination.

Once you have a solitude poem, or a story, or an essence line, you are on the way to developing material that you can form, craft, develop, and edit into a piece you may decide to perform.

✪

Robert
Priest

poempainter.com

A literary poet in the tradition of Neruda and Mayakovsky, a composer of lush love poems, and a widely quoted aphorist, Robert Priest is a mainstay of the spoken word circuit both in Canada and abroad. Also known as "Dr. Poetry" (CBC's Wordbeat), he is the author of 16 books of poetry and numerous CDs. His most recent book, *Reading the Bible Backwards*, rose to number two on the *Globe and Mail*'s poetry bestsellers list. Robert has performed his exciting mix of poems and songs all over the world. His words have been debated in the legislature (see video at youtube.com/greatbigfaced), turned into a hit song, posted in the Transit system, broadcast on MuchMusic, released on numerous CDs, quoted by politicians, and widely published in text books and anthologies.

Priest's work includes the spoken word video/single *Congo Toronto* which received nation-wide airplay on MuchMusic for over three months in 1986; *Rotweiller Pacifist* (1988) a collection of 20 spoken word pieces, many of them accompanied by tracks and beats; and his collection of poems, *The Mad Hand* (1989), which was the recipient of the Milton Acorn People's Poetry award. Robert's third spoken word CD, *Tongue'n'Groove*, was released on EMI's Artisan label in 1998. Robert lives in Toronto where he is a freelance cultural journalist for *Now Magazine*. ✪

Photo credit, Ann Collins

133

Money/Mommy Meme Splice

Just give me mommy
I work hard for my mommy
You need mommy to get by in this world
You have to to save your mommy
Let your mommy grow
But don't let mommy take over your life
Don't get too attached to mommy
Mommy can weigh you down
Use your mommy wisely
Keep your mommy in a safe place
Mommy is just a tool
Mommy is a symbolic system
We are in a mommy obsessed culture
Mommy hounds
Slaves to mommy
We spend our whole lives scrabbling for mommy mommy mommy
Filthy mommy, blood mommy
Hypnotized by the power of mommy
We are all in the pocket of big mommy
Good mommy bad mommy
What is this insane lust for mommy
Mommy is being driven down devalued
We have not been very smart about our mommy
When interest rates are low mommy is cheap
Just throw mommy at it
Mommy changes everything
I have no mommy-sense
I'm bad with mommy
Mommy burns a hole in my pocket
I have to go begging for mommy in the streets
I hate mommy
I reject mommy
Mommy is the root of all evil
But it is so hard to live without mommy
I'm trying to hold on to my mommy
But everybody wants my mommy
What happened to our mommy?
We took huge risks with our mommy
And we lost
We are completely broke
We totally wasted our mommy

— Robert Priest ✪

First appeared in *Reading the Bible Backwards*
2008, ECW Press

Humankind and the word go back a long way. I used to have a romantic picture of some genius ancestral group making up language from scratch, but the truth is more complex than that. Evolutionary science suggests that language originated from human music, which began as display behaviour—a way of courting. The evolutionary rationale for this is that the wild dancing and extreme vocalization involved in such courting functioned as a kind of advertisement for good health and the bounty of a robust and flexible body full of lots of reserve energy—not to mention any lyrical/aesthetic qualities which might also have been expressed.

And so natural selection favoured those with better singing equipment. The better our singing equipment got the more there were freak adaptations that enabled more exquisite enunciations in the next generations.

Such gifted enunciators, by getting with the best mates, thereby bred even more enunciators. The more we enunciated the closer we got to the biological prerequisites for speech as we know it. The ability to speak, once established, became a clear evolutionary advantage, and groups with the highest communication skills succeeded over their lesser-endowed cousins. As the lexicons increased and the need for more distinct forms of delineation arose, language shaped the tips of our tongues, the roofs of our mouths, the mobility of our faces. It also gradually changed our mode of cognition—moving from inner projections of sheer imagery to those strings of words which we call thoughts. All of this helped remake our brains. So the truth is, language shaped us as much as we shaped language. We coevolved.

Group vocalization and dancing led to tribal cohesion as well. So poets are justified, I think, in their belief that their works at their best become involved in the evolution of the human spirit. And not just the spirit—the body—the entire being and beyond—the community. Our humanity is inextricably linked with the word on a biological level. Language, once established, enabled further technologies for group cohesion and survival. So stop thinking that poetry changes nothing. Everything changes everything. Forever.

Exercise 1 Poetry Detection Exercise

Take a short, seemingly prosaic statement and see if you can hear it poetically. For instance: "the dog sat down." Maybe you can feel the poetry in it by repeating it in your mind, but say it aloud if you need to. Try different rhythms. Ham it up if you must. In a pinch, add something to it that might solidify it as poetry for you. "The dog sat down/in its own shadow." "The moon came up and the dog sat down." "No one gave an order—the dog sat down." "Hunger stood up, injustice arose, hate flew, and the dog sat down." In a real pinch append some kind of metaphor. "The dog sat down, an avalanche of rickety canine debris." Don't worry if none of these work. If you have to, pick another prosaic phrase and start anew. Don't worry if at first there is no apparent result. Doing the exercise itself is the result. The point is there is a possibility of poetry in all language. Even in single words. Often poetry is deliberately made, but sometimes it just falls into place and has only to be noticed.

Repeat this exercise daily, each day trying a new phrase. Start detecting the poetry in the world about you—in the media—notice the phrasing in advertising slogans. Notice the use of imagery in news reports. Check out how many times a day someone in the media says "the irony is...". Listen to the stale poetry present in political speeches and partisan punditry. Listen to the poetry in common speech and particularly in those tarnished little nuggets we call clichés. Notice what makes them work. "It's raining cats and dogs." Surrealism! Always be on the lookout for poetry in the world.

The ultimate goal of this isn't to give you hunting grounds for found poetry (though it would be good if it does); it is to help you develop supersensitive habits of listening to the incipient poetry of your own thoughts—not just your deliberate thoughts but those bubbling up proto-thoughts which precede the feeling of having an idea. These proto-thoughts sometimes emerge from low-level dream matrices that mist up from the bottom of the mind.

Now, see if you can use your original prose line in a poem.

Note: Poetry and the Brain

Knowing how the brain works can provide opportunities and strategies for poets. For instance: when you visit a site on the Web your computer sucks in and stores a lot of information about that site so that if you visit it again it can just pop it up quickly without waiting for the full download of refreshed information. Strangely, it turns out our brains do the same thing. That's why it is sometimes hard to find something that is right in front of you. Your brain is still feeding you the old information. How often does it happen that just as you ask someone for help "Do you know where the can opener is?" you suddenly see the can opener right in front of you? My theory is that asking the question resets the brain—it hits your refresh button, dissolving the old picture to create the new. We tend to take in language the same way—gulping down the whole—often without fresh examination. We don't read by sounding each letter and putting together words—we read whole words or even whole phrases as one distinct unit. As necessary as this may be for the rigors of brain function, it can also bring death to language. The death of cliché. Poetry wants to be fresh. That's why cliché and all other forms of prefabricated phrasing must be deliberately eschewed by poets. Clichés just give you the old picture of the room. The mind is very comfortable with clichés but poetry is surely not about making the mind comfortable. That is not to say that poets must never use clichés but I am of the opinion that we must never use clichés the way they are. The trick is to tap into their power and alter it to one's purpose. In that way the cliché can become a kind of Trojan horse slipping some unsettling, puzzling or even refreshing thoughts by subterfuge into the on-automatic mind.

Exercise 2 Micro Poems & Making Up Sayings

Micro poems must, by definition, be brief, but that need not excuse them from the prerequisites of high quality poetry. They are short, but we want them to evoke the great magnitudes. Brevity forever! We want paradox, metaphor, resonance, feeling, and meaning. To look at some techniques, let's examine aphorisms, proverbs, maxims and sayings. You can find lots of examples of these by Googling "proverbs."

Look around you and in the tools and objects of the real world see the forefathers of loads of snappy sayings. What do you see? A tree? The tree is the mother of loads of micro-poems. Think of the "budding pianist"; "the root of all evil"; "turning over a new leaf"; "the fruit doesn't fall far from the tree"; "can't see the forest for the trees"; "if a tree falls…"; "the family tree…".

As an exercise create a short, snappy, micro poem. Pick a real-world object and by examining its qualities see if you can come up with a unique saying, proverb, slogan, slur, joke, premise or maxim. Some that I've made are: "Sometimes it is the book that opens you," and "You can't kiss ass and kick it too."

Once you have picked an object, start thinking about its qualities. I suggest you write each observation or idea down and don't be timid about starting with the obvious and mundane—these can often be roads to the special. As an example, I follow the process below, with some added commentary. I chose a chair.

What about a chair? It has legs. How many? Would it work with only one leg? Zero legs? There is an expression when a product is taking off, "it has legs." Can this be used? Maybe as a joke—he invested in chairs because he heard that chairs have legs; maybe not. Could the chair be made of air? Faith is to sit in a chair made of air. The air is his chair and the stars his table. Hmm. Chairs are supposed to be comfortable. Don't be afraid to be rude—his ass is harder than his chair. How about absurdity—a chair made of bums for instance. He sits in a chair made of ass. Maybe some irony is available? You could burn a chair in order to read a book but then you'd have nothing to sit in. Can you get a snappy saying out of that? Something really awkward like: She who burns her chair for light must read standing up. Not brilliant yet but… can a chair be something else? Can it be a table? A raft? He's such a huge asshole every time he sits down, another chair disappears. Absurdity—a man cannot sit on three chairs at once. Hop on templates from other sayings, such as: He's all chair no table. The chair is only as strong as its weakest leg. ....

AHA! You've seen that one before. But I could rephrase it—One weak leg ruins the chair. His chair is bigger than his table.

Types of chairs: rocking chairs, easy chairs, electric chairs, musical chairs. Just keep turning it round and round putting things into it to see where it goes. He spent all his money on a chair and couldn't afford the table. The chair is a weapon. Opposite it—she sits on the table and eats off his chair. Don't blame the chair for your ass. He's everybody's chair but nobody's table. Combine things: the combination electric chair/mobile throne. Wheelchairs are excellent for sayings. The world is his wheelchair. His table is round but his chair is still square. What does a chair need to function well?—the legs must be of equal length. That sounds promising. Don't be the long leg on a short chair. Close. The egalitarian chair—no one leg longer than another. The chair is like democracy—it only works when all its legs are equal. None of these are really snappy yet but I hear a snap in the air. Where the ass meets the chair. Rhymes. The chair in the air doesn't care. One chair many asses. There is a chair for everyone at God's table. One table many chairs. You've earned a chair at the table. Sad: the empty chair. Defiant: a chair of one's own. Generous: share a chair. Standup: We have a water table shouldn't there be a water chair? The chair at a university. The electric easy chair. The chair is a nose.

It takes four legs to rest two. All throne no king. The march of the chairs. Combination—there is an electric chair for everyone at God's table. A chair sits alone in a room. Armchair generals and quarterbacks. Easy chair lumberjacks. The fifth leg on the chair. The ground is my chair. Lowbrow highchair. If you make the chairs a table will come. Dancing with the chair. To run from one chair to another. The table is a chair magnet. His chair has too many legs. His chair is higher than his table. Who eats from the ground requires no chair. One chair sits in another. I like that! It reminds me of the gymnasium after a concert when all the chairs are stacked up and put away, but it does have a slightly transcendent feeling to it. I think of the Yeats line, "the young in one another's arms." More trees less chairs. A tooth pick does not a chair make. Your thumb my chair. One must bend if one would sit in a chair. I like that! Beware the easy chair. Now that could be the kickoff line for some kind of witty anti-luxury type song. "I told him it was dangerous/I warned him to take care/now he is but a shadow/beware the easy chair." Eclectic chairs. Wind powered electric chairs. Electric chairs that run on solar batteries. Electric tables. Sit down comedians. Sit down Canadians. "Once upon a time there was one chair leg that longed to be longer than all the others." To a chair, time is a series of asses. Chairs have little chairs of their own. Teetering like a stack of chairs on a trolley. The high branch the little swallow once swayed atop is now a chair staggering beneath a weighty glutton about to pop. Her hobby is racing chairs. Sometimes inside a cherry you will find the seed of many chairs. I'm amazed that chair can bear you—I certainly can't. One chair longs for another. Sit—let the chair do the standing for you. The chair is only on the level when one leg equals another. One short leg tips the chair. Hunger requires no chair….

I could go on, and I do, but I think you get the idea. Let the bad lead to the good. Don't be embarrassed. You could even wait a day before combing through the rubble to see if anything glitters. Usually I check afterwards on the Internet to see if any of my new sayings are truly new. I see, as I look today, that there are some great metaphors about government being a three-legged stool. But actually there are not many chair proverbs as such to be found. Some of the above come close—tomorrow I might even think some of them are just right—but many of them I will revisit and chip away at. My advice is, whenever you cut off this exercise, keep a writing or recording implement with you because usually stragglers break free and keep coming at you throughout the day. And in future don't feel confined to the noun nature of objects. Prepositions—"to" for instance or "if." If you trance out from such unexpected starting points it can be a good way to trick the mind out of its typical rigidities and into a more flexible associative creative state.

Exercise 3 Cliché Spinning

Find some already existing clichés and proverbs etc. that you like, and start stripping them down and retooling them. One technique is word replacement. "In my father's house are many Mansons." Another is extension—lengthening the cliché in some productive way. For instance: "clothes make the man…poor." Try some "oppositing" and reversal: "dreams have us," or "doom is only mood backwards." You should look at every word in your cliché and see what happens to it if you opposite or reverse it. Strip down and rework a number of sayings until you get one that feels fresh and new.

Take the one that inspires you the most and feature it in a poem or make it a poem.

Exercise 4 Meme Splicing

As a corollary to genes, which are the biological components that get transmitted from one generation to the next, Richard Dawkins coined the word "memes" to represent the other inheritances of humanity which we pass along through time. Most memes are cultural: A wink is a meme; language is a meme; a word is a meme; slogans, aphorisms etc. are mini-memes. So, you are probably familiar with gene splicing: a technique for genetic modification which is carried out by splicing new information into existing DNA and then letting it propagate into a mutation. That's why we have square tomatoes. In my days as Dr. Poetry on the CBC show *Wordbeat*, I came up with a playful riff on this: Meme Splicing. Meme Splicing uses phonetic modification to trigger mutant strings of slogans etc. for the purpose of experimentation. The sample poem included here, the Money/Mommy Meme Splice, was written using this technique. I blew out the N and E in money and blew in two M's to replace them. I then replaced the phonetically modified meme back into its many host memes (oft heard phrases, clichés, aphorisms, slogans etc.) to see what such a mash-up might achieve.

The test for me of a successful meme splice is whether or not it cuts both ways. For instance when I use the idiom "this is a money obsessed culture" the spliced version "this is a mommy obsessed culture" is also poetically true and because of the crisscross, each version of the idiom becomes slightly imbued with the vibe of the other. It's a trick to reroute some old pathways in the brain and make it stand up and pay attention. It's a way of writing two poems at once.

PROMPT
Come up with your own meme splice and then compose a poem. And remember please that a poem doesn't have to observe normal grammatical rules or constructions. A pertinent interconnected list of the successful meme-spliced statements—especially if arranged to cascade forward towards a seemingly ineluctable ending—will work just fine.

Good luck. ✪

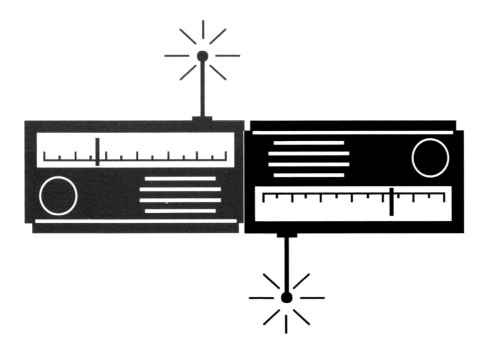

NOTES ON PERFORMANCE

The single most influential performative piece of advice on my own style came from Antonin Artaud, who said, "I have come to give you the experience, not to talk about the experience."

Don't talk so fast. Don't let a poem become more like a sporting event or an Yngwie Malmsteem solo. It loses its groove. There's nothing wrong with space or even silence—give your words at least enough space to activate.

Using a mic. If you're standing at a podium and there's a little mic on the podium about one and a half feet from your face don't bend down and talk directly into it so that your voice comes out all distorted. It's down that far from you for a reason. When in doubt check with the soundman. Always try to find out how far off the mic you should be. Usually two inches is right. If you hear a high-pitched squeal—that's feedback. One solution to this, if there's not a soundman to help, you is to make sure that the mic is not pointed at the speaker. Pointing the mic away from the speaker will definitely reduce and totally nix feedback. Feedback sucks. So does distortion. Get used to listening to your voice coming back at you. If you get that gravelly sound like a radio slightly off channel, that's distortion. It can seriously reduce your effectiveness as a poet. The most immediate remedy is to back off the mic.

♥ **Performance Exercise 1:**
Take your most sincere poem and speak it sarcastically. If you cherish your best sincere poems too highly to do this, then pick one that you don't love so much. Its sincerity is the key.

♥ **Performance Exercise 2:**
Take your saddest poem and recite it as though jesting. If possible use canned laughter after the most tragic phrases.

♥ **Performance Exercise 3:**
If you have a typical three-minute slam entry poem that you sometimes read way too fast, turn off the clock and recite it without the entire forward tilting scurry. Recite it slowly revelling in the words, noticing the interactions and delicious turns amongst the phrases.

Don't give a good message a bad name.

✪

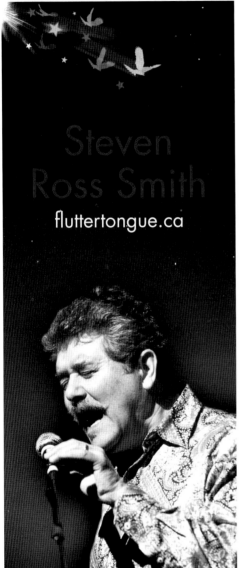

Steven Ross Smith likes to bend, confuse, and disintegrate that which is most popularly straightened, clarified, and constructed in general poetic and fictive practice—language, narrativity, and meaning. A sound and performance poet, writer of fiction and poetry, Smith endeavours to work against convention, especially his own. He has created as a writer/composer/performer, has worked collaboratively with performance poets and musicians, in structured and improvisatory contexts, including the groups Owen Sound, DUCT, and aBANDon. Over 3 decades, he has published eleven books and has appeared on various CDs and audiocassettes, including the compilations *Carnivocal* and *Homo Sonorus*. His recent work: a book-length poem entitled *fluttertongue 4: adagio for the pressured surround* was published by NeWest Press in 2007. He has won awards for his poetry and has performed and/or been published in England, Holland, Russia, Portugal, USA, and Canada. His current poetry-in-progress is the book *fluttertongue 5: everything appears to shine with mossy splendour*. It will be published in 2011. In 2008 he wrote *flown*—his first collaborative, narrative libretto, for a composition by composer Wang Jie. It was performed in Brooklyn in 2009. Smith now lives in Banff in the Canadian Rocky Mountains, where he is the Director of Literary Arts at The Banff Centre. ✪

Photo credit, James Tworow

Declare it Thinly

Razored into skin, a word, a whim, a ticket to fate. Jingle jangle electronic cacophony. The Beats beat it nation-wide, samadhi, satori, with beatific smiles and whoever turns their pages holds in hands the blessèd or blistering steering wheel and spins it like an arcade game in blazing sun or teeming starlight. Late last night, steam from the river could have frozen lungs. Poem, driven through—its air so slight, barely a bump, a ripple. After all, it's twenty-four-seven of hoods, hounds, and Hollywood, all video titillation. Starlets slim as toffee drawn through straws. The plug popped and stopped the car, despite the bulging biceps. Jack declared, in *Chorus 196* Wanta bring everyone straight to the dream, and he did—loaded a generation into his typewriter and hit the keys spontaneous, somnambulant. Tingling skin, all there is between arousal and nothingness. Time's slim ribbon running through slimmer space. Where is radiance? Leaders with fat ambition and anorexic minds build walls and fences or crater them. Everyone abides the drought and steps up for the rain dance. The privileged race that likes to live a cut or two above its station to escape the cloacal trenches. It seems slo-mo, but it's a skinny minute as we drop toward the blade, each sleek side on offer—grace or grit... and oh, the turbulent gyrations.

~

This Ulysses robust, dark green
with enlarged head at the tip
in arousal, constant.

–Steven Ross Smith ✪

First appeared in *Fluttertongue 5: Everything Appears to Shine with Mossy Splendour*
2011, Turnstone Press,Winnipeg

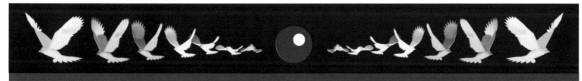

As a teenager, my most extensive exposure to poetry was courtesy of my Grade 10 teacher, Mrs. Columbo, who assigned the memorization of soliloquies from Shakespeare's plays. I was dreadful at memorization, and hence developed an aversion rather than a love of Shakespeare and poetry. But my Grade 12 English teacher, Mr. Strebig, shifted that aversion with his insistence and enthusiasm for poetry and story. Through him, a poet caught my attention—Gerard Manley Hopkins (1844-1889). What impressed me about Hopkins was the way he worked language; he torqued words, hammered and knotted their sounds, and forged meaning in a way that made me think hard. And his rhythms were careful, expressive, and tightly rendered. His poems were about nature, humanity, and spirituality; his themes and his well-wrought language stuck in my mind well after Grade 12.

Here are eight of his oft-quoted lines that exemplify those qualities:

In the late 1960s I began to write poems of my own. I wasn't ready to call myself a poet, but I seemed to be hooked on free verse. In those late '60s I encountered performance art, and innovative new music (Steve Reich, Luciano Berio, and Karlheinz Stockhausen). I also 'discovered' the Beats, Allen Ginsberg performing, Samuel Beckett, John Cage, bill bissett, and more.

But a quintessential moment came in 1970 when I saw Canada's Four Horsemen perform in Toronto. They were a potent and dynamic quartet of writers who had turned to collaboration and ensemble performances. The Horsemen were bpNichol, Steve McCaffery, Paul Dutton, and Rafael Barreto-Rivera. They lifted poetry off the page, called it Sound Poetry, and fired it with dynamic vocal and bodily energy. This was "spoken word" (and nonword) well before the term was invented to define the current "genre." I was attracted and compelled to follow. In 1975 I initiated the formation of a group – at first five guys (Brian Dedora, Michael

```
God's Grandeur
The world is charged with the grandeur of God.
        It will flame out, like shining from shook foil;
        It gathers to a greatness, like the ooze of oil
        Crushed. Why do men then now not reck his rod?
        Generations have trod, have trod, have trod;
        And all is seared with trade; bleared, smeared with toil;
        And wears man's smudge & shares man's smell: the soil
        Is bare now, nor can foot feel, being shod.


  - Gerard Manley Hopkins
```

Dean, David Penhale, Richard Truhlar, and I), then four (M.D., D.P., R.T., and I), then three (M.D., R.T., and I). We called ourselves Owen Sound, after the body of water in Ontario and with a play on "own sound."

This exploration led me to an important node in the history of Sound Poetry—Dada—the art movement that began in the very early 20th century. A revolutionary art practice that attempted to overthrow art conventions in all disciplines, it was often collaborative and performative, and sometimes chaotic. It attempted to create work that moved beyond the standard definitions of art. Many Dadaists have become iconic names in art history. The most notable one for me was Hugo Ball, whose performances engaged chant, meta-language, phonics, syllabics, tones, and costumes—he endeavoured to invoke atmosphere without concern for meaning. He was seeking magical incantation, "the innermost alchemy of the word." The first Dada evening, July 14, 1916 – included Ball, Tristan Tzara, Hans Arp and others —in recitations of prose and poetry, of verses without words ("Verse ohne Worte," also referred to as "Sound Poems" or "Lautgedichte" = loud speaking), and utilizing masks, costumes, and sculpture. By 1917, performances were being held on Spiegelgasse in Zürich, under the name of Cabaret Voltaire. This is my touchstone.

Yet there are event antecedents. As Steve McCaffery writes, "Prior to this there had been isolated pioneering attempts by several writers including Christian Morgenstern (ca 1875), Lewis Carroll ('Jabberwocky'), August Stramm (ca. 1912), Petrus Borel (ca. 1820), Molière, the Silesian mystic Quirinus Khulman (17th century), Rabelais and Aristophanes" (*Sound Poetry A Catalogue*, p. 6). And before these there are the chants, tales, "nonsense syllabic mouthings" (ibid) throat singing and other vocalizations in earlier societies.

As McCaffery continues, "What is referred to as 'sound poetry' is a rich, varied, inconsistent phonic genealogy" (ibid). This genealogy includes art movements or geographically and/or temporally diverse explorations such as Russian Futurism, Italian Futurism, Dada, de Stijl, and Lettrism. And taking us from those times closer to our own, there are myriad later practitioners—Europeans:

Francois Dufrêne, Henri Chopin, Katalin Ladik, Bernard Heidsieck, Bob Cobbing, Paula Claire; and Canadians: Claude Gauvreau, Penn Kemp, The Horsemen, Owen Sound, bill bissett, Christian Bök, Max Middle, jwCurry; that lead us to the present day. It is most interesting to note that there are, today, hundreds of artists around the world who identify and practise in the realm of sound poetry, or related forms with different names. Spoken word is one of those names.

I see spoken word as part of the lineage touched on here, and I see the pursuit of a physical, performative, vocal literary art form as the dynamic edge of exploration that keeps moving forward. I also believe that it is valuable, if not essential, for young "Spoken Worders" to explore the history, and to listen to the recordings. It will enrich your practice.

I have set out exercises whose primary aim is to create situations for you to develop your voice—and by that I don't mean your personal poetic voice, but your actual speaking apparatus, your phonic articulation. And at the same time, these exercises will enable you to move outside your personal content and stretch through the realms of meaning and non-meaning, into a pure state of vocalization, and a discovery of the physical source and dynamic of language in your body.

EXERCISES

Exercise 1

Cut random phrases from magazines, books, newspapers, etc. Do not think too hard or try to relate them to each other. Put them in a hat – draw them out one at a time and type them or paste them down in that order. Read the result aloud three times, each with a different tone – (1) Longing; (2) Anger; (3) Each phrase appropriate to its words. Then arrange the phrases in a way that makes sense to you, and read them aloud as if they were urgent news headlines.

Purpose:

- To get you used to a range of expressive vocalizations.
- To enable random connections of words and ideas to stretch your sense of how language communicates.

Exercise 2

Cut out a bunch of words and letters of different sizes, fonts, colours, etc., from magazines, newspapers, etc., and/or draw your own. Rub a glue-stick in various spots on the paper. Stick those words & letters down randomly, but not linearly – i.e. turn the page, stick one on top of the other, or at different angles, etc.

PLAY.

Once dry, read the result aloud with emphasis. Don't worry about meaning. Sound individual letters and words with variation. Explore rhythm, tone, repetition, and mood. Stretch your vocal capability (but not your vocal cords) by moving the sounds/words around in your mouth, up and down from the tip of your tongue to the back of your throat, to the centre of your chest; play with loud and soft dynamics; puff your cheeks, stick out your tongue, flutter your lips. Don't be afraid of seeming silly. Try to find a form for these vocalizations (e.g. go from soft to loud to soft; or go from sentence to word to syllable, to individual letter sound to hum, then back; or make all sounds with your lips closed, then make all sounds with your lips open; etc.

Purpose:

- To extend your range of expressive vocalizations.
- To begin to bring language into your body in a dynamic way.
- To extend your experience of random connections of words and ideas to stretch further your sense of how language communicates.
- To enhance your sensitivity to the sonics of language.

Exercise 3

Choose your favourite poem. Copy it twice. Now on one copy remove (erase, scratch out or re-type without) all the vowels.

On the second copy, remove all the consonants by the same method.

Now you have two sound texts. Use each as a performance text. Sound each text individually, from end to beginning, giving sonic expression to each letter and where letters are repeated in sequence, use this to help rhythmic variation. Sound the letters with energy ranges, from soft to loud, from gruffly to lovingly. Don't name the letters, but express them with the sounds they make in language (your language and even foreign ones). Use the full range of your mouth, tongue, teeth, and throat, and of course your breath. Try to move the sounds up and down through the diaphragm. Create these as if they were compositions with a structural flow. Repeat the exercise and listen and feel the differences.

Purpose:
- ➡ To begin to understand the qualities of vowels separate from consonants, and vice versa.
- ▶ To learn what power nodes exist in the elements of language.
- ↳ To further extend your range of expressive vocalization.
- ⇨ To further bring language into your body in a dynamic way.
- ➔ To extend your experience of how language, and elements of language, can communicate even without words.
- ↗ To further enhance your sensitivity to the sonics of language. ✪

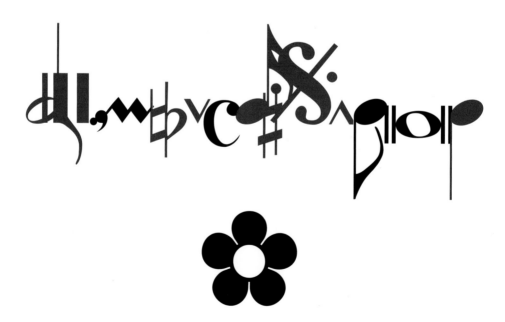

Quincy Troupe is the author of 17 books, including eight volumes of poetry. The latest, *The Architecture of Language,* won the 2007 Paterson Award for Sustained Literary Achievement. He received the 2003 Milt Kessler Poetry Award for *Transcircularities: New and Selected Poems* (Coffee House Press, 2002), which was selected by Publishers Weekly as one of the 10 best books of poetry published in 2002, and was also a finalist for the 2003 Paterson Poetry Prize.

Troupe is Professor Emeritus of Creative Writing and American & Caribbean Literature at the University of California; the founding Editorial Director for *Code Magazine*; and former Artistic Director of Artists on the Cutting Edge. He was the first official Poet Laureate of the State of California, appointed by Governor Gray Davis. He is currently editor of *Black Renaissance Noire*, a cultural and literary journal published by the Africana Studies Program and the Institute of African American Affairs at New York University.

Troupe is the recipient of a 2010 Lifetime Achievement Award from the Before Columbus Foundation's American Book Award, as well as two other American Book Awards: *Snake-Back Solos* (Reed & Cannon, 1979) won in 1980 for poetry; and *Miles: The Autobiography*, Miles Davis with Quincy Troupe (Simon & Schuster, 1989) won in 1990 for non-fiction. In 1991, Troupe received the Peabody Award for co-producing and writing the seven part radio series, *The Miles Davis Radio Project*. He is a two time Heavyweight Champion of Poetry (1994 & 1995) at The World Poetry Bout of Taos (New Mexico); has been a featured poet on two PBS television series on poetry: *The United States of Poetry* (1996), and Bill Moyers' *The Power of the Word* (1989), for which Troupe's segment, *The Living Language*, received a 1990 Emmy Award for Television Excellence.

A screenplay version of his book *Miles and Me: A Memoir* (University of California Press, 2000) is scheduled for 2012; *Hallelujah*, on the life of Ray Charles, is scheduled for 2012; his new book of poems, *Errançities*, will be published in late fall, 2011; and his book of non-fiction prose, *Crossfertizations*, will be released in 2012. He is writing his first novel, *The Legacy of Charlie Footman*, and an auto-memoir in three parts, *The Accordion Years: 1965 to 2010*. Troupe lives between New York City and Goyave, Guadeloupe, with his wife, Margaret. ☉

Photo credit, Rohan Preston

Seven/Elevens; a new suite of poems

Untitled 1

words are dice thrown across floors,
gambling tables, where language circumvents who
won or lost, comes down to bets
lost in chips when snake-eyes dooms your first throw, though
turn a seven, eleven
after bones stop rolling you dance as though great
music, love entered your soul

Untitled 2

living in the world is mostly about chance,
the draw of straws, or cards dealt
in a game of poker, it's all about nerves,
how your eyes react in tight,
cold-blooded moments of chicken, will you fold,
cave in to raw fear, pressure,
will you become an improviser with chance,
probability living
inside this new moment offered you singing
as solo, the notion fresh
thoughts can carry art to new, profound plateaus

Untitled 3

walking beside a building
offers possibility of a falling
brick cracking your skull with death
coming in the blink of an eye, a dice throw
unfavourable to you
in that moment, the fickleness of chance, odds,
is an opaque, feckless risk

Tomas

tomas came whipping in suddenly, winds howled
through wet morning darkness, wings
of cold rain, drenching voices swirling anger
from a roiling, angry sea,
tree branches kneeled down as if they were blessing
snapped sugar cane stalks, whirlwinds
tossing leaves, switch-backing currents, closed hands held
tight together as in prayer,
benedictions raised up to God to spare us
holy terror like this one
whipping hurricane winds in from Africa

Untitled 4

eye hear cold voices whipping
my language of poetry wet with snapping
syllables, flying off white
pages full of dreaming, whirlwinds of rhythms
trying to create a form
history can walk through as pure poetry
rooted in language of place

Untitled 5

poetry is form drawing from nothingness, song
seeking language to create
metaphor, meaning, a vehicle through which
words shape themselves into sound,
local elocutions mapping bird calls, grunts,
slippage of puns, word-plays, jokes,
the march of history's impact on tongues, words,
the chance mixing of races
splices jambalaya voices, tongues simmered down
in pots of Creole culture,
food we eat today is language won or lost

Untitled 6

throw the bones again to see
where the dice stop rolling through life's chief moments
of chance, do they roll stopping
with snake-eyes, seven-eleven turning up
inside luck, ability
raised up from cultural fusion, risk, fresh modes,
language echoing the new

—Quincy Troupe ✪

Great art has been said to be a mirror that reflects the daily life of the culture of a society. If this is true—and I believe it is so—then great art in the United States must reflect the diversity of the culture that it grows from, while at the same time mirroring the authentic regional geographic root-place it springs from. This is a complex task, but all of us live in a complex time in a hyper-complex modern world, whether we understand it or not. In contemporary times all places in the United States—and, I might add, in much of the world—are cross-fertilized places because of the pervasive growth of mass media across the globe. This cross-fertilized mode of local expression provides a subtext, a dialogue of sorts with nationally recognized and celebrated artistic expression, which it feeds—whether acknowledged or not—and makes it distinctive. In music the socalled national genius of rap, jazz, rock n roll and blues in the United States all have their most fertile and creative roots in local modes of expression. The same can be said about visual art and literature. The poetry of Pablo Neruda, the fiction of Gabriel Garcia Márquez, the visual imagery of Pablo Picasso, and the music of Miles Davis and others extend beyond local national borders and reach an international level of communication and stay there for decades; artists like Shakespeare, Beethoven, Mozart, Van Gogh and others have been with us for centuries. This is a rare achievement indeed, especially if this achievement is lasting, like some of the artists I listed above.

Let me explain.

Pablo Picasso is an artist who first came to prominence excavating images from his home town in his native Spain before moving on to France and more modernist tendencies, which included absorbing the sculptural, exaggerated style and language of sub-Saharan African modes of expression, which deepened his art and gave it international thrust. The same can be said of the fictional art of Garcia Márquez, who went outside his Columbian heritage to borrow from the American writer William Faulkner and Pablo Neruda, who also borrowed from another American, the poet Walt Whitman; Miles Davis, the great American trumpeter was influenced by African and Spanish musical forms. All, however, remained faithful to their own indigenous cultural roots while expanding into other cultures that broadened the reach of their art.

Other contemporary visual artists like Romare Beardon, Jacob Lawrence, Robert Rauschenberg, Jose Bedia, Frank Stella, Jean Michel Basquiet, Elizabeth Murray are examples who borrow from other sources while remaining faithful to their own roots. In literature we can point in this century to William Faulkner and the way he raised the local language usage of black and white Mississippians to a national and international plateau that influenced the likes of Ralph Ellison, Gabriel Garcia Márquez, Carlos Fuentes, Milan Kandera, Toni Morrison, José Donoso, Miguel Asturias and many others. The same can be said of the 19th century American poet Walt Whitman, who influenced a slew of 20th century poets, including Pablo Neruda; Langston Hughes; Muriel Rukeyser; Allen Gingsberg; Sharon Olds; William Carlos Williams and me. I learned from Whitman that the oral, everyday voice of people who surround you could be raised and transformed into the high artistic language of poetry, that those rhythms and cadences one hears on a daily basis are the ones that inform and enrich the greatest poetry throughout the world.

I learned this primarily from Pablo Neruda, who directed me toward his mentor, Walt Whitman. I had read Whitman earlier but wasn't prepared to take him seriously as I didn't realize I was going to be a poet. But I wanted to become a poet after reading Neruda, which pointed me back to Whitman. I read him again with fresh eyes and saw the richness there. The same thing happened with Emily Dickinson, and the African-American poets Langston Hughes, Sterling Brown, Jean Toomer and Gwendolyn Brooks, all of whom I had read earlier but only understood their importance after deciding I was going to write poetry full-time.

My first artistic hero and mentor, however, was Miles Davis, who is one of the fountainheads of 20th century American — and world — music. Miles was born in Alton, Illinois, the same Midwestern region of the United States that I come from; the area around St. Louis, Missouri. Miles was raised in East St. Louis, which is across the Mississippi River from where I was born and raised. St. Louis has produced a significant number of great artists in the United States during the 20th century: T.S. Eliot, Marianne Moore, Tennessee Williams, William Burroughs, Chuck Berry, David Sanborn, Clark Terry, Oliver Lake, John Hicks, Lester Bowie, and Redd Foxx are just a few who come to mind. When I read or listen to these artists I never fail to pick up some of the native cadences and rhythms indigenous to the area in the voices of these artists, especially in the music of Chuck Berry and most notably Miles Davis.

I am not a practising literary critic, but I do have definite ideas and opinions about what is being written in the whirling, fast-changing worlds of poetry today. In the United States there are many different styles of poetry being written; there are formalists, language poets, jazz poets — though I confess to not knowing exactly what that term means; does it mean poets influenced by jazz music? There are a lot of those poets around, though when the term "jazz poet" is used it always seems to mean African-American poets when there are plenty of White-American, Asian-American, Latino-American, Arab-American poets influenced by jazz music. On the flip side of this coin, when John Ashberry, or some other notable White-American poet says they are highly influenced by so-called European "classical music" no one calls them European "classical

poets." There are performance poets, poets influenced by rap, cowboy poets, confessional poets, beat poets, black nationalists poets, and the list could go on and on.

What interests me beyond all the manifestos and positions, stances all schools of poetry take — and throughout the world — is how much do their poetics worry the status quo, rather than fit neatly into a position that up holds the status quo? For example, many language poets profess a desire to work against the narrative of history, because in their opinion history has been written mostly by white men and is distorted from their point of view. That's fine, because it's true. The problem is that the overwhelming majority of language poets are white, and American, and it's a political position that they are taking. That's all right, too, for them. If they want to cancel out their narratives because of the barbarous acts of conquests and evil their ancestors inflicted throughout their recent history, and try to begin anew that's all right also. But so-called people of colour all over the world cannot cede the writing of their own history to anyone but themselves, because it was erased in great part by the conquering white Europeans and white Americans, and so they have to reconstruct historical narratives that will serve their own individual societal purposes; they must leave legacies for future generations that will truly reflect, from their perspectives, what happened to them, who they were, who they are now, and who they will become in the future.

The same operating theory that applies to so-called people of colour throughout the world applies to African-Americans in the United States, because we have had much of our history erased too. This is a fact. So we African-Americans have to write and reconstruct a true history that will reflect our journey throughout the last four centuries in the New World, and we must link this relatively recent history — 400 years is but a drop in the bucket of the history of timewith that of ancient Africa, where we first came from as slaves to the United States, and the Caribbean, Brazil, Columbia, Mexico, Central America, Uruguay, Peru and the other New World locations where we were taken.

With this in mind, as an African-American I cannot fully embrace the rejection of historical narrative as many language poets do, because of what I have stated above; it is imperative for me to reconstruct a history through my poetic voice that will serve to mirror the savage but beautiful journey black people in the West have travelled throughout the last 400 years. It is a very painful, though glorious, triumphant journey we have been on, one full of much tragedy, but wonderful accomplishments too. It is an historical record very worthy of restoring, and it one that many can learn from.

My poetry is strongly influenced by music and the visual arts, especially painting. It is a poetry always searching for new ways to balance musical and visual impulses with poetic and philosophical ideas. That's why a robust figurative language is a very important tool in my work, because the modern world is in a constant state of flux and change (even as it remains the same in some areas like humankind's inhumanity to humankind, which never seems to change, as does our insatiable greed, racism, and religious intolerance) and these debilitating areas of human life have to be "imagized" and given a rhythm. That's why music and the visual arts are so important as active ingredients in my poetry: I want the reader and listener to see and feel the rhythm of what the poem is attempting to address. Sometimes it works and sometimes it doesn't, but the journey, for me, is always exhilarating.

There are other strong influences in my work, like the poetry of Aime Cesaire, Cesar Vallejo, Jean-Joseph Rabearivello, Derek Walcott, W. S. Merwin, Sterling Brown, Robert Hayden, Amiri Baraka and others. My poetry is not a dialogue with someone else, other writers, poets, painters, musicians but is a conversation with myself, and it is one that is constantly seeking innovation, risk, rather than one dialoguing with tradition. What I'm involved with in this artistic enterprise is an art that seems to always pull me, and my poetic voice, toward magical seduction, towards the undiscovered path rather than toward the path which is known. I love discovering surprise in artistic expression rather than settling for the known or the safe in creative expression. That's what my poetry struggles with every day I sit down to write. That's why I embrace music and visuals arts, but especially certain genres of music like so-called jazz, some rap, and even newer hybrid American form — again created by young African-Americans — that is sweeping the entire globe even as I write.

But jazz is the classical music of the United States, though many European-Americans refuse to acknowledge this fact, because jazz is a creation of African-Americans and its greatest artists are undeniably black. It's pure racism that many whites in America refuse to really acknowledge the important place jazz music occupies in this country and the world. But whether they accept it or not, jazz is a truly original mode of American musical expression and it is relatively new, having been birthed in the 20th century. On the other hand, poetry is an ancient art form, probably as old as human history on earth. Now, during the latter half of the 20th century, probably dating from the 1940s, the marriage of poetry with jazz is an exciting new creative mode of expression, and it has influenced the phenomenal growth of the newer hybrid musical form called rap.

As I said, my poetry has been primarily influenced by jazz, but rap has also impacted my writing. Rock 'n roll and the blues have also impacted my writing. One of the primary reasons music has had a large influence on my poetry is because of the elements of improvisation and surprise. These elements are basic ingredients in great music, especially jazz, and to my way of thinking they are also crucial in crafting important contemporary poetry.

—Quincy Troupe ✪

Seven/Elevens

I grew up in the inner city of St. Louis, Missouri, and I watched older and younger people—mostly men—gambling when they played the game of dice. Some were killed because one of their adversaries perhaps thought they were cheating, though sometimes it was for winning a great deal of money, which made their opponents mad. So in my mind playing the game of dice contains within its mandate an essential element of risk and chance.

Seven/Elevens is my attempt to create a new form based on the roll of the dice and the elements of chance and risk embedded in that game. To put it simply, the form goes like this: in the "seven," the poem is seven lines, with alternating seven and eleven syllabic lines, beginning with a line of seven syllables. With the "elevens," the poem is eleven lines of alternating eleven and seven syllabic lines, beginning with an opening line of eleven syllables.

In my view of the form the series of poems opens with the seven form, with the next form being an eleven, though I don't see the form necessarily conforming to this strict configuration. For me the idea is to write poems that address risk, chance, as the throw of the dice does when someone is gambling, because in my view life and living is always about taking risk even if one approaches life conservatively—because there is no way to predict what will confront you while passing through the daily activity of breathing and living.

With all of this said, I also think of "Seven/Elevens" as poetic form open to possible improvisation when performing these strictly syllabic, written poems. How can this happen? One might ask. Well I think if the poet/performer internalizes the music/metre of the seven/eleven syllabic count, in the same way an actor memorizes written lines, then perhaps it might be possible to construct on-the-spot sentences, riffs of the same syllable durations in the manner that a musician plays notes—for instance an accordion player creating solos through "reeds blown by bellows and played by means of keys and buttons"—through the manipulation of the poet's voice.

Anyway, I think of this as food for thought, or poetic creation if you will, because I have always found it fascinating what an artist can do when creating in the air, on the spot, like dancers, painters, actors, and musicians do every day.

In the end, poetry is very close to those of the above-mentioned artists' way of working and creating, especially when employing the techniques of surprise, improvisational practices, which can lead to the profound mysterious, magical way the trickster operates, which brings to mind the art of Picasso, Miles Davis, Jimi Hendrix, Gabriel Garcia Márquez, Prince, James Brown, The Beatles, Michael Jackson, Heath Ledger as the Joker, and others, when the high level of creation constantly challenges the audience, which is precisely what great art is supposed to do.

Poet, performer, professor, editor, and cultural activist, Anne Waldman is the author of over 40 books of poetry, including the recent book-length hybrid narrative poem *Manatee/Humanity* (Penguin Poets, 2009), and the *Iovis Trilogy, Colors in the Mechanism of Concealment*, her 1000 page epic (Coffee House Press, 2011). She is also the editor and co-editor of numerous anthologies, including *Civil Disobediences: Poetics and Politics in Action*, and *Beats at Naropa* (2009) (both Coffee House Press). Her books include *Fast Speaking Woman* (City Lights), and now in multiple language editions, *First Baby Poems, Marriage: A Sentence,* and *In The Room of Never Grieve.* Her 800-page epic *Iovis* will be published by Coffee House Press in 2011. She is the co-founder (with Allen Ginsberg) of the renowned Jack Kerouac School of Disembodied Poetics at the Naropa University in Boulder, Colorado, where she is Chair and Artistic Director of The Summer Writing Program. She is the recipient of grants for the National Endowment for the Arts, the Foundation for Contemporary Performance Arts, and has been awarded the Shelley Memorial Prize. She has been a fellow at the Rockefeller Foundation's Center in Bellagio, the Civitella Ranieri Center in Umbria, and a fellow of the Emily Harvey Foundation in Venice, and she was the resident poet at the Women's Christian University in Tokyo. She has been one of the prime movers and creators of the "Outrider" experimental poetry community for over four decades. She has recently been appointed a chancellor of the Academy of American Poets.

Currently, she works collaboratively with her son Ambrose Bye, a composer and musician. Their CDs include *Eye of the Falcon*, *Matching Half* (with Akilah Oliver), and *The Milk of Universal Kindness.* Her play *Red Noir* was directed by the legendary Judith Malina and produced by the Living Theatre, running for over two months in New York City (2009/2010). She is also the co-writer of the script *Entanglement* (2009), with her husband, Ed Bowes. ✪

Photo credit, Greg Fuchs

from Matriot Acts

"Women are the weapons of history, we are the symbolic representations of compassion and decency."
-Carrie Mae Weems

invoke the hyena in petticoats!
laughing hyena, spotted hyena, striped–
all stalk the charnel ground amidst
microscopic & telescopic worlds
a step ahead of what is to come in lineage
in gratitude, in naming las madres
las mujeres,
look for reclamation, sniff it out…
in a voice not my own but all of them
the wizened ductile face of slumbering female memory:
beginning of time, the timepiece of time
she who was the mother of a ghost ship
Ship of Locked Awe and subjugated dream
she who learned from all the male poets
she who could never be reduced to a "gender issue"
she who announced a talismanic bond to planet
who saw vole tracks in the snow once on the
        radical poet's tiny death plot
Lorine, Lorine! you can come out now…
who salvaged a blow dryer for the art people while
they sold the rights to textures of paper, of glass
(touch me, touch me with crenellated beauty now)
particles in the sunlight, a democratic grace
who documented all hurts and slights & transmuted them
to poetry, to flesh, to the wink after sex
she was a challenge in my heart, the penultimate mother
did you have any animals around you from the start?

did you enjoy yourself a lot?

how old were you when you started this running around?

what was your mother tongue?

was it in a language that translates "ocean of bliss" to a seed syllable?

she reports a tabula rasa and a grandmother who cautions

"Denial Silences Violence"

"Remember the Suffragettes"

or considers William Blake's schema of Los representing

Imagination in Action

who then tries to create forms so they can be recognized

who then gets deluded that it created the universe and can thus control it

and then whose zones split into genders

genders lost in realms of jealousy & fractal time

battling the projected others

seeing one's own imagination in a pool produces a double

while another character sacrifices herself to the sun...

—Anne Waldman ✪

First appeared in *Outrider*
2006, La Alameda Press

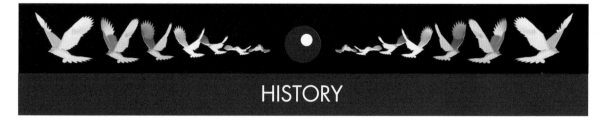

POETRY AS POLITICAL ACT

Poets have been involved with political acts for centuries. And in many cultures and societies with fewer freedoms than we take for granted in the West, art— especially written art—is a form of rebellion, resistance, protest, even redemption. In many countries with repressive governments or regimes, poets are considered dangerous, and may be censored for their views.

Allen Ginsberg's poem **"Howl"**—in spite of a notorious trial that exonerated the poem which is a *cri de coeur* for humanity—may not be played on the radio in the United States during daylight hours. The language of poetry might be visionary, and so embracing of an alternative reality advocating peace and justice and fairness and individual experience, that it threatens those in power, who live by narrow-minded or in some cases, autocratic rule. Those who fear any mention of antiwar sentiment, anti-capitalist, or pro-Middle East sentiment. Those who do not acknowledge women's rights or gay and lesbian and transgendered rights. Those who do not understand the subtlety of poetry, and its role in the collective imagination. Who do not comprehend Walt Whitman's lines: "Do I contradict myself? Very well, then I contradict myself, I am large, I contain multitudes." Or almost a century earlier, the poet John Keats's notion of "I is another." Because poetry may present both sides, "I" is always the bigger mind, the bigger view. Poetry may embrace the contradictions and then allow the audience members to think for themselves. It is not always about "preaching to the converted." It is the "minute particulars" (William Blake's term) that we need to pay attention to, the details and tangibles in our world, in order to present a larger view.

When I wrote my own long hybrid poem "Manatee /Humanity," I was inspired to present a meditation on another life form, an endangered species. I chose the manatee to stand in for other endangered creatures. The manatee goes back 60, 000 years and has the elephant as its closest relative. It was a land animal first before it took to the sea. Its name comes from "manitou"—breast—in the Taino (Caribbean) language. I investigated the biological history of the manatee and in performance, with my son composer Ambrose Bye, we used actual recordings of the manatee song in our "Manatee Suite" composition.

The Manatee

...the manatee is a migratory animal
the manatee is gentle and slow-moving
the manatee moves in slow moving rivers slowly...

It is always helpful and salutary also, to invoke the Romantic poet John Keats's original definition of "negative capability"—to be able to hold disparate thoughts in the mind "without any irritable reaching after fact or reason." To live inside the contradictions and yet see clearly a way through to greater tolerance and inspiration.

Langston Hughes and other African-American writers, including poets Audre Lorde and Amiri Baraka—and many other holders of their lineage—have been instrumental in expressing the outrage and historical experience of slaves and the continuing incipient racism that has permeated the culture for many years. Resistance and freedom have always been the battle cries.

The many decades long Festival de Medellin in Colombia, a country consumed by fratricide and on-going civil war, considers poetry a necessary act; a political, even redemptory act; in that it represents a way to express an alternative reality of peace, kindness, love, and collaboration. Making art is in itself a political act, whether or not the content is overtly "political." It establishes creative expression as a supreme value for humanity. There is a notion that poets cannot be bought, do not compromise their ethics or values. Magical efficacies of language are ways to "hold the space."

Poetry is generally marginalized. But I have also seen acts of poetry that have made a difference. Allen Ginsberg reading his "Plutonian Ode" at Rocky Flats Nuclear plant in the 1970s. We were both arrested there, doing our protest poems in the mid-1970s, along with Daniel Ellsberg of Pentagon Papers fame. I chanted:

Mega Mega Mega Mega Death Bomb—Enlighten!

I dedicate this day to mega-death
This plutos-wealth
plus archia-rule
This rule of the wealthy
This plutolatry
This worship of wealth-I spell away!
Mega mega mega mega mega

Mega mega mega death bomb—enlighten!

Junk plutonium
Love it?
Hate it?

We'll all be glowing for a quarter of a million years!
Teeth glowing
Underwear glowing
Pages of words glowing
Ah the third lumbar glowing in pain...

With 20 years of protest we helped close the plant down and many local residents are still "on the case" — working to keep the site of toxins off-limits to local residents.

Poems might lead to internment, the mental ward, even death. I think it is important to have an historical perspective about the power and efficacy of poetry in the social realm.

Because we live in a culture where poetry — considered primarily "literary" — persists in academia, in institutions, we forget that poetry has a whole other range of importance. It asks the fundamental questions: What is language? What is life? What is a life in language? We live in a consumerist reality but it is difficult to "own" poetry.

Adrienne Rich has called the revolutionary poem a "wick of desire." Diane di Prima wrote a whole book of poems entitled *Revolutionary Letters*, which gave advice on survival during times of political unrest in the 1960s.

There are poets who have covered the spectrum of social outrage, from Paul Celan, who wrote in German (and whose family was destroyed by the Nazi holocaust); to the great Russian poet Anna Akhmatova (a victim of Soviet Russian censorship & repression).

As writers, we should be informed about and investigate the "causes" we wish to inhabit and hone our skills for, and also know the history of our own literary activists — ours and the rest of the world's. We are part of a larger community that wishes "to keep the world safe for poetry," and in doing that we keep it safe for an ethos of imagination and tolerance.

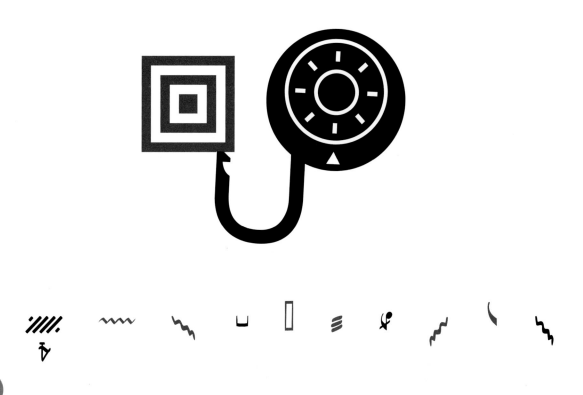

Perspective for Performance

My practice has always been to let my texts and poems themselves guide me into performance. There is often a particular phrase or refrain that works as a gateway or entry into a longer piece — or an image or an idea. Or I am called upon to participate in a particular gathering or occasion.

It is first useful to consider and work with the three "poeias": the *phanopoeia*, or "image cast on the mind's eye"; the *logopoeia* or the intellect or "dance of the ideas"; and the *melopoeia*, which is the inherent sound — down to the phones and phonemes — of the language you are invoking.

The word "poesis" means "making." You are making a piece of writing for performance with language; and with your voice; and its attendant inflections, tone; and with your body. You might also choose some accompaniment with music, or other voices, or the inclusion of images. Or you might be working in more ambitious modes including dancers, and so forth. There are myriad possibilities.

Ponder your own tendencies and propensities.
Ask yourself:
Am I more of a sound poet?
Am I an image poet?
Or is it the ideas that motivate my work?

Of course, any text combines all three poeias, but it is important to work with your strengths.

I have trusted my ear a good deal over the years and in creating some of the anaphoric or chant poems, I have started with a phrase that builds as it repeats.

I am putting makeup on empty space
All patinas convening on empty
Rouge blushing on empty space

Painting the eyelashes of empty space… etc.
I cup my hands in water, splash water on empty
space
Dancing in the evening
It ended with dancing in the evening
I wanted to scare you
The hanging night, the drifting night,
Daughter of troubled sleep

The idea for this poem, "Putting Makeup on Empty Space," was generated from a notion in Buddhist psychology, however. This is what the feminine principle does: creates atmosphere, dresses up the phenomenal world, and so on. The masculine principle is involved more with action or skillful means. The feminine principle adorns. So the poem is a ritual enactment of that process.

But the way *in* is most exciting. It was that initial flash, and as I came up with the first lines out of the phrase, "makeup on empty space." I started to gesture as if I was in fact applying makeup to my own face. This gesture informed my poem. I imagined standing in front of a mirror.

In one of my poems entitled "Corset," I conjure up the historical figure Emma Goldman (1868-1940) who was an anarchist, free-thinker, and advocate for women's rights, who had a lively and fiery life "in the struggle" for social issues. She had worked in a corset factory as a teenager in St Petersburg. I was inspired to write this piece after seeing a documentary about John Lennon who had been hounded by J. Edgar Hoover, who was the head of the United States CIA. He had also hounded Emma Goldman earlier in her anarchist career. I was amazed by the span and long reign of this repressive figure and wanted to create an homage to Goldman and also declare my own "imaginative ever-free of the imagination of J. Edgar Hoover," who still lurks as a symbol at the edges of the continuing invasive surveillance of activist citizens. My motive was to create a piece that would be a

161

"history lesson" and also be relevant to the times. It was written during an anti-war protest in New York City, when a blimp overhead was monitoring protestors on the streets below:

What is it to be corset maker binding the bone and cotton in a daily sweat of labour and purpose what is it to know the sweat of all you my sister workers of daily living surviving an economic purse-string purpose what is it to be declared the most dangerous of purpose when J. Edgar Hoover has your number and what is it here now in St Petersburg hungry and anxious and soul-stirring for surviving my purpose what is the cause of insomniac passion my further disillusionment in your systems in your many systems in all the systems that bind the bone in this labour to you who will always profit off the labour of Emma's hands sewing binding aching toiling bone and cotton in the class struggle a dangerous purpose you want to call it that why you can call it that and it's so much more but do call it that and you will I'm sure call it that and most dangerous of violence and terror too and you want to call it that? Why you can call it that and it's so much more but do call it that and you will I'm sure call it that and most dangerous of violence and terror too and what of a Spanish Civil War I'll call wake up all minions! I'll call: Arise!

I used the repeating "what" as an inquiring goad for the piece and the refrain "you want to call it that why you can call it that." I read the piece with a building intensity, with a sense of urgency, rushing the phrases. But the rhythms in the piece are also meant to echo the sound of factory machines, and the need to produce the item quickly with a maniacal energy.

The piece continues:

and would cast in a daily sweat of labour a struggle a sweet edge that way for it's an energy of daily sweat and toil to be free of the fascisms of how and when and why and why o never free of J. Edgar Hoover but my imagination ever free of the imagination of J. Edgar Hoover who will surely most certainly have your number in his fractious labour and psychopathic toil even now when he the ghost of fractious J. Edgar Hoover is stalking haunting the work places the meeting places the "commune" of all my sweat and purpose…what is it to be a large woman be-speckled and intent in my libertarian socialist moment you want to call it that? Why you can call it that and it's so much more but do call it that and you will I'm sure call it that and most dangerous of violence and terror to incite a riot what is it to be thus called trouble and to be forever "unpopular with authorities" to be watched and goaded and arrested and in lock-down what kind of terror moment is this

and ends with the lines:

will the ghosts of Haymarket stalk the Union Hall still in that old purpose and will that will now sisters break the corset that binds the moment?

The heave stress is on **"break" "corset" "binds" "moment."**

When I worked with composer Ambrose Bye to make this a musical piece, he opened the piece with my voice singing, "Arise! Arise!" And the music speeds up and builds during the "you can call it that" sections.

PROMPT
- Create a text of your own, based on an historical figure you admire. Do some research.
- Select key phrases to amplify.
- Let the piece guide you to your vocal moves and rhythms.

Seen/Unseen

Think about the contrast between what is "revealed" in language and voice and gesture and images, and what is "concealed." You might consider masks or props in this work. This was inspired by my experiences in studying art and performance in Bali, Indonesia.

Create a text that is bifurcated on the page. Sliced across the middle.

Create the upper half of the page with images, phrases, list of things seen—what's obvious, visible, what you may have witnessed.

Write in tangible phrases.

Name places, describe these various realities.

Paint with your words.

Push your mind to see the pictures clearer, as Jack Kerouac might advise.
Work with your sense perceptions.

On the lower half of the page, create a similar list of what's hidden; what is secret; or what is the dark underside of the realities riding above. You might want to put your lines into brackets to visually suggest they are less available or less obvious, or dangerous even.

You have several choices in how you might perform such a text. You might want to create a space in which there is a screen or a doorway to stand behind. You could be hidden. The hidden part of your text could also be spoken in a whisper. You might also work with two voices, two bodies. You could go back and forth between the lines of each section or read simultaneously. But the point is to make a clear demarcation between these different realities. You can also project the text on a screen, or think of other ways to bifurcate the space for performance. The hidden parts could be performed in darkness.

Temple rituals in Bali work with the layers of what's seen and unseen in subtle ways. You can conjure different realities through placement in the space and through pitch of voice. Masks are often used to denote characters from different realms. Human/ghost, peaceful/demonic and so on.

Be sure that the words come through

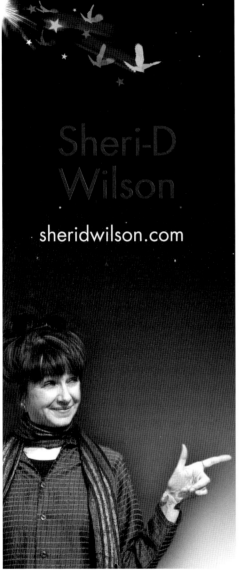

Sheri-D
Wilson

sheridwilson.com

The Mama of Dada
Poet, performer, film-maker, educator, producer and activist

Sheri-D Wilson has seven collections of poetry; her most recent, *Autopsy of a Turvy World* (Frontenac House), followed *Re:Zoom*, which won the 2006 Stephan G. Stephansson Award for Poetry, and was shortlisted for the CanLit Award. She has two spoken word CDs, and four award-winning VideoPoems including: *Airplane Paula, Spinsters Hanging in Trees*, and *Panty Portal* (BravoFACT). In 2009 Sheri-D was chosen as one of the Top Ten Poets in Canada by CBC Arts, in 2007 *Heart of a Poet* produced a half hour documentary about her, and in 2003 she won the USA Heavyweight of Poetry title.

She has performed all over the world, with highlights which include: maelstrÖm 2010 (Brussels), Blue Met 2009 (Montreal), Voix d'Amériques 2008,'05 (Montréal), Bumbershoot 2003, '99, '92, '91, '89 (Seattle), Vancouver International Writers Festival 2007, '02, '00, '95, '93, '90 (Vancouver), Taos Poetry Circus 2002 (Taos, New Mexico), Poetry Africa 2001 (South Africa), WordFest 2008, 2000, '95 (Calgary, Banff), Harbourfront Reading Series 1993 (Toronto), Small Press Festival 1990 (NYC).

Since founding the Calgary Spoken Word Festival in 2003, Sheri-D has worked at quantum velocities to present one of the most respected spoken word festivals in Canada. Since 2008, she has been Director of the Spoken Word Program at The Banff Centre.

Sheri-D Wilson is the editor of *The Spoken Word Workbook: inspiration from poets who teach*.
calgaryspokenwordfestival.com ✪

Photo credit, David Johns

165

Sexy Madonna from Florence

for Raffaella D'Elia

Sexy Madonna from Florence
stands before me, in the after-hour
street lamp torch, on cobbles of curb,
in that crazy Bard-o-space twixt theatre and life;
she stands opposite me, on stones of ancient lane
rife with Lorca in her veins —
and the gypsy flamenco clapping
and plumes of palmas dust rising
and the zapateado heel snapping, and the deep song
shadow of Duende blood rapping —
ghosts around and between us, cante jondo,
like a dancing spirit, it
hangs over our heads,
like the agony of an animal with three spears
in its side, it hangs over our heads
like a blindfolded poet with seven rifles aimed
at his heart, it hangs over our heads, like the single
word: Fire!   coup de grace   execution's devolution
assassination of desire
the air is charged with an omphalos hit —
What a powerful show! she says,
I can hear Lorca's cries, rise from the grave

Sexy Madonna from Florence
wears the hanged man
on a long chain of devastated pearls
shock-wave around her neck,
like a High Arcana boa constrictor
I think: Woman strangled by her own pet Tarot
card poisoned by a traitor's elixir: *asp, asp, asp*

Sexy Madonna from Florence
stands restless in a spotlight
of Belgian moon, full of early spring
as she waits all a-jitter
for her lover to finish his smoke,
in his black trench coat, tête-à-tête baroque
loquacious, no end to his talkfest in sight;
she shivers, with a shutter   shifts from foot to another
swathed in a light blue cashmere shawl
I think: *She's a chrysalis stonewalled*

Her lover continues his smoke as she smoulders frail,
so I lift her stole from her shoulders to her head
as a hood, or a veil; and that's when I espy —
the perfect tail of her black liquid liner, how she draws down the moon

with her eyes—I am close enough to see inside
she's more than Cleopatra's disguise
she might even be Isis
eyes so deep they make me afraid to fall into them—

I freeze, for her eyes would need an expedition; they are
Marianas Trench, challenger deep
36,000 feet, they mesmerize
so suggestive, they are a swinging pocket watch,
they induce hypnotic sleep, entranced—
I submerse myself slow, rip current undertow,
sense of time-space slips away
am I an astronomer, I don't know?
in mind's eye—I am Leonardo da Vinci's last
brush-stroke of her eyes,
and she is the grand-great-grand-great granddaughter
of Mona Lisa, her eyes her demise
for they will drive men mad with longing
and mystery, they are the impossible placebo—
I dream of being the surrealist in Paris
who plots to steal her eyes from the walls of the Louvre
so I can look into, Santo Spirito forever,
for she is a Mesopotamian magnum opus heiress
older than the stones on which she stands,
her eyes a direct line to the original amulet
essence of earth, pyramid of seashell and sands
she whispers: *I will tell you my secrets…*
I fall further   scrying   can't help myself
she says: *…and my dreams*   dotdotdot

Now maybe it was the shock of the Lorca show
that shifted her shadow so, I don't know
but as she speaks of her dreams
in Italian whisper-low, her breath lifts from Cave of the Crow,
like she goes to Point Nemo, divines herself
and returns, with a crazy Nostradamus after-glow;
forward in time to realise who she is,
like she looked into the eyes of unknown;
and her hanged man swings across her belly
there on the cobblestone,
in the chill of eve's air; as the caterpillars
look down on us from freezing branches
their beings transform, as if warmed
by this Madonna's inner sun,
who breaks through, spiral spun—
incredible, she gives birth to herself

before me in the nocturne
her head a halo as she lowers her eyes
and sees into her own vision
her own apparition, in which she flies
morphing-mystic
we could be in a play, and then
her lover advances, breaks the spell, puts his arm around her
It's time to go, are you cold?
she replies: *I am warm now*

And I return to the words of my teacher who said:
You have entered the realm of gold
and now I know what she meant—
I would crush a priceless pearl
and drink it, to stay in this moment
for time: *zingaro   zingaro   zingaro*

—Sheri-D Wilson ✪

First appeared in *Black Renaissance Noire*
2011; E-zine; Canada Speaks commission

LEARNING TO HEAR HISTORY

I remember when Allen Ginsberg asked me, "Who are you influenced by?" At the time, I was deeply offended because I thought he was asking, "Who are you copying?" or, "Who are you emulating?" I couldn't understand why he would ask such a question, and now I know my hearing had deceived me. In my youth I was under the distinct impression that I was utterly original, the first, the one and the only—to write the way I was writing—and for that reason my hearing was limited. Until you realise you are part of something larger than yourself, you will not be given the curiosity to hear.

Truth is, the vibration of every poet who ever lived resonates in all poets that follow (like a collective prayer)—we are part of something bigger than ourselves—a voice, a universal sound, a frequency—a cog in the wheel of poetry-time.

Prompt
In point-form please answer the following questions:
※ What sounds do you hear?
※ Whose footsteps are those?
※ What does history mean to you?
※ What do you have to learn from those who came before you?
※ Can you hear them if you listen?
※ What are they reading, or listening to?
※ What has been passed on to you? And what do you pass on?

I am part of a lineage: a collective voice.

Prompt
One history which influenced me was the "Beats," so I ask myself, "Who were they inspired by?"
☀ Read/or listen to one poem/tune by:
William Blake, Hilda Doolittle, Billie Holliday, Marianne Moore, Charlie Parker, Wallace Stevens, William Carlos Williams, Walt Whitman.

Mental Note:
Count the number of women who have been left out of history.

Listening to History

The oral tradition—or spoken word—is not about speaking, it's about listening. So we listen. And as we learn to love words, sounds, and forms of communication; we listen some more. When we hear the words "look it up," what does it make us think? Oral history predates the concept of "looking it up." So we go back, waaaaay back and think of what we might do instead of "looking it up." Where do we look? Do we find it? Do not answer these questions.

Looking for the Meaning of History

What does the word "history" mean? Look it up—try a good juicy dictionary. There are many words surrounding the word "history"—words that precede it and words that follow it. It is part of a continuum.

We may see: historian, historiated, historic, historical, historically, historicism, historicity, historicize, historico, histories, historiette, historify, historio-, historiography, historiographer, historiography, historiology, history, histrio, histrion, histrionic, historionical—

Prompt

❋ Where does history begin?
❋ What does it mean?
❋ Who keeps history? Who is history written by? Whom is it written for?
❋ If you were the word "history," what would come before and after you?

Prompt

❖ There is an oral tradition in most cultures.
❖ Discover yours—what stories were you told and how were they told?
❖ Dig.
❖ Now excavate your own story.

Where do you begin?
Perhaps you will track your stories
starting at your first epiphany.

Teachings in History

When I attended The Jack Kerouac School of Disembodied Poetics at Naropa University, Anne Waldman reiterated Charles Olson's sense of the poet's job vis-à-vis history, and she asked us to consider the word "istorin" (the root of "history") which means "to find for one's self." This is the root of a more investigative poetics. Wow, what a concept! Not to depend on received knowledge but to trust one's own probe and experience. Pass it on. Trust yourself.

Prompt

Read everything Anne Waldman ever wrote or edited about poetics. Her ideas are astonishing! Find "Outriders," and read it until you know it by heart—in your heart.

Grave-site Observation

Think of a poet who came before you
Now find out where she is buried and visit.
I have acute reverence for Guillaume Apollinaire
I visit his gravesite at Père Lachaise Cemetery, Paris
Create a ritual to take to them
And see what you find
(I find a love poem engraved in the stone of him)—his headstone, over-plot
When I am there it is like two worlds join, mortal and im-
he is alive and I am the ghost inside his poem "Zone";
After,
Listen
Write
Listen
Write
The description of what happened at his grave
becomes "Panty Portal"
Later I come across Ginsberg's poem
"At Apollinaire's Grave," and realise
I am schooled from his grave's grave—
history repeats itself, skips a beat;
Apollinaire versed Ginsberg, sweet.
They are my history, my present, my future,
continuum. Beatnik. Surrealist. Eros. Life.

Prompt

❋ Think of the top ten epiphanies of your life — give each one a title.

❋ Without thinking, sketch details of the event in point-form.

❋ If epiphanies overlap, let them.

Prompt

❋ Read one poem by:

   Guillaume Apollinaire, Allen Ginsberg, Langston Hughes, Sylvia Plath, Dorothea Tanning.

Prompt

✍ Who were the **Surrealists**?

✍ Who were the **Beats**?

Prompt

Write a letter to a poet you love.

✪

Is it important for you to be an historical figure? If it is, don't write. All there is, is all there isn't.

GET LOST!

But if you love to write for the love of writing, then write! If your burning desire is to communicate, write. If you think you have something to say, write. If you need to express your truth, write. If you long to document the beauty of this changing world through sound, poetic vibration, and frequency — fabulous — write. If you're dying to express a social injustice, speak — and speak out now. Et cetera… right!

Once you have decided to write, write with everything you've got! Write with your entire being: your body, your gut, your soul, your heart, your spirit, your madness, your sadness (deep song sorrow), your intuition, your vision. Write on the edge, scare yourself. Find your authentic self and get drunk on ideas (like Baudelaire). Write until you're exhausted, and then get up and write some more. Write until you sweat, until you're speechless, and then write about that. Live inside writing, and let writing live inside you. There's no separation between how you live and what you write. Live inside poetry-head (where everything becomes poetry). Everything you experience is fodder. Always assume your intelligence — don't prove it in poetry. Be curious and discover what is really there, never take anything for granted, and then write. Be humble and don't preach — leave that for religion, they're good at that — and then write some more.

SKETCH!

If you think you've got nothing to write about, sketch with words — like Kerouac said — like you're painting a picture — describe in detail what you see. Write.

Prompt
Describe what's in your fridge.

WAKE UP!

Prompt
Every day, in the morning, write your own epitaph, in case you die that day.

Note to Self!
Always carry a notebook. Find a book you love to write in and write about everyone you meet and everything you see. Write about the freak with the disposition to bully. Write about the oldest woman you ever met. Tell her story. Listen. Listen some more, and then write. Write it down as fast as you can. Write about the voices you hear.

With No Judgement!
Don't judge yourself. As Micki Maunsell once told me, "There is no right and there is no wrong — there is doing and there is not doing."

When I teach I often meet people who say, "I always wanted to be a writer, but I got too busy with life." The only way to write is to write. It's never too late or too early to speak, to tell your story, to live in the rapture of the imagination. So just stop making excuses and pick up a pen and write with all your might. Write. Always do what you always wanted to do.

SHAPE SHIFT!

Are you an animal? What animal are you?

Prompt
Write from the perspective of that animal.

EPIPHANY!

An epiphany a day will keep somnambulence away!

Prompt

Have incredible sex, and then write, write.

First thought—best thought!

(à la Kerouac)

Prompt: First-time eyes. Tomorrow when you wake up, drink a glass of water, go outside, walk, see everything as if it's the first time, like you're seeing for the first time. Wonder what things are, where they come from—then write, write it down. Then sleep on it.

AND DREAM!

Prompt

When an idea wakes you up in the middle of the night, get up and write!   Always make the choice to write!

DREAM!

Prompt

When you wake up in the morning write while you are still half-in-and-half-out or half-out-and-half-in.

BUT WRITE!

Now what is your poem about? Don't tell me what it means, tell me what it is about.

Prompt

Write down what your poem is about. THAT is your poem.

Stay on topic. What is your poem about? Remove the bits that divert you from the poem and file those lines under "later."

Who are you speaking to in the poem? Write. Trick yourself by devising three projects. Write the one that captures your attention. Write.

SET A DEADLINE!

Prompt

Find out where your local readings are. Go listen. Find out where the open mic's are. Go listen. Set a date when you will read—no, perform.

READ!

Read: all poetry, fiction, dictionaries, erotica, technical books, science journals; read books about: Dadaism, surrealism, hermetic transformation, alchemy, Buddhism, et cetera. Read.

Prompt

Take notes. Listen. Where was the author sitting when she wrote the book? Read. Listen. Make notes. Read. Listen. Make notes. Write. Make believe. Make love. Make notes. Read. Make coffee. Pray. Meditate. Write. Make notes. Listen. Make time. Release fear. Eros.

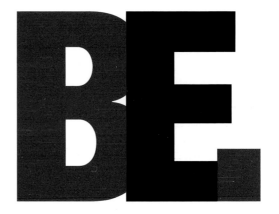

PERFORMANCE STARTS IN THE MIND

Years ago, when one of my students announced she wanted to enter a citywide speech contest, and win gold; it signalled red to me. In fact red flags appeared out of the blue! Then she told me the category was poetry, which started to capture my interest. But it was when she said she could choose any poem that she had me. Pow! I knew exactly what poem she had to do: "Deaf Mute in a Pear Tree," by P.K. Page—one of my favourites, I love that poem.

We worked on the poem for months and when the time came for her to compete, I told her the following: "If you can be inside the poem and stay inside the poem for the length of the poem, you will have achieved one of the great accomplishments of oration. If you can embody the poem, without stepping outside, letting the penny of the poem drop, you will have achieved gold. Assume the gold because you receive 'gold' when you fully experience the poem."

It doesn't matter what other people think, or even award you. All that matters is your own experience. The resonance, the feel in your mind, body, spirit when you truly hold a poem is the kind of gold that cannot be awarded to you, for you can only give it to yourself.

So when you say a poem, assume the gold because that is what every poem has the possibility of sharing with you. The vibration of a poem in your body as you speak it (share it) occurs on a frequency that is the base line of transformation.

Performance Prompts

1) Print your poem so it's easy to read—& get a pencil. (A poem's never finished).
2) Stand in the middle of your practise space. Imagine an audience before you.
3) Read your poem to the audience (not at them) 10 X's.
4) Observe the flow—& your breath—when there's a bloop in the tire, change it, so it's smooth.
5) What are your verbs? What are the stakes of the verbs? Try different verbs and see how it sounds.
6) Try saying the poem with different intentions & tempos. Play with the sounds. When you get dizzy, sit down and drink some water.
7) Who are you speaking to?
8) What is the poem about? Say the poem with this intention.
9) Improvise the poem, and see what you find.
10) Where does the poem live in your body? And the sound?
11) Create gestures—to aid the flow and punctuate your poem.
12) Observe yourself and keep what feels good in your body.
13) Communicate with your eyes. Say the entire poem with your eyes, just your eyes.
14) Ground yourself.
15) Visualize your images.
16) Tape yourself. Listen.
17) Say the poem at least 100 X's!

Now to the reading

1) **Wear** something you feel comfortable in.
2) **Breathe** — in relaxation — breathe — out tension.
3) **No** judgement — you're five years old — instant forgiveness.
4) **Assume** the gold — experience the poem.
5) **What** do you communicate beyond words?
6) **Remember** this is for all poets who ever lived — and all poets who will ever live. You are part of a continuum.
7) **Stay** out of your head and inside your body.
8) **Don't** get too attached to your own voice, but love yourself.
9) **Don't** go overtime.
10) **Observe** the vibrations of oration.
11) **Speak** truth — your authentic self.
12) **And listen** — everything you need is with you.

The biggest question you can ask yourself as a poet is:
What am I giving to my community?

If you have difficulty answering this question,
Remember

poetry can never be lip service!

Blessed be. ✪

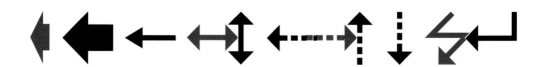

d'bi.young

dbiyoung.net

d'bi.young is an afrikan-jamaican-canadian dubpoet, monodramatist, and educator who is internationally recognised as a visionary, an innovator, and a leader in the development of arts education. most recently recognized with a *resiliency award* from the *canadian national health organization* for her uncompromising dedication to community, she is the published author of two collections of poetry, six plays, and six dubpoetry albums. her profound new creative-performance methodology, called the *sorplusi method*, is making shock waves through the global arts community as a radical paradigm shift in artist training and practice. she has worked with theatre companies, universities, cultural organizations, social institutions, and individual artists across north america, the caribbean, europe, and africa. in 2008 she founded anitafrika! dub theatre in toronto canada and proceeded to design and facilitate two cost-free twelve-month national residencies for emerging artists, instructing them in her biomyth monodrama model and assisting them in formulating their own solo performance shows. her own monodrama trilogy, *sankofa*, featuring the plays *blood.claat*, *benu*, and *word! sound! powah!* toured extensively in 2010, playing to critical acclaim and garnering awards in canada, jamaica, england, and south africa, and is due to be published in 2011. she is the recipient of two dora mavor moore awards, the canadian km hunter theatre award, the toronto mayor's arts council award, and numerous best solo artist awards. having recently completed her first year-long international tour of her latest album *wombanifesto*, in december 2010, she is presently writing her premiere theoretical text on the *sorplusi method* and has founded the pan afrika performing arts institute (papai) — a cultural movement committed to the holistic development of continental and diasporic multi-disciplinary afrikan artists. d'bi.young resides in cape town with her two sons, moon and phoenix. papainstitute.org ✪

Photo credit, Chris Young

177

rivers and other blackness between us

for joshua and cape town

who among us carry the sage-secrets of loving?
who among us carry the sage-secrets of loving?

what elders and children
walk with old-time knowledge
of a courageous love
an unapologetic love
an uncompromising love
a healing love

tell me who
and I will sit studently
by the rivers of their feet
washing away all the unknowing I have come to know
relearning a language of integrity honesty passion
scribed on our heart's tongue
by the ancients
whom I have forgotten

somewhere between a dream and a time-less-ness
across di ocean waters
black sons and dawtahs
black moddahs and fadahs
black auntie uncle sistah and breddah
stretch love fabric
thick and thin
so now we trodding
trying to heal these scars
of broken fibre
that stick up inna wi like macka

who among us carry the sage-secrets of loving?

what elders and children
walk with old-time knowledge
of a compassionate love
an unapologetic love
an uncompromising love
a healing love

tell me who
and I will sit studently
by the rivers of their feet
washing away all the unknowing I have come to know
relearning a language of integrity honesty passion
scribed on our heart's tongue

by the ancients
whom I have forgotten

forgive us for not having loved you relentlessly
in all cases fear has been our worst enemy

were fear not here
I would kiss you
and feed you food from my mouth
stop you from aching and share a smile
maybe even wait with you
by the roadside for a while

were fear not here
I would give name to these unnamed
spaces of accountability
and responsibility
that flow like rivers between us
sometimes silent but always deep

were fear not here
the full moon radiance of your
vulnerable warrior spirit
washing over me like the sun
bathed in blackness
could mirror and you would shine
and I would shine
and we all could shine brilliantly

who among us carry those sage-secrets of loving?

tell me
where are our elders
where are our children
who walk with the old-time knowledge
of a courageous love
an unapologetic love
an uncompromising love
a healing love

tell me who
and I will sit studently
by the rivers of their feet
I want to unknow all this unknowing that I have come to know
I want to relearn a language of honesty
a language of integrity
a language of compassion
these were scribed on my heart's tongue

by ancient ancient ancient ones
who somehow I have surely forgotten

please forgive me for not having loved you relently
in all cases fear has been my worst enemy

I cannot promise to love you fearlessly
but I will love you courageously
in spite of my fear
I will love you compassionately
honestly
and with integrity

this love is a healing love
re-branching herself like the iroko tree
roots reaching beyond
the wounds of yesterday
arms outstretched to the promise of tomorrow

you and I and we
the community
the people
we can choose
to stand firmly
in love
one love

—d'bi.young ✪

First appeared in *rivers and other blackness between us*
2007, women's press

biomyth monodrama & the sorplusi method

objective

to explore the creative process of *biomyth monodrama* using d'bi.young's *sorplusi method*, culminating in a series of monologues originated by program participants. these monologues provide the backbone for possible future biomyth monodramas.

the theory

the *sorplusi method,* which grounds the program, provides the participant with immeasurable life skills that include self-esteem building, critical analysis, collaboration, and conflict resolution. the lesson is based on the premise that everyone is a storyteller, whether professional, amateur, or neither.

participants get the opportunity to reflect on their lives while developing a personal creative system that they can utilize when they need to generate art. this system is primarily concerned with developing a sense of accountability, responsibility, and integrity on the part of the artist's work, and for themselves within the work. the artist is always implicated in their story and the dialogue between them and their audience is always open. the *sorplusi method* trains artists to be socially conscious human beings.

definitions

biomyth

my use of the term *biomyth* refers to the abbreviation of the words biography and mythology. I first encountered the term reading audre lorde's *zami*, which she refers to as a *biomythography*. in my appropriation and reinterpretation of the term *biomyth*, biography pertains to the accounting of one's own lived experience; mythology, in this context, pertains to a. the poetic reinterpretation of the lived experience, and b. the use of orature, folklore, myth, and magic in the process of reinterpretation. *biomyth,* therefore, is the poetic space between what we interpret as real and what we deem make-believe.

monodrama

is theatrical solo performance work. *biomyth monodrama* is a mythologized autobiographical play told by the story's creator/performer, using the eight *sorplusi* elements as the foundation of the creative process and to weave the story together. poetry, music, magic/ritual, monologue and dialogue (primarily with the audience) are biproducts of the *sorplusi method* and are crucial stylistic, aesthetic, and technical considerations. a theatrical fourth wall is rarely present, as the performer erases the divide between audience and storyteller, real and make-believe; the stoyteller-audience relationship is crucial in biomyth monodrama storytelling, encouraging biomythicists to constantly explore and expand the relationship with themselves, their communities, and their belief and practice in art as a tool for social transformation.

sorplusi method

the word *sorplusi* is an acronym I originated, based on the seminal dub theory work of my mother, pioneer dubpoet anita stewart. the acronym represents eight considerations of creative thought and practice, which are *self-knowledge, orality, rhythm, political content and context, language, urgency, sacredness,* and *integrity*. in my developing methodology these ideas form a comprehensive eco-system of accountability and responsibility between the storyteller and the communities that gather to hear our stories. the *sorplusi method* is meant to be taught as the foundation of a *biomyth monodrama* training course. in the course, the artists meticulously excavate each *sorplusi* principle, always interpreting their findings from a critical-analytical, self-reflective, oppression-aware point-of-view. the storytellers and their stories grow simultaneously as they uncover/recover themselves within the magic of storytelling and community.

outline

♥ session one

laying the foundation
what kind of storyteller am I?
how to be oppression-aware

begin the session by asking everyone in the circle to describe what a storyteller is, and how they feel in their personal experience that they are storytellers. ask them to answer the following questions using a few clear and concise sentences per answer.

the storyteller's integrity/resource questions for learners

1. how would i describe my life/art practice(s)?
2. why have i chosen this life/art practice?
3. how do i define integrity?
4. how does this practice feed me/my soul/my integrity?
5. what role does my art practice play in community?
6. how do i share my art practice in community?
7. what role does community play in my art practice?
8. how do i define accountability and responsibility?
9. what is the relationship of accountability and responsibility to my personal integrity?
10. how do i practise integrity in my life/art?
11. how do i hold myself accountable to a. integrity and to b. community in my life/art?
12. in what ways do i ground my life/art in love and transformation?
13. how do i define success?
14. a. what choices do i make in life/art in order to become successful? and b. how are these choices related to my personal integrity?
15. how do i identify myself in community?
16. what voices do i possess in relation to these identities?
17. a. how do i define appropriation? b. in what ways do i appropriate?
18. does community participate in the shaping of my art?
19. what are my expectations of community in my life/art practice?
20. what are my expectations of myself as a storyteller/human being?
21. how does my ancestry and ethno-cultural context influence my art?
22. in what ways do i want to develop professionally?
23. what kind of professional development program would help me to develop professionally?

✳ introduce anti-oppressive terminologies/ break into groups to explore some of the terminologies/make tableaux representing some of the terminologies

understanding the language of discrimination: definitions

stereotype, discrimination, prejudice, race, culture, racism, ethnocentrism, systemic discrimination, linguistic discrimination, homophobia, dominant group/culture, disability, social power / social privilege / people of colour, white / first nations / transsexual / islamophobia / class / equity / transgender /diversity / justice / equal rights / poverty / ageism / gender / sexual orientation / socialization / nationality sexism/misogyny / homophobia / body politics / hair / aesthetics / brownin / high class / marital status / family name / what school you went to / education / area branding / occupation / political affiliations / parenthood / degrees/graduation/street smart

♥ sessions two & three

sorplusi principles: self-knowledge, orality, rhythm, political content & context, language, urgency, sacredness, integrity

- ⟿ ask the learners to define for themselves what each sorplusi principle means. use the bullet points under each term to inform the discussion
- ⟿ ask them to explore how each principle informs their creative process and why
below are some suggested points regarding each principle, that can be used to stimulate discussion

self-knowledge
knowledge of water/knowledge of self/humans are made up of over 60% water
ancestral knowledge/knowledge of ancestors
self-awareness
self-care
self-analysis/self-critique
self-discipline
self-love
self-growth
self-esteem/self-worth
food
breathing

orality
the oral
the spoken
the voiced
with mouth, body, spirit, or a combination
orality is verbal, vocal, utterances of communication
stories are told every day to our parents, lovers, children, and friends
peoples who have been uprooted, survived numerous atrocities and lived to tell these stories due
   to the power of the oral traditions
how the body remembers
memory stored in cells
eye contact

acknowledging your village when they gather to hear you speak

letting the audience know that you love them and that you are honoured to occupy the storytelling space

using your entire body as a way to communicate orality is a reciprocal process moving through and past the fourth wall

the storyteller is implicated by the community and vice versa

rhythm

rhythm is the heartbeat

rhythm is the moving energy of both the medium and the message of the story

afrikan peoples who were transplanted from their homelands on the continent and dispersed throughout the world, were not allowed to bring anything along with them, other than their bodies

rhythm retains memory

rhythm is everything

rhythm also speaks the symbiotic ecosystems we participate in, ie. the cycle of the moon and her relationship to the ocean

if we consider the heartbeat to be the first word, the first sound, the first powah, it becomes clear that rhythm communicates certain energies that language sometimes cannot. storytelling is one of the ways we can reconcile our relationships with our bodies. rhythm also represents music and the power of music to speak and communicate in ways words cannot.

political content & context

"politics," in this context, simply translates into 'of the people'

the personal is political

the political is personal

micro is macro

macro is micro

choosing to "speak" is a therefore a political act

what then do we "talk" about and not "talk" about

do we talk about the things that are actually important to us? the things that move us? the things that we feel passionate about? and is there a connection between those things and community? what i am feeling as a person may also be felt by other members of my community: how does it feels when you're left outside in the cold, when you feel like you give so much love and it goes unrequited, when you've been betrayed, or when you're really being loved properly. those emotions and spiritual energies that move in us are a part of our collective reality. it's necessary always to look at the content of the work and how it affects our communities.

language

oral lore, pithy sayings, parables, proverbs, and riddles

legitimization of a people's lived experience through words

the working people's language in a neo-colonial system

new languages that grow out of colonial systems

speaking the people's language as a celebrated and acceptable way of telling stories

speaking the people's language as a political act

speaking coded language to avoid persecution

the language of the body

the language of music

using language to reinforce bigotry and oppression

reinventing language

creating accessible language

urgency

oya is an afrikan goddess in the yoruba religious tradition who is responsible for revolutionary change
    she governs the wind and the lightening and the thunder
how are our stories urgent
why would we need to tell stories that are urgent
why would we need to tell stories that are important to us
what stories can we tell that urgently convey that
what stories am i going to continue to tell now that i know that unrenewable earth resources
    are drying up
what do i need to learn and what do the people need to learn
what do we need to find out together so that our children survive
urgency is the fire infusing our work
it is a part of recognizing what is happening globally, within our communities, within ourselves,
    and exploring the relationship amongst all three

sacredness

sacredness and religiousness do not necessarily mean the same thing
what do we consider sacred
what do we honour
what do we treat with respect and love
for the things that we do not consider sacred, how do we treat them, interact with them
is storytelling sacred
is the storytelling space sacred
how do we relate to the story and the telling of it
how is sacredness related to spirit and spirituality
what does it mean to honour the word, people, ourselves, the earth
storytellers weave the fabrics of reality and document these fabrics into people's, especially young
    people's, hearts and souls and minds
what is our responsibility to look at what is sacred
sacredness also speaks to the role ritual and the (re)presentation of ritual play in our storytelling
    represent systems, processes, and methodologies
rituals can also be mediums of magic
how we engage with them can have a profound effect on our storytelling and our understanding of
    the sacred

integrity

any dialogue on change, on the way that our work affects people, has to consider our relationship to
    our very personal integrities. these standards or circles of accountability are something that we
    each have to negotiate as part of our process as storytellers.
what does integrity mean to you
can we identity integrity and a lack of integrity within our ourselves
what does that look and feel like
can we identify the violent perpetrator within ourselves and hold ourselves accountability to a more
    liberating and loving standard
integrity allows us to be implicated in all processes of community growth and development

exercise 1
mirror exercise connecting with childhood self
➡ connect with our seven-year-old selves
➡ brief meditations / individual visualization / dialoguing with the young selves we all walk with
➡ share mirror findings

meditation
okay. let's begin. (pause). so. just sit down. get comfortable. we begin with the breath. just find your breath. become aware of it, as you breathe in and out. I want you to let it go. kind of like being at the edge of a river maybe. a calm river. where the water is flowing slowly. and then there are these images that come out of the water and appear to you, and then they flow downstream. i want you to go back to something you were doing last week. anything. the image rises up out of the water. you look at it. and then you let it go. let it flow away down stream. and keep breathing. and i want you to think of something that happened last month. and it comes up out of that river and you look at it. no judgment. you just let it go back into the water. now i want you to think of something that happened last year. anything. last year comes up out of the water, and then it rolls back into the water and it flows downstream. now, i want you to go a bit further back. think of life five years ago. what were you like five years ago? who was that like? where were you five years ago? the memory comes up out of the water and then goes back in the water. then think about 10 years ago. where were you 10 years ago. and what were you doing? and then you let it go back into the water and it flows downstream. now think about 15 years ago. and let it go back into the water. and now, i want you to look into the water, and when you look at your reflection in the water, you see the youngest, youngest, youngest memory of yourself. your youngest self stares at you from the water. and you look. and i want you to ask your youngest self... how are you feeling today? and if your younger self is able to speak, i want you to listen to her. listen and observe, as you look into the water.

♥ session four
shape mirror monolgues
✿ rework mirror monologues using the sorplusi principles as guides

♥ session five
refine monologues and animate them
✿ memorization, body language, gesture, physical movement, physical ideas around storytelling
✿ revisit the sorplusi principles in relation to the theatrical aesthetic and stylistic choices you have made in your monologue.

♥ session six
basic rehearsals and presentation of monologues
✿ learners work to fine tune the monologues
✿ presentation of monologues

✪

Eugene Stickland grew up in Regina, where he eventually worked on an MA in English at the University of Regina. His studies were interrupted when he went to Toronto to complete an MFA in Playwriting at York University. For a number of years Eugene wrote plays in Toronto for the Act IV Theatre Company before moving to Calgary in 1994. While in Calgary, Eugene enjoyed a 10-year stint as Alberta Theatre Projects' playwright-in-residence, writing six plays for the company, and others for other theatres across Canada. Upon leaving ATP, Eugene became a feature columnist for the *Calgary Herald* for five years. His plays have been produced around the world in many different languages. He is currently working on several new projects, including a poetic novel, which he has read from at various spoken word events around town. Eugene was recently appointed playwright-in-residence at Calgary's St. Mary's University College. Photo credit, Janet Woolgar

Have You Heard:
The spoken word and the Absurd Theatre

A few years ago, I began working on a series of poems inspired by the death of a girl friend and the sudden and recurring presence of a beautiful young woman in a coffee shop in New York City. I was actually writing a novel about a man sitting in a coffee shop in New York wondering what would become of him, now that his muse was dead. Was the lovely girl who also wrote in a journal and smoked cigarettes meant to be his muse?

The pondering kept me amused. For the month or so that I was in New York, nominally chaperoning my daughter who, at 14, had somehow become one of the top models on the planet, I wrote a series of poems and feeble attempts at narrative to join them all together.

It was lovely, and it was fun. And if you're curious, here's one:

> My psychiatrist pokes
> around in my brain
> Like an unemployed scholar
> Performing a lube job
> On a rusting Volvo
> station wagon
> In the rain.

None of these poems really mattered in the big picture of my life, or so I thought at the time, because I am a playwright. They were a diversion —a pleasant one, but nothing I thought would ever lead anywhere. They were written perhaps for the best reason I know of: to write a poem, which is no reason at all, actually, beyond the sheer love and exhilaration of creating something from nothing.

I make this distinction because I am of an older somewhat quaint generation that was taught to believe that drama was one thing, prose fiction including the novel and short story, another thing, and then poetry was different again, all different and distinct things. Almost like writing was based on the medical model that was evolving at this same time, giving rise to the era of the specialist. Sore throats over here, broken ankles over there. Sonnets to the right, novels to the left, and all the rest of it.

When I finally returned to Calgary from that extended trip to New York, I had the nagging sensation that I had promised someone I would give a reading for them, although the details weren't clear in my mind. All I knew for sure was that I was expected to show up at the ubiquitous Auburn Saloon with something to read. I typed some pages from my New York journal and headed down for what I knew not.

It's hard to describe what they had going on that night at the Auburn, and do it any kind of justice. Whereas I walked in thinking I would encounter a sleepy, tweedy disaffected group of half a dozen people with nothing better to do on a Saturday night, when I arrived the joint was packed and it was jumping. It was full of dancers and dj's and rappers and spoken word hip-hoppers and hangers-on-ers and videographers . The room was not just eclectic but electric, there was a mad energy surging through the place that was palpable and I don't ever remember having felt anything like that with anything having to do with the arts, although a few of my opening nights at Alberta Theatre Projects may have come close. But I'd never felt anything like this associated with "poetry." Or whatever this was.

Whatever it was, it was new to me and it was real and it was like a big steaming train had pulled into the station.

I was suddenly scared by all the energy in the room. This was all new to me. Would I be eaten alive by this younger and wildly enthusiastic crowd? One doesn't want to think one has outlived one's usefulness, but I admit I was apprehensive if not terrified going up to the mic that night. Unlike the other readers (or performers), I had not memorized my piece and so had to read. Being of a certain age, I needed my reading glasses to accomplish this. While all the others were hopping and jumping and dancing around, I sat down.

Maybe there was something about this older man with the glasses and wild hair actually read-

ing that seemed in an ironic way somewhat avant garde. Happily, the audience were actually very kind and attentive.

And so in this trial by fire I was introduced to the spoken word movement. My background, and why I would had the cachet in the past to be asked to read, was in the theatre. Over a twenty year career, I had also been writing poetry. I think all writers do. Probably everyone does. But it was because I had made a name for myself in the theatre that I was reading at this event. I'm sure everyone attending that event was surprised that I actually had some poems to read.

I was asked recently to read some of my poems at a more conventional reading, a non-spoken word event, if you will. As has been my habit, I grabbed my box of poems (which resulted when I rode a wave of enthusiasm following the reading I described above) and headed down to, where else, the Auburn Saloon. On the surface, it seemed like exactly the same activity as the spoken word event, only with different organizers and a different audience. Or so I thought. It turns out I was very mistaken.

The poems on index cards in my little cardboard box are brief. Another example:

Normally, brevity is a virtue at any performance—at least in my mind it is. On the night in question, I was asked to read first, which I did (although reluctantly; I usually have enough status at such events to read last), with no real idea of the nature of the event or the intentions of the other readers. Whereas my brief poems have always been enthusiastically received at spoken word events, after reading them this particular evening, what I can only describe as a pall settled over the usually convivial audience in the Auburn Saloon. I took my seat to tepid applause in something resembling shame. It was going to be a long night.

The next reader up read something that was, shall we say, more substantial. Certainly it was lengthy, although as we are all aware, length and substance are hardly the same thing. He at least tried to inject a little humour into the proceedings, but fared little better than I had as he sheepishly took his seat to a smattering of clapping.

A few readers later and we had a young woman reading a short story, and not a short short story at all—by the time she was finished it seemed that we had collectively endured an entire novella. Oh, how I wished I could be anywhere but where I was. On and on she read. And on. I had no idea. All I can say is that it was an ordeal which I must have survived for here I sit at my kitchen table writing these words. But tough sledding, to say the least.

And yet, and this is the amazing thing about it, the audience seemed to hang on her every word, listening intently to this reader who had no clear sense of drama or theatre about her. She had written a short story and she was going to read it, all of it, come hell or high water. These were just the words, with very little variation in pace or dynamics.

But if the audience's response to me had been tepid, its response to the short story reader was relatively enthusiastic, maybe even wildly so. I suppose what was so notable to me that evening was that despite the absence of theatrics from her reading, the audience had been engaged.

From these experiences, along with a few decades of reading early drafts of some of my plays in public, I was able to make some inferences about the relationship between spoken word and the theatre, as well as to more conventional poetry. Ironically, it would seem that spoken word owes much more to the world of the theatre than to the word of conventional poetry. At the same time, in performance it seems to owe very little to the public activities of playwrights reading from their works in progress.

Theatrical techniques such as memorization, movement, song, rhythm, dynamic variations and even costuming all contribute to the performance-based nature of spoken word. An evening of spoken word poetry is an evening of intense energy and performance. Ritualized rejoinders from the audience, sacrificial readers and often sardonic hosts give the event a very distinctive celebratory aura, where one can't help but feel enthusiastic and even optimistic about the future of the artistry and elegance of the spoken word in our postmodern often inarticulate culture.

The other night I was at the theatre and remarked to a friend who works there that it didn't seem to be too crowded. My friend sighed and said, "It's a sign of the times, I guess. No one seems to want to come to the theatre anymore." I walked around the lobby for a few minutes. I remembered opening nights of my own plays in the same place and felt that the anticipation and excitement we had created around those plays seemed to be gone somehow. Audience members shuffled around the lobby clutching glasses of wine, speaking, if at all, in subdued tones. It almost felt like I was in a funeral home.

When I got home at the end of evening I turned on Facebook. On the news feed, I saw that several of my friends (most of whom I don't know, but that's another matter) had posted a short video clip of a young woman performing at a spoken word event. Over the next few days, more and more people shared this video. By then it was being carried on You Tube. As I have more than a thousand friends who could potentially see this clip, and as many of my friends have a like number of friends, one can do the math and get a sense of how many people have viewed this clip.

I don't believe that other forms of poetry and performance are moribund. I certainly hope not. But as a youthful and enthusiastic hybrid of poetry and theatre, spoken word has surely emerged as the dominant literary/performance event of the beginning of the 21st century.

I believe that all poets and playwrights, as well as producers and publishers, need to be aware of the spoken word phenomenon that we might inject some of the life and enthusiasm one feels at a spoken word event into our own endeavours.

And so now, as I don't want to run the risk of being called a rat bastard bitch who has ruined it for everyone by going on too long, I will close. I hope my little essay has been for my reader, as it has been for me, welllllll worth it. ✪

Richard Harrison has read at the Calgary Spoken Word Festival, the Hockey Hall of Fame, WordFest, the Saddledome, and at libraries, coffee shops, bars, and classrooms across the country. His work has been featured on "Morningside" and "Adrienne Clarkson Presents." A Governor-General's Award finalist, his poetry has been published in six books over 25 years, and has been appeared in five languages, including Portuguese and Arabic. His essays on poetry, hockey, and the comic and graphic novel have appeared around the world, and his work on the hidden origin of Superman was presented at the 2009 San Diego Comic-Con. Acquisitions editor for Frontenac House's 2011 Quartet poetry books, Richard teaches English and Creative Writing at Mount Royal University in Calgary, where he lives with his wife, Lisa Rouleau, and their children, Emma and Keeghan. Photo credit, Lisa Rouleau

Fandom Performances

1.

I'm here because of the Joker—and a poem I wrote using his advice. I wrote it to try my hand at the challenge posed by *FFWD*, Calgary's weekly arts magazine, to write a poem which either used only one of the five vowels, or in which one of the five vowels did not appear. The winners of the challenge got to read as part of the celebration of Christian Bök's new edition of his oulippian masterpiece, *Eunoia*, a book devoted to the first, more restrictive version of poetic confinement.

The Joker and I took door number two; his poem was deprived of the letter "I"—a fair move given that the Joker's main problem has always been his lack of self beyond the deformity that made him Batman's mirror image: the Joker is pure surface, an effect that long ago consumed its cause. Here's the poem:

Joker (No I)

All a poor clown ever asked for, truth to tell, was to be seen. Lucky for me, that was easy on account of my blanched up features, green mop of fun, ruby mouth, loaded gun, n'all. Now my face appears on TV every day. Yay! And yet, you weren't happy. You wanted more. But what could a man become who has no past (at least not one he remembers day to day), what could such a man become but a leaky vessel of gargoyle selves he offers up for your amusement, only to have them make a mess when they pour out between the cracks? Why do you people want more than what appears? Why can't you be content to have all that anyone can show? What's your problem? Oh? Memory needs an anchor, you say? A slender letter to hold together what falls apart even as you get your eye real close and try to see? Sorry – we're out of stock. You should only speak of yourself when you know who you are anyway. The dead could do so; there's no more guesswork for them. But they can't talk! That's the gag! Why don't you laugh? Why so somber?

I liked the poem. I liked writing it. I liked that it opened up words between poetry and comic books, two worlds that had been separate but side by side in me but that I had never been able to bridge. That year I had just come back from the San Diego Comic-Con where I'd given a paper that traced Superman's origin story through the hands of its various authors. It actually took 11 years for the full account to take shape, and become the one we think of as Superman's beginning. In my paper, I argued that the crowning, and tragic, touch, Superman's understanding of himself as a castaway alone in the universe, had been written by Bill Finger, the under-appreciated genius who also gave us the traumatic origin story of Batman himself as the orphan child of murdered parents in *Detective Comics #33* in 1940.

My study of comics filled me with their language, and in San Diego I had found a way to take that filling up and pour it into an essay. The re-launch of *Eunoia* gave me a place, writing it slant, to take that filling up and put it into po-

etry. I kept going. For Batman's poem, in answer to the I-less rant of his arch-enemy, I confined the caped crusader to words that used the letter A, the only vowel in his name. Here's what he told me:

Batman (All A)

Say what any has, all at war fall by war at last— that's a fact a man can grasp. My flat mandala traps sky at dark. My sharp hand, a batarang, fancy car, a castaway lad, all act my avatar. And a Barbary grammar blasts back: Bam! And Zap! Kablam! and crash! And … and what? All drang and raw drama; a black palm hangs an arm span away—Smash—a bad man sags, all rags and mass. Glad, all afar clap as at a play (any hand can smack away all that damns). Apart, an ark sans an Ararat, a man stands at an abyss and an abyss asks, *Why? All fall anyway as ash—all happy and all sad; all angst, all calm as a man that prays all day. All tasks. All plans. All Adam's clay.* And Batman? A man may pass as man and mask: a half that falls, a half that stays.

And by then, Mr. Freeze had something to say. So did Two-Face, Catwoman, the Penguin. "The Gotham Monologues" was born.

2.

When I came back from Comic-Con, I presented the Superman paper —with its accompanying collage of comic book images—at the university where I teach. To set the stage, I gave a short talk on Comic-Con itself, with photos of the best costumes the Con is famous for. There were people there dressed meticulously as Green Lantern and Superman, and Spider-Man, of course. There were several Iron Men, one wired so his chest plate and the palms of his hands glowed when he raised them. There was a Bumblebee from Transformers so completely rendered that until the person inside moved, I thought I was looking at a studio-produced statue. There were people dressed as superheroes who just acted normally —after my talk, Robin the Teen Wonder (as he corrected me) engaged me in a five minute discussion about the research in my paper without ever taking off his mask. When I accidentally bumped into an enormous body-builder outfitted and body-painted as Kratos from the supremely vicious God of War video game near a t-shirt booth, he gently said, "Oh, sorry man, do you want to look at these?" and let me through. There were those who never left their personification. One of the Borg from Star Trek walked the length of the comic-trading floor and never said a word to anyone. There were those who occupied a middle space: the Golem who only snarled and hissed at passersby, but wore a watch and stopped posing in her cave to answer her cell phone. And there were some who occupied a different space yet again—those who could never match the physiques of their superheroic ideals, but who wore their identifying garments anyway. Wonder Woman was most like that—Wonder Women of all shapes and sizes—as if Wonder Woman had done what no other superhero had done, and become symbolic beyond her body type.

Many in my university audience were more intrigued by the costume part of the talk, so we spent a lot of time on it in the Q&A session. We discussed the way the free play of outfits and make-up served the purposes of a fashion show, allowing creators to vie for bragging rights as makers of the most accurate and impressive real life versions of cartoons, paintings, and video-game graphics. It was a psychological statement, the way some say that that superheroes themselves represent how their creators and fans want to be seen: a way of being open about an otherwise overlooked aspect of yourself. It was concealment, too, a submerging of the everyday identity in a dramatic mask. It was theatre, it was Mardi Gras; it has its own term, "cosplay," a sometimes contradictory dialogue between who the costume wearers are in themselves and who they portray within the safe zone of the Con—but not just there: the whole of San Diego became a cosplay zone, with Thor, or Harley Quinn paying for tickets and getting on the trolley with me every morning to go to the panels on the live-action TV drama Lost, DC's animated remix of its venerable Brave and Bold comic line, or Myth-busters, an educational TV show devoted to seeing how many of our fantasies can be recreated,

or not, by the masters of special effects. And that show's stars—Adam and Jamie—got into the act by disguising themselves in the Emmett Kelly masks of the Joker's henchmen from the opening scenes of The Dark Knight and had filmed themselves wandering unrecognized in the crowd. Perhaps the best word for the experience is the one used to describe videos overlaid on top of each other in such a way that the properties of the original works still show, collide or connect: Comic-Con is a mash-up. I loved it. With the Superman essay, I'd attended as "A Professional." In "The Gotham Monologues," I'd found a way to become one of its artists.

And there were lots of them: not only on the panels that featured those who, past and present, drew the official comic book stories of Iron Man, Captain America, and the Flash, but in Artists' Alley, row upon row of fan artists who made black-and-white or painted reproductions of original comic covers and panels, or dramatically rendered versions of their heroes—none of them official, of course, none of them part of the "Real Stories" of characters under the control and care of Marvel, DC and Dark Horse, or, more accurately Warner Brothers and Disney. But there, nonetheless: their work, hand-made, shown, and admired.

3.

I read "The Gotham Monologues" at last year's Calgary International Spoken Word Festival, letting each character speak through me. When it came time for Catwoman to take the stage, Festival organizer Sheri-D Wilson, in cat-ears and with black fingernails, took the microphone. During the reading, I screened the images that I'd asked other artists to create as part of a series of visuals based on the 1966 Batman cards which were themselves paintings showing the Caped Crusader and Robin fighting various villains, some from the comics and TV, some unique to the cards. Combining these images with snippets from the cards, the artists and I came up with a series of works that visually spoke to the monologues: an animator gave me the figures of Catwoman and Batman melted into an eternal Moebius strip; a concrete poet and a graphic artist combined to contribute a portrait of Two-Face, half drawn in pen and ink, half composed of letters; a children's book author/illustrator painted Mr. Freeze trapped in the products of his own mind; my daughter PhotoShopped the Joker as a broken mirror, and Batman as a figure composed of all his conflicts at once. And, as I requested, she made the Riddler me — his catchphrase "Riddle me this!" catching me up and riddling me, reading me, into himself. I was a fan with other fans making fan art — occupying that grey place between work original and not; it was cosplay with images and performance. On stage I was both a poet reading the high art of poems that the audience could later read themselves, and I was performer offering something that you had to be there in order to see.

4.

So what does it say, all of this art, layer upon layer — fan art, high art, art reproducible and art not, visual art and verbal art, art of the moment and art you can always find again — damned if I know. I haven't got an argument yet, but I have some thoughts that might lead to one, or may turn out to be just fun ways of thinking in a discussion that has no conclusion and is all the better for that.

5.

Someone once said that there is no drawing of Superman: Superman *is* a drawing. And that stumped me. Then I thought, Yes. But not just one drawing. Think about the way we understand the "Superman" who acts as the subject of that sentence: the first Superman I saw was drawn by Curt Swann in the early 1960s, but if you started reading in the 1940s, it's the one by Joe Shuster, or Wayne Boring in the 1950s, or John Byrne in the 1980s or Leinil Francis Yu a few years back. Each one of these, to someone, is the drawing that Superman is. All the drawings are equally him. So Superman isn't one drawing: he's an infinite number. The fan as artist asks, Why shouldn't mine be one of them? With Superman's figure emergent on the page, and with

the experience of having Superman to hand become that much more immediate because it is by one's own hand that Superman is there, the fan as artist answers: It is.

And these drawings aren't copies in the way that photos or re-paintings of the Mona Lisa are copies. As John Berger points out, images of the Mona Lisa make da Vinci's original painting more valuable because it is the original of a copy. Fan art reiterates its subject. Drawing Superman is less about making an art object for others; it's about becoming intimate with the act of seeing Superman by creating the Superman you see. For the fan, the Superman he or she creates is no farther away from Superman than the one in the comics. Fan artistry is about doing what the "real artists do" but with less attention to audience. It's about doing what the other readers do but with more attention to the act of taking in. Fan art, and I'll include the performative fan art of cosplay, is a form of self-location; making it says "I belong to the community defined by the character I have made." Fan art reminds us that identity is derivative.

And how different is this, really, from poetry? There are no poets I know who don't owe their love of poetry, at least in part, to the work of the poets before them. Or at least have some measure of their work found in the way it sits next to the poems that came before. As vain as it sounds, I want my best poems to sit alongside my favourites by Dylan Thomas, William Butler Yeats, Sharon Olds, Carolyn Forché, Ted Hughes and Percy Shelley. You can tell a lot about me from that.

And more from this: I learned my love for almost all of those poets in the way their poems poured from my father's lips, filled the air with words he loved but could never have written, and emotions he felt but expressed no other way. Almost all of my favourite poems I loved in performance first — and they kept that quality of being performed, being breathed into life — when I looked at them again in the word-filled silence of the page.

Performance of the poem is the taste of the meal, the scent of the flower, the hearing of the song, the thrill of touching the person you love. The poem on the page, written perfectly, is exactly what Wordsworth said the composing of it was: intense emotion recalled in tranquility. But "intense emotion" is not just about feelings; it's about the intensity of sense experience itself. Performance, too, is a form of belonging: both the performer and the audience are necessary for the experience—both belong to something different for their being there; performance reminds us that identity is social, that our inner feelings are felt differently as part of, or in front of, an audience.

6.

You could say, then, that poets are fan artists of other poets: making their own versions of what has moved them in the works of others: putting out what they've taken in in order to re-experience it through themselves. And to belong to the group that shares that experience. Does this similarity make poetry, or all art, fan art? Or, rather, is there a way for the poet who makes something for the voice that will, it is hoped, be preserved on the page as well, dissimilar to the fan artist? Yes.

And it isn't simply a matter of the difference in audiences. Sure, fan artists are more concerned with showing off what pleases and declares them as fans than with what pleases others or causes them to explore their own selves which is something I think that the arts, like poetry, do. For those who already see and desire this difference in purpose, perhaps that's enough. But I know many poets who say with as much certainty as fans do that they make what they make to please themselves first.

There is, I think, a difference in the object, even as the "Gotham Monologues" address the same figures as fan art does. Whatever else a superhero—or any object of fannish artistry is—he or she or it has something missing, the space into which art can move: an incompleteness which not only allows creative participation, but invites it. Not with so open an invitation that the fan artist can do whatever he or she chooses to do and remain a fan artist, though; a work of fan art

must, in order to belong to the very community that gives it strength, preserve the essential features of its object.

That missing element might be the necessary incompleteness of the superheroic or serialized story: Batman will never find his parents' killer, nor will his childhood vow to wage war on all criminals be concluded. Just as the Joker will always bounce back from defeat, so crime will always be a part of Gotham City. Superman will never lack for opponents, nor can his homeworld be recovered. And yet the stories go on; the superhero never stops trying, or having something left to do. Some might call that a heroic failure, but for the fan artist, the scripted incompleteness of the character is what allows the audience to enter the story.

Or perhaps, or as well, the way in which superhero characters become symbols of human characteristics, almost medieval in their personification of greed or charity, devotion to a cause or despair. If Wonder Woman is women's power through solidarity with other women, then she invites anyone to express their commonality with the characteristic she gives form to.

7.

But as an object of art, the poem demands not just something of the self; it demands the self as part of its existence, even where that poem is about the already-existing artwork of others. For the poems about them, the Joker, the Mona Lisa, and the hailstorm are all the same: they all contain something that demands an original response, something that excites an original making. And what I mean by original can be defined effectively on the subjective side as a different kind of absence: "original" work is work the maker is unaware of having a precedent. An original work isn't about filling the necessary gaps in a character designed to be incomplete. It is one that moves into (but cannot fill) the gaps and hollows in the things that should be complete but aren't yet so: language, knowledge of nature, understanding of the self, of others; faith. In short, all the gaps in life that each of us lives into. How do we know those incomplete things? They are named by our questions, our desires, what we put forward in making poetry, making art, at all—saying out loud what we love, what we wonder about, what we fear, who, as much as we can know we are, even as we make who we are in speaking about how little of ourselves we know. For me, the comic book hero and the poem are parts of both what I know and don't know. It gives me a lot of pleasure to play out that tension in words. And then offer them. The Joker is here because of me. And I am here because of you. ✪

Sarah Murphy** is the author of eight books; the most recent is *Last Taxi to Nutmeg Mews* (2009) a Brooklyn childhood memoir in dramatic monologues, prose poems, one-liners and drawings. While holding an Arts Council England International Artists' Fellowship in 2007, Murphy recorded live her first innovative sound art/spoken word CD: *when bill danced the war*—an hour length dramatic monologue, also performed in full throughout the UK, and in Ottawa at First Women, First Voices. In 2008, Murphy received the Calgary Spoken Word Festival's Golden Beret Award, and in 2003 the Howard O'Hagan Award for her inter-media book: *die tinkerbell die.* Murphy has performed, published, and shown widely in Canada, the UK, the US, Australia and Mexico and also instructed in art and creative writing—or a combination of the two—in Canada, Mexico, and the UK. Of Choctaw, Irish, English, Hispanic and German heritage, Murphy has resided in the three largest countries of the North American continent and continues to write of all three. She grew up in Brooklyn and now splits her time between Calgary, where she has resided for over 25 years, and the shores of Passamaquoddy Bay, Maine.

The Story:
That Cutting Edge

Stories that have beginnings should have endings. That is the condition of a story, the reason that we tell it. Stories should have middles too, apparently, we are told, at least if we write them. That's not so important, though, really, not for telling, over drinks at the bar, or after class, or over coffee in morning with the neighbours, or down at the Bingo Hall, or over the phone. Then it's really the beginning and the end that count, and they should match somehow. The middle can be interminable, full of questions and answers and acknowledgements, small little

First appeared in *Fast Forward Weekly*
2009, FFWD

"Uh-huhs," and "Ah-hahs," and "Really's," and "You don't say's," and even more indefinite clucks of the tongue; but somewhere in answering to *Well*, or *And then*, or *What exactly do you mean by that*, the problem will come up: that basic coherence between the beginning and the end, the beginning's ability to determine that end, to determine somehow the meaning—If not of the story, then of the teller's intent.

But what if there is no beginning, no clear place of starting, and certainly no clear end? What if there is just this moment, only this one, the one now with her standing, standing there with the knife; there, just there, her hand raised her face set, neither beginning nor end but just that middle, that cannot be a middle without beginning or end, so that it is just now, now, NOW, now and her standing, there with the knife. And standing there with the knife because it is not beginning or end, because it is somewhere muddy like this in the middle, it is as if she has always stood with the knife, a life spent standing with a knife, spreading out around her to past and future, while it is only this moment, the making of this moment because it is knowing this moment and standing here in this moment that makes this moment forever, forever and only this moment and standing here this moment with this choice, with this knife, this choice, this moment, that is neither beginning nor end, but choice, that chooses forever from this moment beginning and end, this moment this cutting edge, this forever that is the question the choice standing here with the knife, the question that she cannot ask, there is no time to ask, it is the question that answers itself, that if she chooses her beginning right now, if she chooses it, then will the end fall into place, the next movement of the hand, of the knife, the one that will end it, will it be chosen by its beginning, by whatever beginning she chooses, or is it the end, the movement of the hand, that will in that moment in ending, just in ending, that movement, choose a beginning? From this moment, standing there standing. With the knife. The knife.

Or does it all somehow come together at once, beginning and middle and end, on the cutting edge of the moment, this moment echoing, choosing compressing, beginning and end both implied in the gleam of the light off the edge of the knife where it has been honed and honed, sharpened and re-sharpened over the years, waiting for this moment, the edge and the gleam too, in hers in the man's eyes, all his all her being all the emotion there in the eyes, is that all there has ever been, this moment determined forever? And perhaps it would be hard to say, terribly difficult in fact, to find all the elements and make them come together, but still if we must have it, and we must, we always must, that is the story. The Story.

But it will be hard to find. Probably terribly difficult. Maybe later it will seem easier, but it cannot seem easy now, not with her, caught in the eternity of the moment.

I wrote that once. A long time ago in fact. And you must all recognize it, of course, if you've already heard or just read my poem on the connected website because, yes, of course, it's that incident referred to at the end, the one where I chased the man through the Central Park Zoo, after pulling the knife. My knife. And I think, too, that I had a marvellous conceit, in the baroque poetic sense, of course, one that I really liked, that followed so strongly from my belief in story that I thought I could structure it into a novel based on a series of matrices, as in matrix algebra, use that as a method to pick the starting point, letting a beginning, middle or end fall out of memory to dictate action, at the same time as it would give me an excuse to write each possibility down. To form a whole, but variable, in which you, the reader, would have the task of making my character's decision, of figuring out what she would, what she must, do. Only what I figured out, instead, some seventy-five or a hundred pages later, was that this could not be a fiction. And I left it, to start the work, the headlines, the headlong speed, that would become another form of work, leading to all the *Nutmeg Mews* pieces, and eventually, the small incursion of this story again in my poem on the connected website.

Because I do like it, of course, not that moment of rage standing on the stairs in the Central Park Zoo my knife in my hand, but what it says here about story, what thinking of that incident first told me about story, that the end does determine the beginning as much as the beginning the end, with the middle, some muddled muddy middle or other, most usually the starting point to get to either, like jumping into the centre of a river, and only then figuring out which way you need to swim. Except that the direction changes the shore. And you can see the logic of it, where we end the story will tell us how it began, as much as the other way around. And maybe there are two ways you can argue that, the physics, the mathematics, of time, all those ideas so well established in Borges as well as so much speculative fiction, or just go the simpler way: we are storytellers. And in choosing the structure of story we choose meaning, and in it the salient facts that lead to further action, further story. So that no matter how much the post-structuralists tell us that all reality is discursive reality, that's just their story, the one in which they choose their meaning. While reality proceeds on its merry or not so merry way far beyond our grasp, far too big for us. Story is all. An idea which allows me to further savour my central metaphor, more metonymy really. To let the gleam off the knife stand not for the whole of humanity exactly, but for the constant cutting edge of all human decision, when a smaller entity faces a much larger one, which it can barely predict, hardly know. Finity facing infinity, if you like.

And yes, that one was among the stupidest things I've ever done, and no, I did not catch him. But I have long been overwhelmed by wondering what would have happened if I had. So why not let the moment of her, the her that was me, that matrix of possibilities, structure the imagined novel. The order of whatever popped into mind structure her decision. In simple terms, we could see that decision as easy. For action there could always be only two alternatives—to act to assault him, assault with a deadly weapon, assault with intent to kill, once more the smaller against the larger, the less against the more powerful, the circumstances when you have only one chance of survival and must make good on it, your intent clear, or you are simply giving your one weapon away. Yet, it seemed to me, the alternatives were really four, because the intent of that man too, had to be

taken into account. Morally, anyway. In the universe of meaning.

Was he just an everyday pig, grabbing my butt that way on the stairs into the zoo at nine am, and whispering in my ear, Come on, let's make love? Or did that grab—and they do sometimes grab—signal an intent to drag me into the nearby bushes for a travesty of that act: to rape, even to kill? And did my response, shouldering him to below me on the stairs where I could kick him in the balls, signal a measured response to this intent, or an unmeasured rage at a multiplicity of things in my life: ideas, circumstances, stories, moods, memories, not least of which was the early hour and my groggy uncaffeinated brain? As he went on to say, backing away—the kick, after all, was accurate but hardly powerful—Hey, Lady—and now you could hear the New York whine—I'm already going to have a rough day. To which I replied, as he started to turn away, You're going to have a rough day? Not just New York but Brooklyn in tone, a rough day? I'll give you a rough day—and—he'd turned his back and was running now. I pulled the knife I'd been carrying for years. Truly for a more extreme situation than this, it was a K55 German Army knife, still legal in New York City by an eighth of an inch, with a weak spring my brother had loosened so that I could open it with a flick of the wrist, or slowly, with one hand, inch the blade open inside my purse, to allow me, blocking with my left arm, to stab with accuracy. That's the way I opened it now. Only there was no blocking, no danger. Just giving chase. Furious. Only to lose him.

And to think later, still on edge, back in the subway to Brooklyn, and to keep thinking off and on, to still keep thinking on and on: What would I have done, had I caught him? No, it was not so simple. Because I had acted that quickly, there had been no way to measure his intent, or, for that matter, my motives. I had already multiplied two times two times two. Two times two times two and again. Him me, me him, and again. Action, intent, idea. And again.

If he meant to harm me, the only thing to do was to attack him, and besides, I would be taking a rapist off the streets. If he did not mean to harm me and I attacked him, I would have caused the death of another—because, yes, it is deadly force or nothing—without cause. If I failed to act, and he meant no harm, then we could both let laughter enter our eyes and our bodies until they shook, and then go about our business. Only, if he did mean me harm, and I failed to act, then he could disarm me, and I would be the one to be harmed, perhaps to die. Because, even if something in me, some rage, had motivated him to run, as rage sometimes will, bringing fear or some other visceral need to be elsewhere even in a much stronger opponent, it is unlikely to last if the opponent is trapped, or if he reads doubt in any gesture. So safety, of course, once that knife was in the mix, was in action. Stab first and ask questions later and all that. Worry about the morality after. Because rage protects us often enough, not just from fear but from ethics. Until the incident haunts my dreams.

Because whether you believe me or not, I wasn't just a fighter when younger, I was a good one, had an unearthly confidence and that uncanny ability to feint, and to predict the next move of my opponent. And when it wasn't just any fight, but one motivated by rage, I would not lose control, but become cold, utterly calculating, utterly in the moment, in a way that is perhaps not so good to be in the moment: not a shred of fear left, or morality. Combat ready, in the truest sense. A quality I am happy to believe I have lost over the years, even if still it haunts me: not the fear of being harmed, but of doing harm where it was not merited.

So of course, you can see why this incident structures my thoughts about story. How it moves backward and forward in time, is never one, but many, and asks how, how, do you find it. Not the story you tell, but the cutting edge of intent that can become the story that tells you. The one, in this case, that could tell me why I would act in this way when I so definitely knew better. Because it was not an action without thought, it was an action logic, whose story, when it happened, I failed to recognize. So I wanted to find the centre of that story, the centre of the me that was in that story, or those many stories. And in that, too, in another journey into mathematics, I had to recognize the notion of limit. That a story

is never everything. But a set of things. One's own story never the whole self, but a set of momentary fragments. And that what limits story is precisely that cutting edge moment of choosing. And is contained in the voice that chooses.

To find that voice may be the most difficult task of all. And no, it is not easier later, with recollection in tranquillity and all that, as I thought it would be when I started what was to be the novel. Because it isn't really recollection, you're not collecting anything, just finding your way back into the moment. And that moment is never a fiction. Fiction is the one that collects, that could explain the world to me, allow me to understand how I see the world, but never parse my identity, tell me into story, never let me know what it was in me that had let me do this thing. Because the duty of fiction is mastery and a place in meta-narrative that rings true, not the exploration of the edges of the self where it exceeds the known narrative, becomes new, becomes other. So that, even if I had motivated my character, quite well I thought, within the matrix story I had devised, still, she was not the one with the story that would tell me the one I needed to know.

That's when I entered this trajectory, the one I am still on, not a walk in the park, surely, or for that matter a run, knife in hand, but still that cutting edge that is encountering the story of the self, of the selves, always at their limits, their fragments, where they are not the whole but can inform it. And where too, they are not the ego, the need to impress or to manipulate, to retrofit the story to a formula. To make it safe, a match for one's mental decor, or even to escape a story too unpleasant to look at. But the clearing of the mind as profound, and in its own way combat ready, as that girl with the knife. Only no longer amoral. Because among the gifts of story will always be the gift of encountering the morality which defines us. But method will be important too. Finding ways to enter the moment of true story. And its treasure.

The first technique, one I still use, one I started shortly after writing this beginning, when I could no longer make a fiction of it, was simply to list, one after another after another a phrase, a headline I say in *Last Taxi to Nutmeg Mews*, listing incidents from my life that somehow resonated. And then from there to write as fast as I could, until somehow the phrase led me to the story's ending, or back to its beginning. And sometimes these would be stories I had often told, casually or with intensity or in humour or to prove a point. Yet, seldom in this new telling did that instrumental old story appear. The story would be new, would tell a new me. And sometimes I would find that the story emerged simply and clearly from that first moment of writing, and would remain almost unchanged. Other times that first writing would only hint at something worth returning to hone and to shape, like a master craftsman might a blade until it gleamed with the sharp edge it needed. And always that clarity, that edge, would be a balancing act, between the needed content longing to emerge, and the only form, the only language that could shape it.

It's not only headlines I work with. There are numerous other ways I will find to enter the story, to bypass the hyper-conscious ego that wishes always that the world remain safe, its edges the same. But always, whatever technique I use, it is one designed to let the voice emerge. And it is not always the fast voice that overcomes resistance through speed. Sometimes it is slow, encountered through the mnemonic phrase, its slow rhythm. Something as simple as: This then. This. Or: This is how it will start. Speaking often in the future tense, and addressing myself as "you." As if to some part of myself the voice can inform, and thus, letting go of the I that wishes to justify her. And then sometimes, later, I change it. Though often I don't.

Then too, there are just exercises, like practising scales. One of my favourites is the one where you pick a category. From insects to cars to kinds of clothing, where I ask myself, my friends, my students, to see in their mind, one place one time where there was one specific member of that category, because it is the specific image of the moment that leads to the voice. So it can be anything at all: a praying mantis a terrified man burns by a bus stop, a kitten whose spine is broken in a refrigerator, a tropical sunset while you make love waist deep in the turgid salt water

only feet away from the nearest person. Or sometimes, I am simply haunted by a word and insist on writing it into a phrase which then becomes a story. Like the poem on the connected website—which took me back to that story, asked again why it was, why it really was, that I chased that man through the zoo, my knife drawn. To come up with another element in my equation matrix, another small hint at the answer to the unanswerable question of what I would have done—because who knows which of my stories I would have been then—had there been a moment when I caught him. ✪

Wendy Morton believes that poetry is the shortest distance between hearts. She has published five books of poetry, and a memoir, *Six Impossible Things Before Breakfast*, in which her adventures as a corporate sponsored poet are revealed. Her latest book of poetry, *What Were Their Dreams*, is a book of photo-poems of Canada's history. She is the founder of Canada's Random Acts of Poetry, now in its seventh year, and is the recipient of the 2010 Spirit Bear Award and the Golden Beret Award. For her day job, she has been an insurance investigator for the last 28 years. She lives in Sooke, BC and is a raven watcher. In 2011, she was made an Honorary Citizen of Victoria.

Impossible Things:
Returning A Poem To Its Bliss

In *Alice in Wonderland*, Alice says to the Queen, "There is no use in trying; one can't believe in impossible things." The Queen answers, "I daresay you haven't had much practice. When I was younger, I always did it for half an hour a day. Why sometimes, I've believed as many as six impossible things before breakfast."

I'm a great believer in impossible things. I'm mad for dreamers like Larry Walters, who wanted to fly in a lawn chair powered by 42 helium filled weather balloons, or Bill Lishman who taught geese where to fly with an ultra light aircraft. Annie Dillard says, "You've got to jump off cliffs all the time and build your wings on the way down." And so I built my poetic wings and learned to fly.

In 2001 I had one book of poetry in the world, *Private Eye*, and wondered how I would get known as a poet. One day I asked a woman in my aerobics class, who was having a book published by a now extinct Toronto press, what it was doing for publicity. She told me she'd been interviewed by the Canadian Press. I picked up the phone, got Marlene Habib on the line, and told her I was a private eye and a poet. She said she did articles on lifestyle and aging. I said I was old, and she said, "Ok, let's do it now." The article she wrote appeared in about 30 newspapers across Canada, and gave me a scrapbook full of publicity.

One day, during a long wait in the Calgary airport, I decided to call up WestJet Airlines. I had no long-term plan there; I just acted on impulse and got the marketing director on the phone. I said, "I'm a poet, why don't I read poems to the passengers, write poems for some of them in trade for flights?" She said, "No one has ever asked that before." After some months of letters (including the CP articles) and phone calls, she said "Yes," and for the next six years, I was WestJet's "Poet of the Skies."

I boarded my first flight March 11, 2002. I had no idea what lay ahead of me. I had never read to a captive audience in the sky. When the seatbelt sign went off, I was introduced by one of the attendants, and read them a poem about Larry Walters, called "Flying with Frank." After I read the poem, I told the passengers that I would be delighted to write poems for anyone who wanted one. Dozens of hands went up. As we flew across Canada, I would sit next to them, and the passengers would tell me in quiet voices about their lives and what they loved. I would write them a poem. I wrote poems for dreamers, for daughters, for lovers. As we flew across Canada. And when I read the poems back to them, they often had tears in their eyes; they would grab my hand or hug me. I discovered the power of the spoken word and how it moved people. I began to believe that a poem is the shortest distance between two hearts.

In 2003, WestJet was starting flights to Halifax. I had a new book of poetry that year, *Undercover*, so I arranged for a reading tour of the Maritimes. When I looked on the map, I thought it seemed like a small area, but I thought I'd need a car and didn't want the expense of renting one. So one day, again without any plan in mind, I just picked up the phone and called Chrysler head office, got the vice-president of marketing on the phone on the first try. I told him I was "WestJet's Poet of the Skies," a faithful Chrysler customer and that I was touring the Maritime and wanted the loan of a PT Cruiser (since in my mind PT meant Poetry Travels) for 10 days and I wanted them to buy 50 books that I would give away to strangers. He said, "Yes, right away." And then he said that his guy in the Maritimes would give me a call in three days. I got the call, got the car, got the books, and asked for a decal on the car saying, "Chrysler supports literacy."

My idea was to cross paths randomly with people as I travelled the Maritimes. I thought that introducing people to poetry by having them listen to a poem, then giving them a book of poetry, might help them to see poetry in a new light—take it out of the dark room of their memory (where some teacher had tied a poem to a chair and beaten it to death in grade 10), and see what a new and shining way it was to see the world. When *Private Eye* first came out, I carried it everywhere. It was just that feeling of empowerment that allowed me, standing in line at a bakery, to pull out my book and read a poem to those nearby. Between that and the time I escaped a speeding ticket by reading the officer a poem, I had all the proof I needed. I was convinced of the power of poetry. Something happened when I stopped my PT Cruiser on a street in Moncton, for instance, got out and read a stranger a poem. If there were any barriers, they fell away.

So *Random Acts of Poetry* was born. When I came back from the Maritimes, I thought that poets all across Canada should be able to experience the delight in reading a poem to a stranger. I went in search of funding. AbeBooks was the first sponsor. Then I called up poets I knew all over Canada and explained the project. They would be paid for their 50 random acts, and we would buy 50 books. They were delighted, amazed. For them a poetry reading meant getting a bunch of people in a room in a library or café and standing up and getting polite applause, and then hoping after it was over that they'd sell some books.

This was a new way of doing things in the poetry world. We're now in our seventh year. The

Canada Council for the Arts now sponsors the project. Hundreds of poets from all over Canada have participated and each year we have many new faces.

Poetry does suffer from a kind of public neglect, however. It doesn't often appear to be high on most people's literary reading lists. In spite of substantial prizes, National Poetry Month, and thousands of years of history—poetry rarely appears to make it out of the small and rarefied world of classrooms, readings, and literary festivals. Literary agents often have a notice on their websites not to send poetry manuscripts. But poetry is not a dead or obsolete form. Poetry spoken out loud has a kind of magic.

For those poets who love the spoken word, reading poems to strangers at any time is the best way I know of to bring poetry into the world: at a bus stop, on the bus, in line at the movies. Asking people if they would like to hear a short poem, is rarely met with a no, in my experience. It is reading poetry one to one that brings real magic back into a world that is increasingly impersonal, a world filled with electronic substitutes for connection that has no poetry in it.

All across Canada, I've met people at random who treasure the kinds of delights and impossibilities that poetry offers. I've read poems to priests who then blessed me; to a college president who stopped short, then read me his own poem; to a gas station owner who called his daughter over to hear the poem; to a woman who, after I read her a poem, bought me flowers. Poetry speaks to the extraordinary hopes and dreams we all hide beneath our ordinary lives. Poetry is a way to get everyone to put on wings and fly.

Nancy Holmes, of the University of British Columbia in Kelowna, was part of *Random Acts of Poetry* several times. I asked her to write about her experience:

"Reading someone a poem face-to-face is a surprisingly intimate act. People who stop to listen get a chance to have a poem spoken directly to them and they don't have to find the metaphor and it won't be on the final exam. The real experience of lyric poetry is this intimate listening. Unlike most storytelling, plays, or bardic epics, lyric poems weren't created for a communal audience. A lyric poem is meant to talk to you. The lyric voice is accessible on the printed page because reading is so private; the voice travels down the generations into your own ear: Sappho's voice, Shakespeare's voice, Dickinson's voice. So a *Random Act of Poetry*—intimate words spoken face-to-face, on the street, at the bus stop, in the grocery store line-up—returns the poem to its bliss."

I think that poetry can take the armour that we wear—that we polish to a bright shine to keep the world at bay and to keep our hearts buried—and shatter it. Poetry can connect us with each other as humans as no other art form I know. Poetry is a gift that we can create from whatever life has in store for us. Poetry opens the doors of the heart, the doors of joy and sorrow. Poetry opens the doors to bliss. ✪

Gardenias

He tells me his mother,
at 91, is moving to Toronto
to join a gypsy band to play
the tambourine, wear bells
and birds of paradise.

He's sold her house.
His wife is sick.
His daughter is getting married
in July. The whole magillah:
engraved invitations,
a tap dancer,
grandma's band playing Klezmer.
And a thousand gardenias.

And two friends died.
Just like that.

I want to tell him
about the sunbursts of grief,
the broken mirrors of joy.
Gardenias, I say,
a whole room full of them.

Jamaican born **Klyde Broox** is a veteran, well-travelled, 70s vintage dub poet who first gained significant public recognition as "Durm-I." Broox taught English then worked in the curriculum unit of Jamaica's ministry of education before migrating to Canada in 1993, to settle in Hamilton, Ontario. A former University of Miami James Michener Fellow, Klyde also won the 2005 City of Hamilton Arts Award for Literature. He has published two volumes of poetry: *Poemstorm* (Swansea, Wales, 1989) and the award winning, *My Best Friend is White* (McGilligan Books, 2005). Klyde hosts a monthly hometown Open Mic event called PoeMagic. Steeped in both old and new world oral and scribal traditions, Klyde usually invites audiences and workshop participants to experience poetry as social communion. He is a member of Toronto's Dub Poets Collective.

Dubpoetriology!
Dub, Poetry, & 21st Century "Neoliterary" E-mergings

Dub is the voice that moves the pen. Dub is the pen that shapes the voice. Dubpoetry balances oral and scribal language competence, positioning the oral as preceding the scribal as is usual in the sequence of natural verbal expression. The tag dubpoetry should be written, as uttered, as one word. The practice of writing dubpoetry as 2 words suggests an erroneous academic con/clusion that the dub is separate from the poetry. Dubpoetriology outlines ideas, functions, and dubpoetic practices that extend significantly beyond dubpoetry's much emphasized reggae connections.

The concept of dubpoetriology evolved from the idea of metadub (dubpoetry about dubpoetry). Dubpoetriology speaks from inside dubpoetry, using description to expand the taxonomy of dub to widen its definition to encompass the vast range of capacities and potentialities uncovered by experience, observation, research, discussion, contention, and extrapolation.

DUBSTORY
Bongoman was the first dubpoet Bongoman was the first dubpoet   Revelation unseal to reveal it

It, it, it's really so real, you can feel it
Bongoman was the first dubpoet Bongoman was the first dubpoet

Bongoman, the first dubpoet, did not "perform" poetry but dubbed poetic utterances of empowered parlance out of, into, under, over, and around daily sounds of loud life in constant motion. Dubpoetry echoes the urgency that Bongoman used to dub messages of life, on life, to life, as life goes on.

Dubpoetry dubs the pulse of daily life into poems
Dubpoets dub the pulse of poems into daily life to an emphatic reggae – or any musical - accenttttt!
Colonial-lies-ation included colo-noise-ation. Dub enables decolonialiesation and decolonoisation. Dubpoets did not create dubpoetry. Dubpoetry created dubpoets. Cultural chemistry forged it within the crucible of the Caribbean Basin to dub itself prominently into the story of the "New Englishes." Since the 1970s, dubpoetry has articulated, embodied and demonstrated the resurgence of orality as the first and foremost frontier of universal literary activity. Dubpoetry is an area of anglophonic literatures where the dominant aesthetics are not determined in any ivory, or even ebony, tower.

Dubbing can be read as a "neoliterary" product of the "neolinguality" that resulted from power struggles of the tongue between accents and enunciations from both Europe and Africa in the re/dis, and trans-locations, occasioned by invasions, dispossessions, oppressions, rebellions, uprisings; suprisings and emergings arising from colonial enter/prize.

Orality's literary revival is intertwined with digital developments in electronic technology. 'Dubwisery' foreshadowed - and represents - the evolving 'neopoetics' of a digitized world. Dub(poetry) portrays body as text. It processes word as unit of sound and musical element. Dubbing transcends language barriers, cultural borders, and national literatures. Dub mystique is culturally connected; dub techniques are culture-neutral.

Dubpoetry mainly occupies the domain of English Literature, but also embraces music, straddles theatre, has a foot in dance, and an eye on visual art. Its immediate scribal heritage can be traced to Miss Lou and Edward Kamau along with calypso and reggae songwriting styles. Early Jamaican dance hall artists initiated the idea of delivering spokenverse over music. Most of dubpoetry's oral traditions are derived from body memories, tongue-retentions, drumlines, chants, prayer, worksongs and the dance of resistant slaves. Later influences include repertoires of Black preachers and the spontaneous sermonizing semantics of Rastafarian activists who insisted on ritualizing a blackened version of Christianity centred between the side the edge of the coin of systemized culture.

THE THIRD SIDE OF THE COIN
Every coin has three sides, the head, the tail, and the edge. In reality, orality is the foundation of scribality; both are two sides of the same coin. Dubpoetry resides at the edge of the coin as a bridge around an academically alleged oral/scribal divide. Digitality enables this bridging but is not essentially necessary because dubpoetry's resources and devices are ideal even for purely oral live interfaces involving only body, voice, mentality, and memory without the aid of any form of technology. This is called Ital dubbing. The idea of Ital is as fundamental to dub technique as Dread is to its mystique. Ital means using only natural resources. Ital, at its purest, is the total absence of artifice. Dub functions both as an engine of change and a process of retention. It synergizes the scripting of orality with the oralizing of scribality.

Today, time and technology have circled us forward to the globalvillage campfire via digital camera and Internet browser. Digitality dubs written word as spoken word and vice versa.

The digital re-oralization of poetry finds favour in the eye of the camera. Print was the Internet of its times and it page-trapped poetry for centuries. Dubpoetry demands that poetry must "Buss Out!" of print entrapment. In Canada, pioneer dubpoet Lillian Alllen inspired Canadian spoken word pioneer Sheri-D Wilson.

Upon a page, the best poem of any genre is flattened. Reading dubpoetry is like looking at the picture of a house. Performance takes you into the house itself. Dubbing poets are best experienced audio-visually. Written definitions, descriptions, and audio or video recordings of dubpoetry do give a good sense of the intensity of its energy. However, the force of dubpower, music of dubword and charismatic influence of urgent dubpoemic presence of body demand live experience!

Live dubpoetry actualizes, embodies — gives physique to — the harnessing and unleashing of energy in a manner that is unpredictable, memorable, and unrepeatable outside the moment or content of embodiment.

BODYNOISE!
Listen to dubpoets with your eyes Dubbers gestures stylize body noise as dubwise Word word of body is voice Voice of word in body Body of voice fills word Word of voice echoes in body nuances   Gestures of dancing voices multiply as body noisesisisisisisis!

Dub(poetry) harnesses, stylizes, and unleashes three basic components:
WORD, SOUND, POWER!

Dubpoets compose performative verse that often tracks the beat of an embedded musical accent. Dubpoetry typically blends spokenverse, gesture, song, dance and drama. It tends to historicize the stories of ordinary people. Dub delivers poetry as social communion and usually synthesizes common voices within discursive frames of resistance that contest official narratives and discourses.

Dubpoetry shares features with Romantic and Metaphysical poetry. Dubpoetics also resemble Griotic, Bardic, Dadaist and Beat poetic traditions. Rapso is a type of dubpoetry from Trinidad that mostly trracks calypso beats. Emphasis on orality creates the need to memorize. Versioning, which is integral to dubbing, causes challenges for memorization. Usually, root versions are the editions fully retained in the library of memory.

Dubpoetry combines storytelling with theatre, literature, lecture, and music. It can also be defined by meanings of the word dub. Dub is what is dubbed. What is dubbed is dub, is dub, is dub! Dub is dub is dub is dub.

Dub is Dub: the English word we've all heard that became a much reggaed word as an audio word and a soundengineering word which Oku, or, as some say, LKJ, dubbed as a poetry word.

SOUND!
SOUND IN SOUND OUT sounds all about
SOUND SOUND SOUND
SOUND of VOICE is SPEECH in UTTERANCE
as EXPRESSION!
EXPRESSIONEXPRESSION
EXPRESSION as UTTERANCE in SPEECH is
VOICE of SOUND
SOUND in SPEECH is UTTERANCE of EX-
PRESSION as VOICE
VOICE of SPEECH as EXPRESSION in SOUND
is UTTERANCE!
Dubbing is doubly process and result, means and end. Dubbing can version confrontation into collaboration by dubbing-out negativity and dubbing in positivity!

Dub conceptualization begins by observing that questions are stems of answers. So, when will we get the "One Love, One Heart" of which the mighty Marley warbled?

We will get "One Love, One Heart" when we dub it all together person per person by person to person from generation to generation dubbing it on and on and on beyond the reggae connection.

under the   influence of dub

sweet n sour jerked-around blues, bruise
migrant moods, diffuse a mutative muse
     creole soul; raw soul creole
sudern noise in di nort; sudernoisin di nort

     under the   influence   of Dub
     under the   influence   of Dub

under the influence of Dub
bodyspeakers
demolish language barriers

illuminate ivory towers
accelerate rates of insight
obscurity obliterated by spotlight
     under the   influence   of Dub
     under the influence of Dub
dub, Dub, dub di dub; the the, dub dubbed Dub

dubculture is not shrubculture
nor scrubculture, grubculture
pubculture nor paystub culture
not much of a fanclub culture
dub, Dub, dub di dub; the, the, dub dubbed
Dub is subculture, hubculture
     voice signature, live literature
     altercultural capital
ancestral oracular revival
conquering continual spiral
under the influence of Dub
     under the   influence of Dub

under the influence of Dub
bodies politic talk louder
utter to camera, arouse browser
transmit wit in gestures, engender
close encounters of an oral kind
     open windows to new states of mind
     a neoworld can be designed
under the influence of Dub
     under the   influence of Dub
dub, dubbin di Dub a dubbed
dubber dubbed in dub dubbin di Dub
dub Dub, dub-in, dub-outtttttttttt

First appeared in *My Best Friend Is White*
2005, McGilligan Books

Trailblazing poet, author, musician and media artist **Heather Haley** pushes boundaries by creatively integrating disciplines, genres, and media. Her work has been published in numerous journals, anthologies and collections: *Sideways* (Anvil Press), and *Three Blocks West of Wonderland* (Ekstasis Editions). She has also directed three videopoems, *Purple Lipstick, Bushwhack* and *How to Remain*. Haley was an editor for the *LA Weekly*, publisher of *Rattler* and the *Edgewise Café*—one of Canada's first electronic literary magazines. She was the architect of the Edgewise ElectroLit Centre, the Vancouver Videopoem Festival and Visible Verse at Pacific Cinémathèque. Her own works have been official selections at dozens of international film festivals. Haley has gained renown as an engaging performer, sharing her poetry and music with audiences around the world. Most recently she toured eastern Canada and the US in support of her critically acclaimed *AURAL Heather* CD of spoken word songs, *Princess Nut.* heatherhaley.com

Sideways

Subversive, sub rosa—sideways—like a snake in the grass—is often how an artist must move, and technology can help cover more ground. I address social issues in my work but I dread dogma as much as cliché. I believe that being an artist is a political statement.

Though founder of the Edgewise ElectroLit Centre, I am not a technocrat. I felt strongly it was vital for poets and artists to have a presence on the World Wide Web, so published—or Web-authored as it was referred to—the *Edgewise Café*—one of Canada's first electronic literary zines. I'm not a technophobe either, just a poet struggling to be heard, via "any medium necessary," as my Telepoetics friend and colleague Merilene Murphy used to say.

I employ myriad media to advance my art, including the Internet. Democratic, even anarchistic, the Internet provides a powerful alternative to print as publication in print becomes more difficult, but also less critical. Musicians have adapted well, learning to cultivate an audience online though social networking. Adapt or die. Brutal. Darwinian. Natural. Some writers, dragged into the 21st century kicking and screaming, are beginning to think outside the book, beyond text and adopting the DIY—Do It Yourself—edict. Be your own agent, publicist, and publisher.

All these changes can be viewed as dismaying or liberating. I for one will be relieved when we are free of the gatekeepers. Then we will do it our way, according to our own individual circumstances, style, and vision. Opportunity abounds.

But I must confess. Though I'm a well-adapted digital immigrant, I am still a page baby at heart. It is safe to say that when I was a child my dogs and my books saved my life. I am thrilled each time I manage to get published and still consider the book to be a valid technology. At the end of a long, hard day I am only too happy to abandon the screen and curl up in bed with a good novel. Recall, too, that the demise of painting was predicted when photography came along, and then movies, and television. There is much fevered talk of the book's extinction but I've been noticing a backlash not unlike the slow food movement. Popular lately are elaborate volumes replete with illuminated text much like the books of yore. In any case, I try to think beyond media, because what is most fundamental is voice.

One of the most useful aspects of the Internet is the personal website or blog. A website is an effective showcase and more versatile than ever before. Images, video, and music players, podcasts, and Internet radio stations can be incorporated without much difficulty. I've had a website for a long time but was reluctant to begin blogging. I instinctively resist trends, but eventually I overcame my trepidation. My blog, *One Life*, has forced me to be more productive and helps to keep my writing chops up. I was afraid of the pressure, the unspoken law that dictates daily entries, but I have found there is no giant ham-mer that drops from the sky onto my head when I don't, or can't. It's a journal, and I often post poetry as well. I like to include photographs and graphics and provide as many links as possible, because of course the more links, the more traffic is driven to the site. I use WordPress but Blogger and LiveJournal are popular and user friendly as well. I promote my blog primarily through Twitter, Networked Blogs, and Facebook.

Another vital medium is video. I believe Jean Cocteau was the first poet to employ film. In 1930 he produced *Blood of a Poet*, usually categorized as surrealist art. Then there were the "film poets" from the West Coast abstract school, James Broughton, Sidney Peterson, and Hy Hirsh, the latter two collaborating with John Cage in 1947. In 1978 Tom Konyves of Montréal's Vehicle Poets coined the term "videopoetry" to describe his multimedia work. Rather than get bogged down in semantics, I'd like to point out that I think in terms of moving images, and don't make a huge distinction between film and video. I work with digital video because it is accessible and affordable, important considerations for most poets. A high definition camera can now be acquired for approximately $500. I don't have to settle for a lower quality image, either.

Though most of us in the West are visually literate, it is brave — foolish, some say — to adapt the oral tradition to a medium where image is metaphor. I'm drawn to video because of its populist nature. It lends itself to hybridization and its history of experimentation is a fundamental aspect of the medium. Video is a natural fit for me, having grown up with television and cinema. According to my mother, I was enthralled with movies and always viewed them with my mouth gaping in awe. It's a powerful medium and I still can't resist its lure. In 1999, as one of the curators of the Vancouver Videopoem Festival, I defined videopoem for a journalist as "a wedding of word and image." Achieving that level of integration is difficult and rare, however. In my experience, the greatest challenge of this hybrid genre is fusing voice and vision, aligning ear with eye. Some poets like to see words on the screen. The effect can be exquisite, but I find that film and video don't accommodate text well. We are busy listening to the poem with our eyes, as-

similating it through our ears. I prefer spoken word. Voice is the critical element, medium and venue secondary considerations. Unlike a music video — the inevitable and ubiquitous comparison — a videopoem stars the poem rather than the poet, the voice seen as well as heard.

As for criteria, for me the words must have true literary merit. Approaches to production are as diverse as the poets, but in terms of execution, I prefer to take a cinematic approach. Using the poem as script, I start with a shot list and storyboard. I see it as an adaptation process, adapting voice and text to video. Preparation is crucial. Choose your crew wisely. Get everything in writing. I pay artists half their fee up front and the remainder when the work is completed. Invariably videopoems are produced despite zero budgets; one must be inventive and resourceful.

Speaking of voice, it's the other thing that saved me. Singing. Performance. I grew up listening to folk and country music and sang in choirs at school and church, the only reason I attended. I would get very excited donning our robes and making our "entrance," only to drift off to sleep during mass.

In my book, poetry evolved from the oral tradition. Long before Gutenberg, people gathered together to share stories. Verse was devised as a way to preserve myth, to pass it down generation to generation. By breaking the story into lines and stanzas people were better able to recall them. Rhythm and rhyme are powerful mnemonic devices, as is melody, song evolving for the same reason.

And speaking of song, music can be a powerful vehicle. It's entirely possible to find and develop a rapport with a guitarist, cellist, accordion or banjo player — according to your own bent — to accompany you and your words. In my *AURAL Heather* work, which I call "spoken word song," I collaborate with musicians in several ways. They might compose melody to accompany my words, or I will write poetry to go with their music, improvising and experimenting along the way, a fusion of spoken word and song our goal.

Advice I wish I'd received along with Read and Learn your craft:

Find your voice. Be true to it. ❦

As for the future, I can imagine a growing awareness of spoken word and video poetry, more cross-pollination between disciplines, genres and media, currently manifesting in media and music as the **mashup**. I envision rampant experimentation and innovation, with nearly universal access to necessary tools I can see, and hear, a melding of poem and music, a blurring of the distinctions between song, verse, music video, and videopoem. Perhaps a **renaissance** in poetry is inevitable. I'd like to think so, but I'm an incurable optimist, daring to imagine a utopia where everyone is a creator.

Three Blocks West of Wonderland

The murders mattered
only because they went down
in my sweet pea-with-a-bent-stem friend
Daisy's neighbourhood. We could be sisters,
sharing obscure origins in *la belle province*. I foisted
Daisy adopted, blossoming into a blonde
Jewish princess. Beguiling kook. Fatal Brooklynese accent.
Two transplants to Los Angeles. I dipped in Silverlake.
Solo act. Daisy regal atop Lookout Mountain Avenue,
Three blocks west of Wonderland. Aspiring director boy toy
in tow. No gun clubs on their map of LA. Leery elkhounds
patrolled the property. Litter box kitties safe from coyotes,
rabid coons. One morning LAPD prodded creeping sage
ground cover. Rats? No. We're searching for body parts.
Clues. *Wonderland*, the movie based on a true story.
Val Kilmer still too hunky to play geeky
John Holmes, decidedly Joe Blow as appearances go.
Might explain his appeal though.
Everyman identified, despite the grotesque cock.

Coppola wannabe split. Mattress and pillow a prairie of down.
Daisy bought a Colt .45 to dream on. *Statistics, shamistics.*
She had a plan to scare off intruders, to shoot up
into the rafters where the petrified red rosebuds hung.

—Heather Haley ✪

First appeared in *Three Blocks West of Wonderland*
2009, Exstasis Editions